*Influencer Creep*

# Influencer Creep

### HOW OPTIMIZATION, AUTHENTICITY, AND SELF-BRANDING TRANSFORM CREATIVE CULTURE

Sophie Bishop

 UNIVERSITY OF CALIFORNIA PRESS

University of California Press
Oakland, California

Library of Congress Cataloging-in-Publication Data

Names: Bishop, Sophie, author
Title: Influencer creep : how optimization, authenticity, and self-branding
  transform creative culture / Sophie Bishop.
Description: Oakland, California : University of California Press, [2025] |
  Includes bibliographical references and index.
Identifiers: LCCN 2025013809 (print) | LCCN 2025013810 (ebook) |
  ISBN 9780520402713 cloth | ISBN 9780520402706 paperback |
  ISBN 9780520402720 ebook
Subjects: LCSH: Cultural industries—21st century | Social media—
  Influence | Internet personalities
Classification: LCC HD9999.C9472 B57 2025 (print) | LCC HD9999.
  C9472 (ebook) | DDC 338.4/7306—dc23/eng/20250716
LC record available at https://lccn.loc.gov/2025013809
LC ebook record available at https://lccn.loc.gov/2025013810


GPSR Authorized Representative: Easy Access System Europe, Mustamäe
tee 50, 10621 Tallinn, Estonia, gpsr.requests@easproject.com

34  33  32  31  30  29  28  27  26  25
10  9  8  7  6  5  4  3  2  1

# Contents

# Acknowledgments

I'll start by thanking my spirited and supportive PhD supervisory team at the University of East London—Julia Dane, Stephen Maddison, and Helen Powell. Thank you for your attention, guidance, and kindness. I also want to express my appreciation to my PhD research participants and the organizing teams that permitted me to attend their influencer events (lipstick on my teeth and all).

During work on my dissertation I particularly benefited from attending the Oxford Internet Institute summer program; I appreciate all the amazing people that I met there. In particular, I want to honor the memory of Niko Hatakka, who was a great researcher and a very nice guy, and who once wrote me a beautiful song about all the merits of buying a Deadpool hat on the internet.

Thank you to Elaine Sedenberg and Meta for funding the initial stages of my artist research project. Thank you, especially, to Elaine for everything else—you have spent way more time in the North of England than anyone who meets you would ever expect. Thank you to all the artists who generously gave up their time to speak to me and to Laura Plant for offering truly excellent research assistance during this project.

Thank you to my colleagues in the Department of Digital Humanities (DDH) at King's College, London. During my time at DDH, I grew a lot as a scholar, becoming an adult (at the age of twenty-eight) who was finally able to shop at COS. This department is full of great folks—I particularly want to send good, thankful vibes to mentors Elisa Oreglia, Zeena Feldman, Jennifer Pybus, Alessandro Gandini, and Tobias Blanke. Thanks to my colleagues at the University of Sheffield, especially to Ysabel Gerrard. We have seen far too much together and somehow we are approximately one thousand years old. Also thanks to Sheffield pals Alexandra Woodall, Dave O'Brien, Mark Taylor, Tim Highfield, and Kate Miltner. After leaving Sheffield, I have finally reached my most powerful form in my new role in the Department of Media and Communications at the University of Leeds. I love it here so much! Thank you, Bethany Klein, for giving me this opportunity, and to all my colleagues, especially Bondy Valdovinos Kaye, Ludmila Lupinacci, Cindy Ma, Maitrayee Basu, Marcia Allison, Miriam Kent, Joanne Armitage, Yuan Zeng, Holly Steel, Raquel Campos Valverde, Sara Tafakori, Anamik Saha, and David Hesmondhalgh. Also thank you to my friends and colleagues at the University of Utrecht—Catalina Goanta and Taylor Annabel. With you both in my heart, I will always treasure and honor the rights of the consumer.

Thanks to the attendees and organizing committees of Algorithms for Her? 1 and 2. Their contributions have informed and shaped the early chapters of this book. Many of my favorite academic people are now neatly tucked into the new Content Creator Scholar Network (CCSN), so thank you to all of you guys. I particularly want to send a shout out to Zoë Glatt for organizing the CCSN and being a fabulous parallel-life haver, scholar and friend.

Also thanks to a miscellaneous bunch of academics for offering particular support and reading drafts of my book project or adjacent ones: Brooke Duffy, Lee McGuigan, Brendan Keogh, Thomas Poell, David Nieborg, Vilde Schanke Sundet, and Marika Lüders. Thanks also to my editor Michelle Lipinski at the University of California Press for all the encouragement and support.

My heartfelt thanks go to the group chats for being the very stuff of life itself: GOT (Char, Fran, Jen and Maddy), Dessert Arms (Julia, Leah, Phil, Gráinne, Jen and Lorna), Family (Mary, Gary, Lucy and Dan), Usher Usher (Dan, Beth, Ross, Alice and Hamish), NCL-MCR crew (Jesse, Luisa and Dan), Cribbage (Phil, Collette, Nikki, Elsie, Tee, Dan, Rachel and Ben) and The Bishop Girlies (Tom, Lucy and Mary).

Thank you to Imi for being there since basically forever, and always chatting about this stuff with me—it always helps! Let's open a bottle of cold champagne!

One of my most heartfelt and most sincere thank yous has to go to the ladies of the *Real Housewives of Salt Lake City*, the *Real Housewives of New York*, the *Real Housewives of Miami*, the *Real Housewives of Beverly Hills*, and the mixed groups of *Summer House*. Thank you also to the cast and crew of the following *Below Deck* franchises: *Below Deck*, *Below Deck Down Under*, *Below Deck Mediterranean*, and *Below Deck Sailing Yacht* (you'll notice this is all of them apart from *Below Deck Adventure*, which I did not care for).

Thanks to Blue and Meryl. You will never read this book but I appreciate you and your impact on my life. Thank you to my in-laws, the Josephs, for your curiosity.

Thank you to my parents Mary and Gary for supporting this project and many others before it; it may not always seem like I appreciate you, and that is because I might not always appreciate you, but I do love you both. Thank you to Lucy B Yoga for being an excellent sister-friend, for facilitating some early research workshops, and for offering inspiration for the early project that became *Influencer Creep*. Thank you for always labeling your sponsored content with the upmost care and transparency.

Thank you to Daniel for your radical positivity, patience, and innumerable contributions to *Influencer Creep* and much of my other work. Life is ferfect with you. Thank you to Romy for arriving late, just in time for me to finish this book. This whole thing is completely crazy—I love you both so much.

# Introduction

In early 2024, I received an email from Caroline Mimbs Nyce, a journalist working at the *Atlantic* magazine. Nyce wanted to speak to me for a story concerning the ways in which people post about the rescue dogs they foster on social media, hoping to increase the chances they will be adopted. She was getting in touch with me because I had recently published a piece in *Real Life* magazine called "Influencer Creep,"[1] which was about the ways that promotional social media practices have become increasingly central to the ways we all live our lives online.

I define influencer creep as a process where strategies developed by influencers are being taken up and used in everyday life. The phrase "mission creep" describes how a military campaign's objectives gradually expand until they entail unanticipated commitment beyond the mission's original objectives and scope. Influencer creep, then, captures the ways that influencing extends beyond a small subset of online power users and becomes central to more forms of work. It is a concept that helps us explore how influencer practices and pressures penetrate more deeply into the lives and psyches of workers. It recognizes that influencers are specialists at navigating the technical requirements of platforms, capturing the attention of an audience, and growing brand value, and that this work is highly skilled. So instead of dismissing influencers as frivolous, vain, and consumerist, we should see them as sophisticated architects of some of the very strategies that shape life as lived on social media today.

In the *Atlantic* piece, Caroline Mimbs Nyce used the concept of influencer creep to articulate the pressures that she felt in sharing content about the dogs she fostered. She found herself routinely taking pictures and writing pithy captions to ensure the dogs appeared as cute and engaging as possible.[2] Nyce writes that the time investment, expertise, and effort spent dog-posting made her feel like a "pseudo-content creator." Influencer creep helped her describe how she experienced anxiety about the risks of posting about the dogs—including a flurry of cyberbullying and criticism—as opposed to the risks of not posting, her fears being that her foster dogs would miss out on finding their best possible forever home.

"Influencer creep for dogs" offered up a particularly unique example, but after the *Real Life* article was published, people wanted to talk to me about the ways influencer creep resonated with their own experiences. Nyce and I had spoken before for a different *Atlantic* piece, about how individuals working in blue-collar industries grew a loyal audience by sharing their working day on TikTok live. Line cooks, for example, filmed their work on the griddle, waxing lyrical about their egg- and French toast–flipping philosophies[3]. Streaming while working afforded these individuals a secondary income, but it also demanded significant effort and personal risk. My friend Hamish told me how influencer creep had changed the sport of rock climbing, and how creating a variety of climbing content (and courting social media sponsorships) was now the only viable pathway to make a living as a climber.

I was particularly inspired by the experiences of my sister, an actor-turned-yoga-teacher who originally started an Instagram account to advertise her yoga classes during the early COVID-19 pandemic. While she didn't start out aspiring to be a professional content creator, she quickly amassed 75,000 followers—landing her in the tractor beam of a passionate and demanding audience, negotiating sponsorship requests from brands, and making difficult decisions about how much of her own personal traumas to share. When she came to visit my husband and me during the Christmas break, we plotted ideas to create content to help keep her engagement up over the festive period. We brainstormed a playful Instagram Reel, in which she performed different yoga poses with a message about banishing body shaming from family members. We struggled to drag our tree across the room and light the room to help her grab the needed shots, which she then edited, added a voiceover to, and set to Christmas music. The reel now has 50,000 views—not bad!

My research has shown that influencer creep is complicated. Generating content ideas can be creative and fun. By building an online presence, you really can connect to an interested audience and sometimes even make some money. If you are competitive (like me), winning at the visibility game[4] can feel euphoric. But at the same time, influencer work is labor-intensive, anxiety-inducing, and reliant on the whims of a social media platform that you don't have any access to, control over, or channels for support. Underpinning every view are the doubts: How will content be received? How many views will it get? And how long will your audience stay interested? There are also risks: social media is a double-edged sword and attracting the wrong kind of attention can have significant consequences. This book is an attempt to capture these moments of ambivalence—tracing the histories, as well as the promises and anxieties of influencer creep.

## Researching the Influencer Industry

My journey into studying influencers started in 2012 while I was working at a digital marketing agency in the United Kingdom. My job was to identify bloggers who were suitable partners for our global fashion and beauty brand clients. I trawled through hundreds of blogs every day by searching Google, tracing who was friends with whom, and hopping hyperlinks across blog networks. Blogs mostly featured a mishmash of personal diary-like writing, accompanying mirror selfies documenting outfits of the day identified using the now-deceased initialism #OOTD. Blogs also featured beauty instructions on how to create the ever-elusive smoky eye, and (what would now be considered career-endingly scathing and honest) reviews about beauty and skincare. When I found a suitable blogger, I would add their details to an Excel spreadsheet. At the end of the day, I trotted over to the marketing manager to get him to approve my choices. I wanted to get as many of "my girls" approved as possible, so I learned to assess these blogs with a commercial eye, taking stock of popularity markers as well as the professionalism and quality of their writing and images.

After my blogs were signed off, I could email the blogger to offer them gifted products in exchange for a posted link to a client's website, or sometimes in exchange for a product review. At least in my agency, there was rarely any question of payment for this work. This was mostly because the individuals we were approaching weren't aware of the value of their audience, which (at the time) I saw as a positive. We rarely approached bloggers with talent agents or managers, who would know how much they should be charging. Despite bloggers often having a significant audience reach, the marketing men I worked with basically thought they were doing these young hobbyists a favor. I remember several marketing executives at my agency being floored when they heard a rumor from a client's in-house team that a popular influencer had turned down an opportunity to interview Vivienne Westwood at London Fashion Week, citing an insufficient stipend of (I think it was) £20,000. Where, they wondered aloud, did she get off? I should say that ten years on, this influencer is still working online as a successful "mommy creator" and charging upward of £10,000 for an Instagram story.

While I worked, I was struck by the gendered, commercial, and unequal nature of the blogosphere. I thought the internet was supposed to be an open horizon where anyone could be anything, the barriers to creating your own pathway to creative stardom all but eroded. But in practice, everyone I found looked the same. Most bloggers were white.[5] The outfit ideas, makeup advice, and navel-gazing (often about heterosexual relationships) seemed to be directly ripped from the pages of mainstream fashion and beauty magazines. I was also witnessing firsthand the ways that brands were carving out spaces for themselves within blogging industries. Even when they weren't paying bloggers for partnerships, free products were coveted and offered a legitimizing stamp of approval from the beauty industry. Brands decided who was taken seriously.

Eventually, I did what any sensible person would do with a little industry access, a master's degree in gender studies, and a healthy lack of interest in financial security: I decided to parlay this experience into a PhD project. My first scholarship application in 2014 was rejected because the awarding institution did not think that beauty and fashion content creation would merit a full PhD study; in other words, they didn't think it would be sufficiently serious or long-lasting. This was perhaps the first, but definitely not the last, experience of the hurdles involved in getting influencer culture to be taken seriously in academia, policy, or even marketing industries.

This prelude offers an introduction to my research on influencer industries, which I began in earnest in 2015. At the time, the bloggers I was tracking in my marketing work were engaging more consistently with YouTube, producing early beauty instruction videos, product reviews, and "day-in-the-life" content, which overviewed the highs and lows of the previous seven days, compiled into the "weekly vlog." So I undertook an ethnography of the YouTube side of the industry. I followed key YouTubers and systematically started watching their YouTube content. I attended public and private events held at YouTube, Twitter (now X), and YouTuber conventions like VidCon Europe and Summer in the City. I also conducted interviews with creators, talent managers, and platform employees.

During my ethnography, I also attended events specific to beauty content creation, which typically went as follows: Attendees would talk shop over free samples of syrupy, canned sauvignon blanc, take outfit pictures against silk flower–gummed walls, and gather to listen to panels where a rotating cast of characters would discuss the state of the industry. Brands helmed display tables arranged in a horseshoe around the meetup space, often decorated with elaborate balloon sculptures. Like conspiring second cousins in a Jane Austen novel, attendees would then take a turn around the room. They would approach each brand to network with them, and then collect their allotted sample of product. After the events, brands would track who covered their content in an engaging way, and potentially would approach attendees for paid work. So these interactions crackled with the promise of a longer-term relationship. Everyone attending events took them very seriously. At one point I was sent to a dressing room by an aghast organizer, who instructed me to fix the lipstick smudging my teeth before I would be permitted to return.

My ethnographic work on the influencer economy has helped me to understand the development and professionalization of influencer culture. In this book I navigate the ways that a messy, distributed industry became increasingly formalized, co-constructed by a range of intermediaries like managers, agents, brands, software developers, and platforms. Many of the inequalities I noticed in 2012 related to visibility, pay, and participation remain central to the way the industry functions.[6] This book offers an ethnographically informed story of influencer cultures, economies, and strategies.[7] But to carve the specific pathway toward influencer creep more clearly, I have structured the book around three specific practices, which came up again and again in my research as core tenets of influencer culture and, latterly, the foundations of influencer creep. I write about *optimization*—the affective strategies of maximizing visibility and minimizing risk for those relying on platformized visibility. I identify the practice of influencer *authenticity*, which brings together an amateur aesthetic and a performance of emotional vulnerability. Lastly, I outline the specific tweaks to *self-branding* that have taken place within influencer culture: moving the self toward a consistent identity, with an orientation toward brand safety and commercial suitability.

## Art Worlds and Influencers

This book is about influencer culture but, as I have outlined, influencer creep isn't (just) about influencers. The book unites my influencer research together with a second project that I began in 2020, looking to study the way that art worlds have been transformed by social media. Sociologist Howard Becker popularized the term "art worlds" to move away from the idea of artists as independent, individual geniuses, recognizing the "complexity of the cooperative networks through which art happens."[8] Art worlds include the individuals who come up with the ideas for artistic projects, who produce materials, who find cash, who clean and organize artistic studios, and who assign critical value. To understand the full scope of artistic activity, I immersed myself in online art worlds following galleries and critics in popular presses, trade presses, and any other social media output that were adjacent or relevant. The data gleaned from this ethnography were woven together with interviews with female and nonbinary artists whose practices include illustration, fine art, textile art, silversmithing, and sculpture. Those I talked to made a full-time income from selling art objects. I wasn't particularly concerned with definitions of what makes a professional a high-art artist as opposed to a commercial one—the likelihood that someone will even claim an identity as an artist is stratified by gender, class, and race.[9] I've used Becker's useful overview of art and craft as "folk categories" that are used contextually, with their own "ambiguities and contradictions."[10]

I was not expecting my influencer project and artist project to be quite so compatible. I thought I was owed a break from influencer culture, and my research was headed into a brand new direction, away from the oppressive influences of brands and beauty. I was quite happy to step away from a milieu in which I was physically ejected from an event for (perceived) scruffiness. But as I began my interviews with artists, they mentioned the same topics over and over again—the very same anxieties, experiences, and concerns that influencers had raised with me just a couple of years prior. So the concept of influencer creep was born.

I conducted most of the interviews for this project during the economic downturn and mass unemployment prompted by COVID-19 (between 2020 and 2023). This point in the pandemic affected artists in different ways but nearly always by pushing them toward heavier use of Instagram. Some of my participants made their part-time artistic practices full-time, since they had been laid off from their other jobs. They used severance packages as start-up capital, and deployed the social media expertise they had accrued through their work experience in fashion buying, visual merchandising, and marketing. Some of them grew an impressive presence on social media pretty quickly. For artists already working professionally, trade shows and in-person art markets were canceled, as were their additional income streams, like workshops, teaching, and opportunities and open studios. These individuals looked for alternative ways to show and sell their work, and they found audiences on Instagram that were shopping from home and looking for ways to make their own domestic space more aesthetically pleasing.

It's not surprising that a time of economic risk brough a rise in entrepreneurial artistic creativity. Cultural theorist Angela McRobbie has drawn attention to ways that creative work is often held up as a method of "novel job creation,"[11] heavily promoted by policymakers at times of economic risk, since it is "self-invented work" that can take place without "interference from the state."[12] Aspirants expect creative work to be individualized and competitive; creative industries have glamourized the rough reality of poor wages, long hours, and scant social protections. Creative workers are used to taking on, and strategically managing, economic risk.

I don't know why, but I didn't expect Instagram to be so central to the management of this risk—to artists' thought processes and relationships, to the way they understood their careers. I didn't think artists would approach social media so strategically, or that it would take up so much of their time, or affect their practice so keenly. Just as within influencer culture, platforms afforded an affective atmosphere of anxiety for artists. I am inspired by the way that cultural theorist Lauren Berlant considers affect in her book *Cruel Optimism*, where she describes the "affective structure" of an "optimistic attachment" in which people find themselves "bound to a situation of profound threat that is, at the same time, profoundly confirming."[13] Berlant's idea of cruel optimism captures the impossible promise of a medium like Instagram. Many of the artists I spoke to had early experiences of the platform that were utopian. When artists first promoted their work on Instagram, they found themselves growing audiences quickly and garnering healthy sales. This early bump inspired confidence; they quit their jobs, moved to bigger studios, and invested in artistic materials. Instagram represented an ability to lead a good life, to connect with an audience interested in art works, to share ideas, and to make a steady income. But the platform then became a site of diminishing returns. Artists were uploading the same amount of content for less visibility. They second-guessed their art work, fretting about whether or not it was suitable to be shared by Instagram's visibility algorithms. They worried about being perceived as a real and legitimate artist by an assortment of audiences, and about creating their professional self-brand and performing it consistently. They had become dependent on a precarious platform, as an "optimistic object" over which they had no control.[14]

I chose to research the experience of women and nonbinary individuals in particular because I have long been inspired by the critical academic work that examines gendered inequality in creative work.[15] In art worlds, women struggle to make their creative processes, skill, and expertise visible. The same challenges exist in influencer economies. As Emily Hund writes in *The Influencer Industry*, the market epitomizes "longstanding tropes" that "women are primarily consumers and that using social media is for fun and not work."[16] In this sense, influencer creep causes a multiplying pressure for women looking to be legitimized within creative industries. Throughout this book, I show how influencer creep rewards practices like invocation of the personal or emotional, which can shape valuations of expertise and craft that are crucial to art worlds, valuations that are already struggled over by women.

Monopoly social media platforms have extended the individualization of creative industries, by doubling down on cultural calls to *be creative*. Instagram's creator resources are peppered with encouragement to "be creative to connect to your world," as well as with statements like "you were made for this," "be yourself and your fans will follow," and that Instagram can help you "make money by doing what you best." Media studies scholars David Nieborg and Thomas Poell have captured the ways that social media platforms have transformed creative industries—a process they have influentially termed "platformization."[17] Together, Nieborg and Poell point out the ways that social media platforms have wrought "economic, mental and infrastructural" changes in cultural work, shaping how that work is distributed and compensated.[18] Platforms have had dramatic institutional effects on creative industries. Winner-take-all markets mean the majority of producers remain invisible. Platform governance subjects producers to platform rules. Producers must account for a distribution platform's infrastructure—their "algorithms, data services, structures and interfaces"—when preparing cultural artifacts like music, writing, and artwork.[19] Social media scholar Brooke Duffy has written with Poell and Nieborg about the ways that institutional effects are shaped by how creative practitioners negotiate them. In this sense, the "practices of people" shape the "routines, experiences and expressions" of the platformization of cultural production as those same people attempt to navigate the unpredictability and changeability of platforms.[20] A growing, valuable field of platformization research has tracked the ways cultural producers of all stripes navigate social media platforms.[21] Influencer creep builds on these perspectives, specifically by examining the ways that professional platform users both navigate and expand the pressures of platformization.

## Why Do We Say "Influencer"?

The terms used to describe influencer work have changed as the industry has been professionalized, especially as entrants are now required to maintain a presence across social media platforms.[22] For example, the term I used during my PhD was "vlogger," which is now antiquated, and outdatedly attached to a single platform—YouTube. "Influencer," instead, serves as a catch-all term for content creation straddling the authentic and the promotional online—although, as we will see below, its use is contested. Digital anthropologist Crystal Abidin was one of the first scholars to take stock of the multisided influencer economy, mapping the ways that personal videos, images, and posts online were buoyed by authenticity and monetized by the integration of advertorials in their content.[23] Brooke Duffy similarly defines influencers as identifiable by their "significant online following, distinctive brand persona, and patterned relationships with commercial sponsors."[24] Both Abidin and Duffy draw on the earlier work of internet scholars Terri Senft and Alice Marwick, who captured the rise of early "micro-celebrity" practices, which involved capturing "a new style of online performance"[25] that involves the use of social media to garner and reify popularity online to "think of oneself as a celebrity and act accordingly."[26]

In this book, I avoid offering a stable or even a stabilizing definition of "influencer." I instead choose to follow philosopher Sarah Ahmed's call to follow language around to see how the terms used end up helping the world "take shape."[27] Approaching language in this way means examining who is using words and why. So, for example, it's notable that the influencer industry individuals I research very rarely self-identify as influencers, usually opting for a term like "content creator" instead.[28] Social media platforms also keenly avoid using the term "influencer," also nearly always choosing the designation "content creator." Marketers and brands, on the other hand, are very happy to use the term "influencer" to frame their business and raison d'être—which involves engaging with these individuals to help them sell products.

For me, "influencer" and "content creator" aren't really different jobs. They both involve the independent, serial production of content for social media platforms and are remunerated in similar ways, through a mixture of platform revenue-sharing schemes, brand partnerships, and fan-funded models like Patreon. But the term "influencer" is probably more unappealing because influencers are often derided in popular culture. Influencers are dismissed as frivolous because they use self-representations in part to sell products. Detractors thus accuse them of being vain and narcissistic. This framing is (of course) gendered; it's more closely aligned with the feminized spheres of consumerism than other labels are. Using a term like "content creator" dovetails, rather, with "creativity," a word softly humming with warm, positive connotations. In this vein, influencers sit below content creators within the value hierarchy of online culture.

The word "influencer" is still worth using within this book because it's taken hold in the public imagination; it is consistently reached for by journalists, marketers, and policymakers. Following the language around shows the ways that the word "influencer" is often wrapped up in a moral concern: journalists echo such concerns about the negative effects that influencers have on culture; marketers are worried about fraud or scandal; and policymakers often pinpoint influencers for their role in misinformation, antisocial behavior, or undisclosed commercial content.

## How Does Influencer Creep Happen?

You might be wondering, how does influencer creep happen? Are artists copying what influencers do? Or do they just end up navigating social media platforms in a manner that is similar to what influencers do? The short answer to this question is both.

The longer answer could be viewed as a more nuanced response to a bigger question: how does cultural change happen? To answer this, we can look to the "circuit of culture," an influential concept originated by cultural studies theorists Paul du Gay, Stuart Hall, Linda Janes, Hugh McKay, and Keith Negus.[29] The circuit of culture models the developments of cultural moments through five interlinked and connected elements: (1) representation; (2) the construction and formation of identity; (3) processes of technical and cultural production; (4) audience meanings; and (5) associations through consumption and regulation by institutions and governments. Each of these elements informs the others. So, for example, representation of cultural change in the press may convince politicians to take certain forms of regulatory action. Or the ways that audiences take up a certain cultural object may inform how companies develop a certain technology. An oft-cited example of the latter process is the Twitter hashtag, which was developed by users and later formalized by the platform company. The circuit of culture shows us the many complicated ways in which culture gets into things or things get into culture. It might sound cliché, but cultural moments happen both slowly and all at once.

Following the circuit of culture helps us understand the relationship between identity creation, cultural representations, and audience meaning. Influencers are the instructive platform users who set the tone and develop generic conventions for the social media platform culture that we all live with. Of course, influencer content is itself influenced by technological changes and the legacy of regulation within many different creative industries—including journalism, PR, modeling, fashion, and autobiography.[30] But in its contemporary iteration, influencer practice rests on platform viability. Every beat of influencer cultural production is expertly curated for platforms in a way that simply is not the case for other creative industries with offline legacies, like music, art, journalism, or game development. Influencers are the proverbial canaries in the coal mine—an expression referring to the birds used by miners as an early alert to the presence of toxic gases like carbon monoxide. Like these canaries, influencers experience harms first, since they make use of an entire range of platform affordances and sit in the full spotlight of audience attention. Like many (if not all) of us, influencers are looking to legitimize their own identities and to make a consistent livelihood. They do so by bearing the complex cultural expectations of platform success, by developing and deploying strategic efforts to manage audiences, by navigating platform contexts, and by negotiating with industry intermediaries. Influencer practices and strategies have changed the way that many different kinds of work take place on social media platforms, with artists offering just one occupation worth studying, albeit a particularly interesting one.

On the other hand, artists aren't influencers. The circuitous nature of influencer creep means following the interlinked ways that individuals develop responses to the social media conditions they work within. Influencer creep blends into artists' professional milieu and unique working conditions. This book shows how individuals optimize their artistic practice for algorithmic visibility, which changes the process of artistic creation. Expectations of authenticity—to be ordinary, approachable, and emotionally genuine—clash in influencer culture with expectations to be authentic in art worlds, which means to be legitimate and technically proficient. Artists are required to show more of their own personal life, while convincing their followers that they live in ways befitting the romantic ideal of a professional artist. Influencer culture has also informed a commercially oriented expectation of safety on social media platforms, which shapes the works that are considered suitably sharable on social media.

I have chosen to use the term "influencer creep" not to criticize influencers—who I think are often unfairly and boringly derided from many directions within popular culture. Instead, I ask why we are so invested in the distinction between influencer and creator, revealing the long-standing critical divisions between art (seen as organically created) and mass culture (seen as manufactured and dangerous). These tensions are at the heart of many of the discussions in this book—discussions that involve clarifying the pressures involved in many of the ways that artists describe and account for their use of social media. The tensions between art and consumerism are couched in snobbery. Those holding up art as special or magical tend to ignore the ways that it has always been an outcome of collaborative production between a wide range of actors, only some deemed worthy of being officially legitimized and recognized. As Howard Becker has argued,[31] art does not exist outside the market; artistic practice is always heavily influenced by the available means of legitimization, distribution, and compensation.

I'm not really bothered about who, if anyone, is making "good art" these days. I'm definitely not promoting an argument that influencers have made art worlds worse. Instead, this book draws from an analysis of art worlds to show how influencer creep affects artistic production and how art becomes visible to audiences. Looking to the experiences of influencers is valuable because it helps us understand some of the harshest realities of platformized creative work, which I believe will (unfortunately) be useful to those interested in (or implicated in) a wide scope of contemporary labor. More than this: building bridges between commercial influencers and elite art worlds can offer unique opportunities to share experiences, build opportunities for solidarity, and even offer glimpses of hope in the bleak landscape of contemporary platform capitalism.

.   .   .

Chapter 1 builds out the core argument of this book: influencers are innovators of central importance within platformized creative work. I show how influencers develop optimization strategies to negotiate lives lived on risky platforms. Chapter 2 looks to influencer-informed strategies artists use to figure out what is suitable for posting, what is most likely to net engagement, and ultimately what will allow them to make a living working as an artist.

Chapter 3 looks at the specific kind of authenticity that has developed and sharpened within the conditions of contemporary social media culture. I then outline three kinds of authenticity strategies that have been finessed by influencers and that are now central to influencer creep: a performance of amateurism; a comparison with what is deemed to be ostensibly inauthentic; and an emotional performance to negotiate scandal. At its heart, this chapter recognizes the fragility of the concept of authenticity, closely examining who it may or may not hold value for within influencer economies. Chapter 4 outlines the ways that artists use techniques developed by influencers to represent the ways they are working under authentic artistic conditions and living an authentic artist's life while also conveying a convincing emotional performance that comes from their genuine self.

Chapter 5 steps back to examine the commercial pressures of the platform and influencer economy, drawing attention to how advertisers inform the cultural practices we can see under influencer creep. Platforms and brands offer multilayered levels of scrutiny and punishment that overwhelmingly harm marginalized content creators. After recognizing this context, I then explore the contours and conditions of self-branding under influencer creep, which involve editing the self toward a consistent identity, with an orientation toward commercial suitability and brand safety.

Chapter 6 shows how influencer-oriented brand safety efforts have crept into a form of risk avoidance within art worlds. I review the ways that a drive toward commercially oriented self-branding on social media affects artistic production, promotion, and distribution. Rather than proposing art as a worthy exception to brand safety efforts (for example, by reifying the artistic nude over other forms of nakedness), I suggest opportunities for collaboration and solidarity between influencers and artists as they negotiate arbitrary and unclear forms of platform governance and moderation.

# 1  *Influencers*

## The Canaries in the Algorithmic Coal Mine

In the fall of 2016, Jimmy Donaldson dropped out of college to try to solve one of the biggest mysteries in media: How exactly does a video go viral on YouTube?

In the months that followed, Donaldson and a handful of his friends tried to crack the code. They conducted daily phone calls to analyze what videos went viral. They gave one another YouTube-related homework assignments, and they pestered successful channels for data about their most successful posts. "I woke up, I studied YouTube, I studied videos, I studied filmmaking, I went to bed and that was my life," Donaldson recalled during a recent interview.

The piece above was taken from a news article titled "The North Carolina Kid Who Cracked YouTube's Secret Code," about MrBeast (real name Jimmy Donaldson), currently the most followed individual on YouTube: he has 347 million subscribers.[1] Reporting on Donaldson has highlighted the hours of work that go into his elaborate videos, and the cash that he is willing to fork over to make them happen. In 2023, he recreated a live action version of the Netflix show *Squid Game*; in 2024, he stranded himself on a desert island; and, at a different time, he starved himself for a month. He is known for a brash and personalized spin on philanthropy—he regularly hands out millions of dollars, new cars, or (supposedly) his own personal credit card. Mainstream media and YouTubers alike praise Donaldson's analytical and obsessive approach to YouTube production and in particular his skillful ability to navigate the technical architecture of YouTube (a.k.a. the algorithm). His knowledge of how YouTube works is often cited as a key reason for his sharp rise to success. This explanation diverges from earlier writing on popular YouTubers, extolling their unique personalities or their close relationships with fans. For Donaldson, his success comes from a commitment to making viral content. As he puts it in the story, "in a perfect world, I live and breathe this, working 12- to 15-hour days until I die."

Influencer creep helps us to understand a reality where personal and professional visibility is almost entirely contingent on social media platforms. Influencers have long negotiated a life in which platforms determine how, when, and where content is distributed. Platforms capriciously accelerate or limit the reach of individuals' content without a tangible methodology or explanation. Even when influencers have curated a hard-won following, they have no real ownership of this audience; there is no guarantee that content will be distributed to those that have elected to follow them, and much of the time it is not. Because of platforms' acute inconsistency and lack of communication, influencer production is wholly underpinned by risk. Influencers risk their content being hidden from audiences, a decrease in access to their audience, or even total invisibility because of content moderation or "shadow bans."[2] Influencer creep mandates an expansion of personal branding and authentic self-representation into creative work; it unites forms of creation more closely with the inclusion of the self. In this way, influencer creep helps us particularly to understand the personal and affective nature of optimizing practices. Optimization is thus an affective and strategic attempt to maximize visibility and minimize risk.

This chapter builds on the core argument of this book: influencers are innovators of central importance within platformized creative work. As some of the first to exclusively create work that relies on algorithmic media, they've pioneered technically sophisticated optimization techniques to negotiate the kinds of opacity and instability that algorithms bring. They are especially dependent on algorithmic visibility, because their livelihoods are exclusively tied up in growing and maintaining their platform engagement and audiences. Influencers have become dedicated proto-optimizers, finessing launching strategies that are now widely used throughout creative industries.[3]

In this chapter, I will show how influencers develop and deploy two optimization strategies which are now creeping outward into creative work. The first is algorithmic lore—an organizational effort to diagnose and provide smooth and sensible information about algorithms. Experts dealing in lore unite strategies from marketing fields like search engine optimization with personality-driven content to sell information about how algorithms function.[4] They are influencers making content exclusively about algorithms and how they work; in so doing, they shape the conversation within influencer industries. The second optimization strategy is algorithmic gossip—a live, as well as a collaboratively and community-formed, technical response to algorithmic uncertainty and confusing platform messaging. Through tracing these practices (and who is working on them), I show how influencer creep demonstrates a renewed pressure to optimize for creative workers, who must now work on platforms that deliberately or practically obscure how their policies and coded architectures work publicly.

## Introducing Optimization and the "Black Box"

Optimization occurs when influencers deliberately design and craft content to maximize audience reach on the platforms they work across. Practically speaking, this involves orienting work toward the requirements of recommendation algorithms, which are codified step-by-step processes implemented by platforms to afford or restrict visibility. Algorithmic distribution comes in different flavors across platforms: as an algorithmically curated "For you" feed or home page (TikTok, Instagram, YouTube); as an automatic "up next" playlist (YouTube, Spotify); or as a personalized timeline (Instagram, Twitter). However platforms function, influencers must comply with conditional regimes of visibility. Doing so successfully can lead to income and career sustainability. As media researchers Jeremy Wade Morris, Robert Prey, and David Nieborg have noted, cultural producers create content with algorithmic systems of distribution in mind—to "maximise the possibilities for economic or reputational gain."[5] Such an orientation makes sense when your livelihood depends on reaching audiences, near-exclusively afforded by social media platforms.

The main struggle for influencers hoping to comply with platform requirements is that it isn't clear what they need to do. The proprietary algorithms designed and deployed by social media companies are often depicted as being concealed and mysterious—as "black boxes."[6] Following this logic can lead us to believe that algorithmic workings are obscured by platforms for deliberate or practical reasons. Some scholars argue that confusion or obfuscation is an intentional feature of platform design. It is also a practical side effect of the sheer scale and volume of content that platforms host and distribute.[7] However, it is unhelpful to present platforms as inherently more exploitative and evil— or even more secretive—than other kinds of multinational corporations.[8]

Instead, we can see the concept of the black box as a misleading and unhelpful distraction. Media researcher Taina Bucher describes the notion that algorithmic media are a black box that could be simply opened as a "red herring"—a concept often used to describe misdirection in detective novels.[9] Instead, Bucher highlights the many ways of finding information about algorithms and their sociocultural implications. We may be able to glean the logics and priorities of algorithms through our everyday interactions with platforms, as well as with the spectrum of theories and feelings they animate. We can also access a patchwork of official information released by platforms—for example, press releases, blogs, or "terms and conditions" pages. For Bucher, the notions of algorithms as unknowable holds "seductive qualities," leaning on assumptions about their technical complexity and lending them distracting undue power.[10] A simple algorithmic reveal may not be so immediately satisfying or indeed even possible. Recommendation algorithms are developed by diverse teams who may work in different locations, often without interacting with each other. Different versions of algorithms are also tested out for users simultaneously; social media users on the same platform may not be experiencing the same recommendation recipe. Even those who access algorithmic code may find it inscrutable and challenging to understand.

A feminist critique invites us to critically probe the boundaries of the designation of the technical; the imagined person who *does algorithms* is arguably gendered as male, raced as white, and classed as "logical," whatever that means.[11] Throughout this chapter I encourage readers to look beyond assumptions of algorithmic expertise (for example, as the purview of computer scientists)[12] and to take influencers seriously as professional platform users who have built significant bodies of information about how algorithms work, in addition to pioneering tests on how to work with algorithmic media. It makes little sense to study algorithms without the added context of who works with them and how they do so. Algorithmic media are brought to life—and given meaning—in the ways that individuals engage with them. And we will see that influencers are power users who play a central function in breathing life into algorithmic processes, making them make sense. Influencers develop and sustain the platform-wide algorithmic imaginaries, which then become algorithmic realities. I look to influencer algorithmic experts for this reason: because they diagnose and articulate hunches, theories, and strategies. Such influencer optimization efforts shape cultures of use beyond influencer culture. They have given us a blueprint for optimization, which is often designed to provide individualized solutions to manage structural problems.

## Algorithmic Lore

Creative industries were risky long before the centrality of algorithmic visibility. In *Making Capital from Culture*, organizational sociologist Bill Ryan writes about changes wrought to the creative industries by the increasingly corporate nature of cultural production in the late twentieth century.[13] As creative production moved from artisanal craft toward the formalized corporate *creative industries*, creative managers like record executives, Hollywood producers, and editors at publishing houses were required to "produce immediately saleable commodities in an unpredictable market."[14] Ryan described how the management of this uncertainty was achieved through forms of creative formatting—namely, "moves to make creativity more predictable in the face of changing market conditions and tightened conditions of profitability."[15] Creative manufacturers rationalized the creative process; in other words, they confronted and managed the contradictory and complex nature of creative people and their processes.

Outside the realm of social media platforms, creative intermediaries and managers study a grab bag of resources that they hope will foretell which creative commodities audiences will purchase. These data may come from market research, published market information, the trade press, newsletters, psychological studies, focus groups, audience profiles, and information pilfered from their competitors. Focusing on music industries, sociologist Keith Negus shows the ways that workers in music industries want to understand music production through "constructing knowledge about it (through various forms of research and information-gathering), and then by deploying this knowledge as a 'reality' that guides the activities of corporate personnel."[16] This mixture of information ultimately shapes the decisions that management make about how to produce, promote, and position creative products to ensure that "guesswork, intuition or arbitrary inspiration is minimised."[17] While the formalized environment of a major record label might seem a world away from (seemingly) independent influencer culture, this research into how creative industries work reveals a clear precursor to the optimization practices we will consider here. Like rationalization, optimization involves a two-step process: collecting information, and deploying it—to minimize risk and increase visibility.

These forms of corporate bureaucratization are (of course) implemented to maximize profit; but, as creative industries scholar Anamik Saha notes, they also have an "ideological dimension."[18] Managers want to wrangle potentially unruly creative types using layers of technical and bureaucratic rules, which are designed to obstruct forms of collective organization like unions and to prohibit conflict with management. These rules can be explicitly articulated or they can be implicit, wrapped up in a kind of common sense.

Media scholar Timothy Havens has called these implicit rules "industry lore"—an invisible and taken-for-granted kind of sense making that occupies the space between "structural and cultural forces,"[19] designed to make the unknowable aspects of cultural production knowable and manageable. In distributed and individualized influencer economies, industry lore becomes algorithmic lore—a form of commercially based logic, developed and shared by influencers, and oriented around algorithmic visibility.

## Algorithmic Lore, Experts, and Influencer Culture

Algorithmic lore is most readily found in the content made by influencers who make self-branded content about the way the algorithms work. These are algorithmic experts. Such experts create lore from a mixture of research, experiments, and assumptions, and they communicate it with a compelling style and charisma. They hinge their social media presence on their algorithmic expertise. Experts orient their content toward aspiring or struggling creators, giving advice and, importantly, revealing secrets about the way that YouTube's algorithm (supposedly) actually works. These individuals are often influential on social media platforms, garnering millions of followers and shaping cultural production within the influencer ecology and beyond. It is important for us to study the genesis of algorithmic lore within influencer culture; and as we will see in the following chapter, this information is powerful outside influencer culture as well, making it an important tenet of influencer creep.

Algorithmic lore is so compelling (to me) because experts speak with such absolute confidence and certainty on a subject that they, by definition, cannot be experts in. Even the engineers who write the code for these platforms are sometimes unsure about how they work or how algorithms will respond to certain content. There is a strong undercurrent of uncertainty even in assuming that there is just one algorithm working here, but we know that platforms are also testing multiple algorithms at the same time.[20] In the face of all this precarity, how do these so-called experts produce, maintain, and sell their expertise?

In my research, I've found that algorithmic experts often do this by branding themselves as outsider bad boys or adversaries of platforms, able to reveal secret information, often to build their brand or attract followers. A typical example is the ways that experts framed the same publicly available research paper written by a team of engineers working at YouTube. The research paper was published in the proceedings of the Association for Computing Machinery conference in 2016, as well as on the open-access Google Research website.[21] Both sites made the paper publicly available. Despite its easy availability, algorithmic experts hyped up a secretive process of discovering the article. During an industry conference session, one algorithmic expert slyly informed the audience that he was sent the article by an anonymous informant. MatPat, a popular gaming YouTuber who also runs a YouTube consultancy, suggested he came across the article by "trawling through the bowels of the Google research website."[22] Although at least in theory, anyone could easily get access to this paper, experts spin up their unique ability to both source the article and translate it to audiences.

To give you an example of algorithmic expertise in practice, let's look at Paddy Galloway—a youngish, blond Irish man, who has featured as a guest on podcasts episodes with titles like "Meet the Godfather of YouTube Strategy" and "The Man Who Launched a Million Views." In videos published on his own YouTube channel (with five hundred thousand subscribers),[23] Galloway takes audiences through a deep dive of videos made by popular YouTube creators to explain how they have "gamed" the YouTube algorithm successfully, leading to lucrative careers on the platform. He tends toward the hyperbolic: he talks about creators who have "discovered the new blueprint for how to grow a YouTube channel"[24] or "changed the formula for growing on YouTube forever."[25] According to Galloway, MrBeast has found a way to "hard wire the viewer to keep watching."[26] Galloway takes a handful of extremely successful YouTubers and works to abstract a methodology designed to be easily applicable to an average creator.

A typical video considers Beluga, a young American YouTuber who exponentially grew a subscriber base in an impressively short period—four million subscribers in six months. Galloway partly attributes this growth to Beluga's zealous use of sound effects. He includes a short illustrative clip of Beluga's content, which is scored with a series of high- and low-pitched bleeps and bloops. He informs his viewership that the two-minute clip involved "eleven different sound changes," which is a good thing because they "force you to stay engaged."[27] He also reveals Beluga's "sneaky" strategies to encourage the audience to remain active—for example, running text rapidly across the screen, rendering it unreadable. Galloway theorizes the motivations behind this: "you will naturally have to pause—which counts for a longer video duration." View durations are believed, by experts, to be positive signals within the YouTube algorithm.

Paddy's videos engage in abstraction, a method of modeling or generalizing that aims at a simple and reproducible explanation. Abstraction hinges on "data smoothing"—a term coined by historian Dan Bouk. Data smoothing essentially means averaging a problem at a high level, or removing complexity from a data to minimize "chance and fluctuations."[28] In Bouk's work on banks and insurance brokers, he shows how actuaries have historically smoothed "jumpy" market data to calm the public and prevent panicked withdrawals.[29] In banking, smoothing helps to forge certainty and security. In the case of algorithmic lore, algorithmic experts smooth together research, data, and assumption to propagate settled truths about the "black-boxed" YouTube algorithm. For example, Paddy Galloway confidently praises the thumbnail design for a YouTube series by abstracting the color as one reason for its success: "There's a heavy focus on blue and green colour combinations. These colours are often correlated with higher click through rates."[30] This simplified statement is presented without attribution and it is not supported by any sources; all the contextual information is smoothed away. Galloway also underpins his expertise by reframing everyday content strategies using his idiosyncratic technical and theoretical terms. He says that gaining the early attention of viewers is a "growth catalyst"; a thumbnail driven by clickbait is reframed as the strategy of "statement plus intrigue." When a creator first explains something then goes on to do it, Galloway terms this "drip feeding context." When a creator promises to explain something later, they are engaging the "use of a retention sentence." Galloway attempts to further his legitimacy in this risky field by using exuberant technical language.

Algorithmic experts groom creators toward creating the styles of content that social media platforms want; they provide a volume of information about how to comply with preferred standards of cultural production. For example, experts advise their audience to focus on high picture quality, to make clear and catchy titles, to produce compelling content, and, above all, to keep viewers on the platform. In this way, algorithmic experts are one node in the distributed ideological function of bureaucratized media production described by Bill Ryan, according to whom "formatting serves to rationalise the otherwise arbitrary and idiosyncratic play of imaginary creativity and routinely steers artists toward repetition of the particular cultural forms in which companies have invested."[31] Building on this perspective, Anamik Saha captures the ways that bureaucratic logics can inform self-commodification for creatives, where they "[internalize] corporate promotional techniques."[32]

Evoking this perspective, experts recommend that creators fit into existing, profitable niches on YouTube. In one video (about MrBeast) Paddy Galloway says, "Some people say you should only make the content you want to make before anything else . . . but in my opinion it's kind of like saying a business should only make the products they want and not what the market wants."[33] Although he acknowledges that telling creators they shouldn't make the content they actually want to make is "a bit harsh," Galloway doubles down on the necessity for creators to add their own unique spin to YouTube's dominant culture. In this sense, creative management provides the grammar of creative production—although creatives can use these grammars in their own distinctive vocabulary. Ryan's account of formatting can help us to understand the constraints of YouTube creativity while at the same time accounting for the persistent reality of some forms of originality within creator culture.

It might be unsurprising that purveyors of industry lore are closely aligned with the very same social media platforms that they purport to disrupt. Plenty of algorithmic experts sell their consulting services to Google and YouTube and regularly participate in platform-sponsored events, such as the creator convention VidCon. Many experts are also elite creators who are afforded a "direct line" to YouTube through a "back door" and access to a human partner manager who can explain platform decisions and help with issues or experiences.[34] Algorithmic experts do independently sustain visibility and legitimacy through turning research and conjecture into algorithmic lore—but their success is deeply enmeshed with ensuring good standing with the platforms that they create content for. Although experts regularly make sassy comments about "beating the algorithm," the advice they deliver is intended to work with social media platforms, not against them.

Algorithmic lore involves treating the way that platform algorithms work as a stable reality that can be interpreted and ultimately navigated by (potentially) anyone. In this way, lore is abstracted at the level of an ideal, average creator, tapping into the logics of meritocracy that are central to gaming cultures—the YouTube genre that many algorithmic experts come from and use as examples in their work. For gaming scholar Christopher Paul, the "assessment and adjudication of a player's skill" are often viewed as a fair measure of ability and self-management in gaming.[35] For example, Paddy Galloway describes certain YouTube strategies as "meta," which was initially inscrutable to me (a nongamer). After some Googling, I found that out "META" (at least in this context) means "most effective tactics available," the most effective way to achieve the goal of a game. Experts will also conflate skill at YouTube with gaming skill—for example, in using language like beating an algorithm, and making comments like "[YouTube] does have a leader board."[36] However, we already know that social media platforms like YouTube work unevenly; unsurprisingly, algorithmic lore is unable to account for the issues that marginalized creators typically experience within platformized influencer culture. Paddy Galloway's how-to analysis videos deal almost exclusively with male-presenting YouTube creators in gaming verticals. He has made videos describing the YouTube strategy of a slate of men including MrBeast (who makes stunts and challenges), Dream (who makes Minecraft videos), KSI (a rapper and YouTuber, who started making videos about the football game FIFA), PewDiePie (a very popular gaming YouTuber), and Logan Paul (a YouTuber and now boxer). Of thirty-three videos, Galloway has only made one about a female creator. The relationship between algorithmic prowess and gaming arguably has a "gatekeeping" function, underpinning the designation of legitimate expertise on the algorithm.[37]

When the lessons from the top-tier creators ostensibly represent those who have beaten the algorithm, these findings underserve marginalized platform users. Claims and insights may prove incorrect or difficult to extrapolate for parenting influencers, those creating content about their experiences of disabilities, or people making content on lesbian, gay, bisexual, transgender, and questioning/queer (LGBTQ+) themes, to name but a few genres outside the niches I have discussed hitherto. In fact, the advice given by algorithmic experts could actively work against, or even harm, marginalized creators. For example, we can take Galloway's advice for creators to engage in "trend jacking"—anticipating and using viral trends or creators as video topics. Galloway enthusiastically shares examples of this practice—for example, showing that MrBeast grew his channel by making content insulting PewDiePie, or how YouTube creator AirRack gained views by buying secondhand couches from Logan Paul. These videos capitalize on the high interest that big creators gain across platforms, and by "poking the bear" can draw the attention of their (much larger) fan bases.

This is a simple enough practice for some creators. However, for many others, courting viral attention can bring negative consequences. Most sensible people would not want to visit the home of Logan Paul, a man whose content includes gems like giving CPR to a dead fish and tasering rats. But more than this, as social media scholars Brooke Duffy and Emily Hund have shown, visibility can bring "intensified public scrutiny" for marginalized individuals.[38] Creating content to become visible for dominant platform trends can open creators up to forms of platformized hate and backlash, or what social media scholar Alice Marwick calls "networked harassment."[39] Individuals are particularly vulnerable to harassment when they "challenge normative power structures"—more acutely affecting the experiences of feminists and anti-racist activists, as well as gender nonconforming and LGBTQ+ people.[40]

Marginalized individuals do not "read" as politically neutral; they are more likely to receive harassment when creating content about something that would be viewed as noncontroversial, benign, or nonpolitical if it were created by a white man. As Alice Marwick notes, creators who have (often involuntarily) "marked" themselves as outside a hegemonic norm are subject to more attacks—whether these marked characteristics be those of a woman, a transgender person, a queer person, a Muslim, and so forth.[41] What's more, courting the attention of a particularly vitriolic fan base (like those of Logan Paul or PewDiePie) can bring increased forms of risk for vulnerable individuals. Marginalized creators are often victims of coordinated attacks coming from (perceived) antithetical fandom communities. Social media scholar Colten Meisner shows that fans maliciously flag content in a "bad faith" fashion, which can lead to removals and suspensions.[42] In these cases, nefarious individuals flag a video for ostensibly violating policies, leading to platforms hiding, removing, or reviewing this content. This puts a stop on algorithmic visibility and income in the crucial time right after a video is posted.

## Insider/Outsider Lore

Platforms like YouTube are aware of the value of ostensibly outsider algorithmic information that is compellingly delivered by influencers themselves. Following a particularly heady period of creator backlash in 2020, YouTube minted the position of creator liaison, a job designed to "represent creator interests at the platform." Matt Koval—a YouTube comedy star who had been posting since 2008—was chosen as the first creator liaison. His videos epitomize the goofy skits of nascent YouTube culture, complete with quick-paced editing, a sizable collection of bad wigs, and a bunch of nerdy references. Importantly, Koval had *also* been working at YouTube as a content strategist since 2012. In this way, he neatly fell between platform insider (YouTube employee) and outsider (influencer). After Koval left the job to start his own YouTube consultancy (in other words, to become a full-time YouTube expert!), the second creator liaison—tech YouTuber Rene Ritchie—was hired in 2022. Both creator liaisons fit the profile of an algorithmic expert—they are white-presenting men in their early forties who make content in brand-safe, mainstream verticals like technology.

A big part of the creator liaison's job is to interview YouTube employees on camera, ostensibly to increase platform communication and transparency. However, the information relayed is often not particularly new or illuminating; it rarely diverges from kinds of advice given on YouTube's main creator resources or on YouTube product blogs. A typical example can be found in an interview between Ritchie (who was working as the creator liaison at the time I wrote this) and a YouTube employee called Todd. Todd is the director of growth and discovery; he leads the algorithmic recommendations team.[43] The interview is professionally shot in a sleek, white studio, with a potted fern in the background. Ritchie opens the video by asking a general question about the YouTube algorithm and Todd replies: "The way we've designed the algorithm is actually such that we want to give the audiences the videos and other content that they will be most satisfied by."[44]

Throughout the video, both Todd and Ritchie suggest that creators should simply stop stressing about how platform algorithms work, and instead just make good content that their audience will be satisfied with. This perspective absolves YouTube of technical or cultural responsibility, instead suggesting that creators will mostly experience issues with platform visibility because of poor video quality or audience preference. However, a second video on the Creator Insider channel acknowledges the more complicated reality of YouTube's structuring role for platform workers. In this video, Ritchie interviews a different YouTube employee, also named Todd. The second Todd is the product lead for YouTube's short-form video, the TikTok rival YouTube Shorts. In the video, the duo discuss what counts as a view on Shorts. Todd acknowledges that even arguably stable platform features like views are platform-dependent; "across the industry at large," he says, "different platforms count views in different ways."[45] He states that some platforms may count scrolling through a feed as a view; instead, YouTube treats views as "intent for watching that thing."[46]

Here we can see that even something as simple as a view is measured, reframed, and revalued based on platform governance, business strategy, relationships with advertisers, and, as Todd puts it, "a bunch of other logics behind the scenes."[47] This video acknowledges YouTube's invisible hand, showing how strategic decisions made at various levels throughout the company do create real consequences for those who are dependent on these platforms for their income and visibility. He says that YouTube regularly tweaks the formula for counting a video view because "we don't want people to try and game it."[48] In other words, the platform intentionally creates a challenging working environment by deliberately rearranging platform features just as creators grow used to navigating them.

This version of a smoothed-over industry lore minimizes the real issues that many influencers experience with YouTube's affordances and platform features, which meaningfully affect and shape their working lives. Social media scholar Kelley Cotter has described this kind of talk as "platform gaslighting," whereby social media platforms "leverage their epistemic authority to prompt users to question what they know about algorithms, and thus destabilize the very possibility of credible criticisms."[49] Platforms hold all the cards here because of the limited access creators have to social media platforms like YouTube, relying on restricted, intermittent, top-down information. Instead of raising creator criticisms, this video undermines influencers' concerns about algorithmic media, inviting them to rethink their own theories about why content is not working. Platform attitudes reveal long-standing stereotypes of influencers as potential cheats looking to surreptitiously gain attention or views that are not really deserved. Media studies scholars Caitlin Petre, Brooke Duffy, and Emily Hund have described the pearl-clutching nature of platform communications about "cheating," calling visibility-seeking cultural producers "morally deviant and dishonest."[50] They note that such a framing draws on impossible distinctions between organic and artificial forms of visibility. Content is always technically curated by platforms—there's no such thing as an organic form of visibility. Offhand advice from YouTube employees that "good" content will "naturally" rise to the top minimizes the significance of platforms for visibility and career liability, as well as the natural impulse from those dependent on these platforms to try and make this work for them. Platformization has become increasingly central to cultural producers and creative industries; these individuals are simply trying to reach their audience.

## Lore on Instagram

Instagram has also attempted to provide more accessible insider perspectives to influencers and other users, as many communications about platform changes or issues are disseminated through the personal Instagram page of CEO Adam Mosseri. Mosseri originally came to Facebook as a product designer in 2008, taking the position as Instagram CEO in 2018. He has a polished aesthetic that places him closer to designer than tech bro; he wears luxury basic T-shirts and maximalist heavy-framed glasses. While Mosseri uses his page to answer questions from users about Instagram, his Instagram account also focuses on his personal life. His videos about Instagram sit in a "pinned" rotation of videos under the heading "Dad Life," which includes candid videos of his kids.[51]

Although he uses these images of his life to emphasize his authenticity, the main function of Mosseri's Instagram page is direct-to-camera professional communications about Instagram, albeit from domestic and everyday settings. He films these sessions at home, in his car with AirPod audio crackling, during ad hoc coffee breaks in his office. He responds to a wide range of feedback from both influencers and everyday users in these sessions. A typical user question embedded in Mosseri's Instagram story is more of a comment—"Charging creators for reach!?!"—accompanied by an angry face emoji.[52] Mosseri conspiratorially leans into his phone camera with a rejoinder from his home desk: "A really common misconception is that people think that Instagram suppresses creator reach in order to get people to pay for more reach. But it's not in our business interest to do anything like that. . . . If a creator is creating amazing content and people want to see it, it's in our interest to get that content to as many people as possible because doing so means more people will use Instagram more, and then we can advertise that elsewhere. That's fine, that's great."

Mosseri regularly reiterates the seemingly simple truth that it isn't in Instagram's interest to hide or limit the visibility of content creators. But this answer disguises the complex reality that

Instagram does repeatedly prompt creators to pay to increase their audience visibility and reach. For example, in the following chapter I will show that artists are constantly nudged to pay for Instagram advertising through the promise of reaching a wider audience. Moreover, as of 2023, Meta has been testing paid verification features in Australia—which come with increased algorithmic and audience visibility. While Instagram may not directly suppress audience reach, the company is the one designing how this reach works in the first place. They decide and design the conditions that afford individuals access to their audiences; by the same token, they limit this access too.

The question-and-answer posts that Mosseri makes are often met with hostility by invested Instagram users. Scores of comments posted underneath Mosseri's public Instagram videos criticize the attention that he gives to new features. Comments describe Instagram as "broken" or inconsistent. One commenter writes, "it's the changes you DON'T announce that make us nervous," while another writes, "I'm tired of you and your glasses not listening to us." Someone even offers a nascent idea for a collective Instagram strike: "Everyone should just log out of Instagram for seven days, then maybe they will listen to us."

Mosseri's updates are also picked over by the community on r/Instagram, a Subreddit about the platform with over five hundred thousand members. A typical post offers a furious rejoinder to an Instagram video posted by Mosseri, in which he explains away users' decrease in visibility, saying this is because the audience had lost interest in their content. The Reddit user includes screengrabs of Mosseri's Instagram Story, which is augmented with a personal account of their experience of growing their follower base—from thirty thousand followers to one hundred thousand. "Every time

Mosseri does an AMA this question clearly clogs up his inbox. His reply is always in the vein of 'It's because you suck.' The problem I have with it is the reach issue is not unique to me but seemingly most of the people I interact with who use the platform."[53]

This creator has been in communication with other professional users, patchworking together insights that show a holistic trend on the platform beyond individual experience. They make their private, individualized metrics data public, offering screengrabs that evince a sharp decrease in likes despite a growth in follower numbers. Others chime in with a mix of evidence and supportive comments. The frustration is often directed at Mosseri, who publicly creates content as representative of Instagram, denying the experiences that many influencers have personally had. Because these people are not seen or recognized as technical experts, it is easy to minimize or dismiss them. Many professional influencers don't trust platform communications, and they have worked out responsive and technically sophisticated ways to develop expertise about social media platforms and share these resources. I define these collected sense-making processes as algorithmic gossip.

## Algorithmic Gossip

Algorithmic gossip is a collaborative method used by influencers to track, understand, and map algorithmic changes. The way I understand gossip is drawn from the work of philosopher Karen Adkins, who has called it a "feminist epistemology," which means a theory of how we come to know what we know. Adkins positions gossip as a kind of loose, emotionally charged talk, which is often associated with women and dismissed by institutions, organizations, or even scientific disciplines, which "prefer public, neutral, widely agreeable standards of knowledge."[54] However, in practice, gossip should not be seen as separate from the kind of collaborative talk that generally takes place in the "construction of knowledge."[55] To give an example of this, Adkins talks about the importance of loose talk in scientific discovery. Scientists discuss their findings or track down their competitors in the corridors of labs or even at the bar. This kind of talk is not separate from the official communication involved in doing science; in fact, these conversations about problems, ideas, and solutions are productive, generative, and scientific. I have found gossip, understood in this sense, to be a particularly important framework in the context of influencer culture, because it helps us understand how talk dismissed as personal and emotional can actually be highly technical.

Theorists working in science and technology studies have written about the ways in which everyday people develop theories about how platform algorithms work.[56] Such theories can be directive—for example, some users of the travel website Booking.com had a hunch that the platform was artificially inflating the ratings their customers were giving to hotels. They worked together to input reviews and monitor changes in aggregate scores, sharing their findings.[57] Together, they reverse-engineered the algorithm. While this writing about everyday algorithmic theorizing informs my approach, influencers represent a unique case of professionals working in an established, platform-adjacent field. Their income depends on successfully negotiating visibility on proprietary platforms. So while influencers' feminized output often positions them outside the technical, their work is contingent on algorithmic visibility. They develop a sophisticated understanding of social media platforms, inform the culture of platforms, and shape how they work.

Algorithmic gossip involves a mixture of personal experience with directed experiments and tests that fall under three broad categories. The first is multivariate testing—testing a hypothesis by changing multiple variables such as hashtags, video length, or the time of day that content is posted. Creators will often share evidence of these tests using screen grabs of their metrics, showing how engagement or views have been altered in accord with the aims of the experiment. Based on the results, creators hypothesize what hashtags to use, how many seconds an Instagram Reel should be, or the best time of day to post to gain audience attention. A second category of test is account hopping, where creators check the visibility of their content through a secondary account. This may be their own secondary account or someone else's—like a friend or an acquaintance from a forum. Influencers engage in this test by posting ephemeral content like Instagram Stories or Instagram grid posts, and check that this content is promoted to a secondary account that follows the original one. This strategy is also used to check if metrics information (the number of views or likes content gets) is accurate. For example, one creator complained on Reddit about the lack of views from an Instagram Story they posted: "I even watched my story from another account to test if it's showing, and it still says there's been no views. Anyone understand this?" Responses commiserate with their own experiences or offer explanations about a potential time lag in view data. The final genre of test involves third-party tools. These can include software designed to generate unique hashtags and increase visibility or to check for shadow banning, which will ostensibly show users whether their audience reach is being deliberately limited by Instagram or not. The success of this kind of approach is far from settled; the efficacy of these tools is regularly called into question on forums like r/Instagram. The consensus is that they are often ineffective or even fake.

Algorithmic gossip is intimate. It often requires membership in a particular community or group—for example, r/Instagram or other forums and Facebook groups. Talk in these spaces is practiced with care. Advice can be direct and caustic, but a supportive thread runs through the comments and responses. Although it is focused, gossip is nestled within a wider conversation about (in this case) content creation and the everyday life of being an influencer; it hits the "median point between random and agenda-driven"; it can be both chaotic and instrumental.[58] On Reddit forums, in Facebook groups, and in public conversations, individuals gossip because their experiences are minimized, trivialized, and not believed by platforms and official sources of technical information. Information provided by social media platforms—in this case, Adam Mosseri—routinely minimizes and dismisses the issues that are being raised by professional platform users. Gossip is both a strategic and a soft negotiation of a deep power imbalance within platform work. Influencer creep brings an expansion of this inequality and, with it, a necessity for other creative practitioners to draw from strategies raised and finessed within influencer cultures to navigate the extension of platformized creative work.

## Conclusion

Although algorithmic lore and algorithmic gossip may overlap, there are some key differences between the two. While algorithmic gossip is a collective strategy undertaken by those who often describe feelings of powerlessness, algorithmic lore is produced at the meso-level by algorithmic experts who are often ostensibly affiliated with social media platforms. Algorithmic lore is sharp and organizationally focused; advice is designed to help creators efficiently become compliant with platform requirements. Algorithmic lore is a saleable product in itself. Creators produce videos about this lore in order to garner their own visibility and promote their own consultancy, courses, and products. In its association with male-coded YouTube genres, such as technology and gaming, algorithmic lore is information that is about something that cannot be known; however, in its design and distribution, it is widely believed.

Solutions promoted by algorithmic experts are rooted in a unifying meritocratic approach that ignores the diversity of experiences, topics, and standpoints held by creators. They ignore the dismissive or simplistic language used by platforms to minimize the experiences raised by professional platform users, as well as the lack of recourse when issues are raised that deeply affect individuals who have proof of inconsistency and errors. Their belief in optimization is legitimated by the invocation of technical language—which often elides the ways that data are constructed and readied through colonial legacies—and they bypass the "violence, injustice and poverty"[59] that data management and processing systems are predicated on. Influencers have a strong affective reaction when their issues are repudiated using technical language; they are angry because they are often dismissed.

In his work on creative industries, Anamik Saha points out that strategies preceding optimization, such as rationalization and formatting, have long dovetailed with the racializing logics of capitalism. He notes that "what appear as purely commercially rationalized and race-neutral processes are, in fact, deeply racial in their effects."[60] We can see echoes of these effects in the optimization advice given by algorithmic experts, as individuals are urged to follow narrow pathways of acceptable content production dictated by the political and economic relationships between social media platforms, advertisers, and media stakeholders. When individuals share their own personal and individual experiences through the technique of algorithmic gossip, they are dismissed as too emotional or conspiratorial.

Platforms are capricious, inconsistent, and risky—and this increasingly affects our working lives. Engaging in optimization requires time, labor, and hope. Professional influencers have been aspiring to visibility through social media platforms because they must successfully achieve visibility there in order to do their jobs. The following chapter looks at how this requirement creeps outward, how artists use platforms to build an audience, to connect with intermediaries, and to sell this work. I examine the specific ways that optimization is taken up within art worlds, reflecting on the possibilities that algorithmic visibility strategies may afford but also the limited and individualized pathways that optimization really offers through the platformization of work and personal connection.

# 2 *Artists*

## Optimization, but Make It Aesthetic

In 2021, the painter Isaac Pelayo appeared on the *Artist Business Plan* podcast to "share an awesome masterclass" on "how to use algorithms to your advantage."[1] The episode is titled "Six Figure Artist"—an art world term used to demarcate successful artists who sell their work over the threshold of one hundred thousand dollars. Pelayo appeared on the podcast to let the world know how Instagram facilitated his entry to this club.

During the podcast, Pelayo acknowledged that Instagram's visibility architecture can be frustrating, claiming that "the algorithm has been a challenging obstacle." But, importantly, he also saw the algorithm as an opportunity. About a year prior to this podcast appearance, an impromptu change of style in his artwork garnered Pelayo a surprising boost in audience engagement and algorithmic visibility, which caused a permanent change in his practice. He moved from classical portraiture to a newer, Instagram-friendly approach, integrating street art, pop art, and expressionism. He said, "I ran with it, which has been wildly successful." Throughout the interview, Pelayo mentions the familiar tenets of influencer creep—advising listeners to create more artwork more frequently and to engage heavily with their followers and fans on Instagram.

However, the point that the host of the podcast and the CEO of Superfine Art Fair, Alex Mitow, continually returns to is that Pelayo had the flexibility to change his artistic style according to the bell curve of audience engagement on Instagram. As Mitow puts it, "Part of your formula for Instagram is just making higher quality work. . . . You've landed on this new style that really resonates with people. . . . Every artist listening should take that as a cue. If they are using the tools that are at their disposal on Instagram and they still aren't seeing the results that they're wanting to see, then maybe that's a challenge to think about what it is that people want to be seeing and want to be buying and adapting their work [for social media], evolving their work to reflect that better."

The advice here is that those unsuccessfully pursuing algorithmic visibility should work toward simply making better art. But owing to a lack of platform transparency, creators cannot know whether their work is being poorly engaged with because audiences don't care for it or whether it is being technically suppressed. How can they ever know for sure? Is the problem the algorithm or is it the audience?

This chapter focuses on the ways that artists negotiate this uncertainty and strive to optimize their artworks for algorithmic visibility. Throughout, I show how these techniques often follow the strategies, practices, and tactics developed within influencer culture, including following algorithmic lore and sharing algorithmic gossip. Ultimately, artists work with distribution systems in mind, and they shape their work accordingly. As sociologist Howard Becker observes, "art works always bear the marks of the systems that distribute them."[2] Owing to the platformization of culture and creative industries, art must make sense for Instagram (which affords its distribution) just as much as it must make sense for the consumers who will eventually buy it.[3]

## Algorithms and Taste

The question of what draws audiences to creative work precedes algorithmic media, and sociologists have long attempted to disentangle how taste, preference, and value function in creative industries. Core sociologists working in this area have historically highlighted the role of intermediaries like critics, gallerists, dealers, and marketers in determining what makes art art. Intermediaries pull from their own personal preference, connections, networks, training, and expertise, all qualities underpinned by what sociologist Pierre Bourdieu calls symbolic capital.[4] Symbolic capital is associated with a "distant, self-assured relation to the world and to others which presupposes objective assurance."[5] These intermediaries work to stabilize a highly volatile and uncertain market using their "aesthetic confidence" to leverage and advertise their "superior taste."[6] Bourdieu tracks this forward to show the ways that elites—namely, those who can confidently claim legitimate aesthetic taste—forge the "the social conditions of production in the field of social agents (eg museums, galleries, academies etc) which help to define and produce the works of art."[7] Bourdieu's work shows how artists, organizations, and institutions struggle over the discourse of art as they seek to legitimize and assign value to artists and their works.

Now the grip of more traditional art world intermediaries has loosened, owing in large part to the increasing centrality of Instagram.[8] Incumbents can bypass gallerists or dealers and directly market and sell their work to global audiences on the platform. The artists I have spoken to rely just as heavily on Instagram visibility as influencers do in order to earn a living. Instagram takes up the distanced, objective role of the traditional curatorial intermediary—and creates an algorithmic hierarchy of visibility for artists and artworks. The platform can offer networks with audiences (potential customers and income) or the chance to catch the attention of creative intermediaries who can facilitate career advancement. For example, Klara, a textile artist, told me that she oriented her Instagram toward everyday audiences and the "fashion-promotion sphere"—that is, magazines and designers. Cara, a weaver, wanted to reach both general audiences and top-tier interior designers. And finally, Chloe, an illustrator, directed her attention to visibility for both everyday audiences and commissioning editors working at newspapers, magazines, and book publishers.

At least some intermediary taste-making within art worlds is now taken up by Instagram's recommendation algorithms—automated technical architectures that are (importantly) engineered by humans. Anthropologist Nick Seaver shows that taste is now an "instrumented technique, mediated and organised through countless devices."[9] In his ethnographic study of an algorithmic music recommendation company, Seaver found that engineers who work on algorithms see their role as helping users to navigate an unmanageable glut of cultural products just like art critics before them. Platform workers structure and tend to technical systems—in so doing, closing and opening potential art that users can encounter—exacting a form of subtle power through "modulation."[10]

Algorithmic streaming infrastructure has thus ended up shaping how, for example, music gets made. Artists employ distinct technical and cultural techniques of standing out, oriented toward music streaming platforms.[11] The influence of platform architectures and cultures on artworks has been dubbed by music studies scholar Jeremy Wade Morris "platform effects."[12] For musicians this can mean turning to specific generic conventions, or deciding on a certain length of song or chorus structure. On Spotify, for example, artists are compelled to immediately hit listeners with hooks in their songs to grab listeners' attention as a song opens, and stop them skipping the track. Songs are built around having to keep listeners' interest for thirty seconds in order for Spotify to count it as a listen.[13] The concept of platform effects captures how the architectures and affordances of distribution influence the choices artists make about their work. For artists, their thoughts about Instagram can influence how they size and structure their pieces, what colors they use, or what level of detail they engage with.

However, those who design or enact algorithms may deliberately minimize their curatorial or taste-making role within data assemblages. For example, the engineers Seaver talked to insisted they were in charge of helping natural forms of listener exploration along, "not how the business works or how users behave."[14] This kind of sentiment was also shared by Instagram's CEO Adam Mosseri, whom you may recall from the previous chapter. In a typical question-and-answer session held on Instagram Stories, Mosseri responds to a question about why a creator's reach has been significantly reduced. He minimizes any technical responsibility that Instagram holds in algorithmic recommendation, saying "it's possible that your audience is more interested in other things this week."

I object to Mosseri's point. Actually, platform workers *do* have a significant role in the distribution of cultural products. In practice, there is no such thing as raw data or unmediated access to audiences via a platform like Instagram. Sociologists Anna Jobin and Malte Zietwitz critically probe the use of metaphors—for example, "fresh" or "organic"—to describe certain results from recommendation algorithms. They argue that all results returned from algorithmic media are the "carefully constructed product of design and use."[15] Algorithmic results are coproduced by those who work in strategic management at social media companies, the everyday technical and administrative workers at platforms, the advertisers who fund them, and the platform power users who finesse and shape dominant social media cultures. Each of these groups informs the kinds of work that can be produced and made visible, in addition to the discourse that surrounds the legitimization of work and its value. The algorithmic advice to simply evolve work to better meet the needs of the audience is disingenuous. Artists using Instagram cannot sidestep the platform's curatorial and ordering role. The demands to be visible according to the specific forms of architecture and affordances of Instagram have vastly changed artistic creation for the artists whose stories appear in this book and beyond.

## Optimization and Shaping the Artwork

The artists I spoke to had a wide range of algorithmic gossip about the kind of art that works well on Instagram. Bold and simple content at a high level of abstraction was seen to be most suitable for the competitive Instagram attention economy. Lena, a textile artist, told me the following: "I think, if you want a wide reach, you need to be easily digestible." Artists knew that their artworks would likely blur within a glut of competing content from their audiences' friends, influencers, and brands. Quick access, then, was seen as essential: work had to be easy to identify and engage with during a split-second window of potential visibility. Aoife, an illustrator, considered her blocky, postmodern, large-scale murals to be particularly social media friendly. As she told me, "I would say that because my work is so visual and very colorful, and usually quite bold, that lends itself really well to Instagram and social media and that quick scrolling that people do and like things as they go past." Mary, a weaver, also felt that large shapes translated well because of their simplicity. "What I'm doing," she said, "is . . . drawing a form. It's like I'm drawing a really large-scale thing and I can get really beautiful curves and lovely dark colors, so that is really good."

Participants shared that metalwork was one of the most challenging art forms to represent on social media. Aoife said her murals were easier to engage with precisely because they are not an "intricate piece of jewelry." As she put it, "there's not a lot of detail there to inspect or appreciate," and the work can even look better online than in real life. Similarly, Mary shared sympathy for people who were making "small, fine work," referring to jewelry as "tiny, shiny awkward things." Metalworkers, in particular, lamented the lack of opportunities for ancillary social media content production around delicate work. They found it challenging to engage in the influencer genre of a "flat lay"—that is, a content genre involving taking a bird's-eye photograph of artfully arranged products, popularized by beauty and fashion bloggers.[16] Maye, a goldsmith, talked about how disheartening it was to stylize and photograph her work as a flat lay: "When someone who makes pottery sell seven items . . . it looks like they've sold loads. I sold seven items, but they looked really tiny. They took so much time." The difficulty in visually representing certain work within Instagram's affordances prompted some artists to organize work into an imagined hierarchy of what was postable. Lily, who curates found objects, discussed a range of antique glassworks that she had decided not to post. She said, "I know if someone saw them in person, they'd just buy them . . . but for me to make that look good, they're not worth posting on my Instagram because I won't get any hits." The logics of what kind of details could be appreciated via the image size were determined by the quality of images, which was itself afforded by the technical features and cultures of Instagram.[17] Would audiences be able to appreciate small details on a phone screen? Would the image make sense?

Artists experienced the platform as a kind of push and pull. They felt compelled to upload enough content to consistently engage with their audiences without either irritating them or being punished by Instagram. They didn't want to be seen as spammy—that is, simply being too much, posting excessively, or asking too explicitly for engagement. Engaging the right kind of visibility was a precarious tightrope walk. Artists created their own strategies to help guide the posting process. Lucia, for example, a ceramicist, told me that she makes sure to keep posts below a certain number of images: "I try to do a maximum three pictures, because if you do more, on the third picture you can see people are exiting." Lena, who makes textile art, attributed the push and pull to the platform rather than to her audience. She felt that Instagram wanted her to post a certain number of pictures, which would then be rewarded with audience visibility. After a certain amount of time, however, the platform wanted her to stop, so it would reduce her visibility by not recommending her content across the platform or even to her devoted followers. As she put it, "Always the first one gets loads. So it feels like it's encouraging me. And then

phaedraclothing                                             ...

Liked by **lenniebeare** and **339 others**

**phaedraclothing** Hello! It's me! Taken by my bezzie
@zestinferna ages ago! In the hopes that the algorithm will
look favourably upon me and grant me access to at least 10%
of my actual followers! All in the hopes of letting you know
that my online shop opens TOMORROW FRIDAY 3RD
JANUARY at 6pm GMT!

FIGURE 1. Deva, who makes custom clothing, includes a self-portrait on her Instagram in order to solicit algorithmic attention. Courtesy of Deva O'Neill.

the more I post in that period of time, the more [Instagram] is like, 'no, shut up.'"

Ava, a painter, told me about the effects of Instagram's algorithm on her ability to experiment as well as on her creative process, and how that algorithm had shaped her artistic practice. She told me that throughout her career she had mostly painted landscapes but switched to portraiture (at least in part) because her paintings of faces received more engagement on Instagram and opened her work up to wider audiences. Her experiences now were shaped by her position as a Black artist sharing her portraiture of Black women on Instagram. "This is going to sound really bad," she said. "When I post light-skinned Black girls the response is better. Yes . . . [*laughter*] . . . But I try to put all the different shades and post . . . But even if you go through my posts, you are going to see the ones who have more likes are the ones that are light-skinned."

Ava's lived experiences shaped her understanding of Instagram's regimes of racialized visibility: by scrolling through her own feed she could draw a very simple connection between skin color and the engagement that images received. The increased visibility of images of lighter-skinned women is likely a product of the algorithmic amplification of existing racism and colorism, referred to as "technological microaggressions."[18] Ava's experiences echo accounts from scholars and activists, who have also found that social media algorithms do not offer accurate recognition and visibility to all subjects, often missing or wrongly categorizing people of color.[19] As Daniela Angostinho, a scholar of visual culture, notes, "racializing processes underlying algorithmic recognition have to be taken into account in any reconsideration of what it means to be visible or to claim invisibility under algorithmic life."[20] As Instagram plays a wider role in art worlds, we must investigate how the algorithmic inequalities baked into their technologies shape the visibility afforded to artworks, artists, and art processes—and how this might influence art, practice, and work.

As Instagram becomes a central stakeholder within these interconnected spaces, artists consider what is suitable for posting, what may go viral, or what is most likely to net engagement. Algorithmic lore about what Instagram wants informs the process of artistic production as the platform becomes increasingly central to distribution and networking in art worlds. Against a backdrop of platformized uncertainty, artists seek to create content aimed at social media visibility, although they also complain that optimization strategies make Instagram feel standardized and stagnant. Interaction with Instagram is underpinned by an atmosphere of anxiety, as the artists monitor and chastise themselves for posting insufficiently or too much. As Fern, another ceramicist, told me, "it feels like something has to be presented daily just to remind people that you're there," moments later reflecting on this point thus: "I don't know if that's true, or if that's addiction, who knows?" Like influencers, artists operate under a "visibility bind," where they have to navigate a consistent level of effective exposure without opening themselves up to scrutiny or platform punishment.[21] They have strong feelings about Instagram that point to the centrality of the platform and that guide their participation, as well as their wider practice, in myriad ways.

## Hitting the Content Baseline

Influencer creep means creators must maximize the value of the making process in order to meet a content baseline—that is, what is felt to be an acceptable minimum of content to post. One strategy involves capturing work-in-process content to post on Instagram. Producing Instagram content becomes a priority that is now arguably wholly embedded in the process of making. For the artists I spoke to, the process of capturing ancillary content is far from simple or organic. Rather, it is labor-intensive, and it shapes techniques of making and the embodied artistic process. Particularly when craft is visually interesting, moments of making cannot be wasted. And if a process isn't visually interesting, it needs to become so.

Gertrude, also a ceramicist, told me that she often films live videos from her studio. She feels the format has worked well on Instagram, and reasons that it is also something she would be interested in as a viewer: "I do also enjoy watching people make things." Annie, a metalworker, also uses live videos; in particular, she embraces the interactive features of Instagram to build a relationship with her audience. "I literally have the camera on me whilst I'm making," she explained. "If I'm making something—for example, if I'm making a ring, trying to decide what stones to use—I might have a quiz or a poll and I'm like, 'choose which one?" I try to draw more people in that way."

Illustrators discussed the importance of capturing their processes on video so they could create time lapses, a popular genre on Instagram. Chloe told me that she has a "little arm camera phone thing" that she puts over her work while she draws. Celina goes one step further and wears a head-mounted GoPro while she is working. As she put it, "I was doing a lot of time lapse, because of the kind of interaction and reach that they get. But it gets really difficult to draw. There is like . . . a camera in your head." Content here becomes a valuable secondary commodity produced during the artistic process. Time and resources must be maximized for two

FIGURE 2. Ceramicist Liv Cave-Sutherland documents the glazing of a cylindrical vase in real time. Courtesy of Liv & Dom.

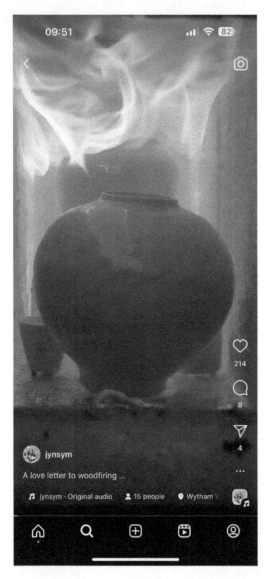

FIGURE 3. Ceramicist Jynsym Ong wood-fires some of her work. Courtesy of Jynysym Ong (@jynsym, jynsymong.com).

outputs—the art and the content designed to promote the art. But this kind of promotional content does not always naturally or organically flow from the production process. In practice, the imperative to create a high-engagement Instagram video interrupts and transforms the physical nature of artistic practice. Balancing the weight of a camera while drawing or being anchored in place by a mechanical arm changes how you work. This is important when creativity is seen by many as a physical process that is widely impacted by the body, technologies, and physical space.

Still, algorithmic lore tells us that we should maximize the value of every day through transforming our simple activities (such as eating and breathing) into content. This is laid out in a detailed handbook published by Laura Bitoui, an algorithmic expert, on how to produce "B-Roll" content for use and reuse on Instagram. In the handbook, Bitoui, who identifies as an "Instagram educator," writes, "I like to think of [B-Roll] as the supplementary content that I mix in with other pieces . . . a personalized stock video library."[22] Her handbook recommends a long list of opportunities for creating this kind of content during the mundane moments of everyday life—for example, walking and moving between spaces, doing one's morning routine, performing one's day-to-day operations and administrative tasks, sitting behind a desk or in meetings, closing down for the day, traveling, or taking a quiet moment for reflection. Bitoui advises that one should be mindful of space, composition, and lighting, and that one should "record a variety of angles and perspectives of the same action."

The handbook frames B-Roll as something a person can grab simply and quickly. Ultimately, though, creating a sufficient volume of well-presented and high-quality content is not something one can do naturally or easily; this is laborious and time-consuming work. People working alone are required to use multiple cameras to get multiple angles or (more likely) to restage the supposedly everyday moments they are ostensibly performing spontaneously. Some of the artists I spoke to had developed ad hoc schedules with other artists who worked in the studio to help them capture content. But for many others, documenting the working process presented real challenges. Cara told me that the slow pace of weaving evaded the kind of exciting transformative content that made Instagram compelling. "You need a lot of time," she told me, "which means it's not so attractive to, like, make videos or many new products easily, where, like, a ceramicist can produce dozens of pots in a week. I can only make one product. So, there is so much process in it and so many steps that it's very difficult to document that in the high-speed social media. Really difficult."

A snippet of algorithmic gossip from Maye captures the challenges of creating and maintaining a content baseline. Maye believed that Instagram's algorithms could determine when she posted work that wasn't freshly made. "[What] I've found," she said, "is that if I post old work, not old pictures, but if I've made an old work and posted it, it doesn't get as many likes as it did then, because I think the algorithm also probably knows. 'Oh, I've seen this object before, so I'm not going to put it on the feed as much again.'"

In their regular, methodical interactions with social media platforms, creative workers may gain a sharper, more holistic understanding of how platforms work than platform designers and engineers. There is evidence to suggest that Maye's theory could be accurate. In an Instagram Story update, Adam Mosseri spoke about limiting the visibility of reshared or reposted content on Instagram: "we are going to do more to value original content more," he claimed. Whether the platform can discern that an art object had been shared before with a different visual, going beyond simply recognizing a reposted image, is unsettled. It is algorithmic gossip—a theory based on Maye's technical knowledge and understanding of Instagram. However, since this theory guides Maye's work and practice, its accuracy doesn't matter. In practice, gossip about capricious and changeable platforms could be right or wrong, but either way, it guides and shapes the way that individuals interact with platforms, as well as the labor, strategies, and efforts this sustains. Maye feels pressured to make newer, fresher work to share in order to garner visibility on Instagram.

Algorithmic experts, who sell commercially oriented educational algorithmic lore, offer sympathy to business owners struggling to maintain an acceptable content baseline. Bitoui's website notes that her job is to "calm the chaos of marketing yourself on Instagram" and to "avoid needless overwhelm."[23] At least in part, acknowledging the frustrations of influencer creep is a sales tactic. The free content Bitoui shares usually involves some kind of upselling—for example, advertising content creation courses or personal consultancy, a kind of time share presentation at an algorithmic Disneyland.

Some artists I spoke to were engaging with these kinds of commercial algorithmic organizations. Annie was a member of a paid search engine optimization Facebook group. For a monthly fee, she could post her questions related to algorithmic issues to the experts in the group, and they would give her suggestions to help resolve her issues. Nora, a goldsmith, had recently hired a luxury marketing firm to help develop her marketing strategy. This was expensive. When I spoke to her in 2020, it cost her upwards of six hundred dollars a month. The individuals who had the budget available for this kind of dedicated or special algorithmic advice were in the minority.

Artists turned to a range of professional arts and crafts organizations and nonprofits that offer specialist social media advice for those in creative industries. Several artists mentioned interacting with the Design Trust—an "online business school" for "designers, makers and professional business owners."[24] In the marketing and social media section of their website, they recommend that artists regularly create and publish blog posts that document their processes, including illustrative images and sketches of works in progress. They also suggest a loose version of trend jacking, discussed by algorithmic experts in the previous chapter, recommending that artists follow "timely" topics to help inspire and structure their content. This means keeping on top of key events in the design calendar—for example, when the color-matching company Pantone releases their color of the year, or newsworthy events, popular TV shows, interest days (like World Book Day), and public holidays. This requires artists to be alert and attentive to social and cultural water cooler moments. In line with influencer creep, the Design Trust's advice also demands the inclusion of what is personal and affective. In a post recommending twenty-four ideas for social media posts, examples include where you live, your role models, your quirks, what's special or different about you, and styling tips. The guidance is always recommending that you do more; it's peppered with needling and provocative questions, such as "Do you post your blog posts and product pages?" with the provocative follow-up: "Consistently?"

Although there is a lot of detail on the Design Trust's pages, their social media advice seems curiously out of step with the contemporary strategies used by influencers. For example, they talk about blogs *a lot*. Their website suggests that artists publish blog posts using trending keywords to answer client questions, and pitch guest posts for other people's blogs. After reading this advice, I was struck by how long it was since I had come across the phrase "guest post," which, to be fair, was a very common visibility strategy in the early days of the blogosphere. Bloggers would write a post to share their niche or expertise for another blog. The host blog got some free content out of this exchange, and the guest blogger got exposure and grew their own audience. The premise of audience sharing continues to be used by influencers, who use collaborative posts with peers across platforms to consolidate audiences. But the platformization of the influencer industry has led to a decline in the use of blogs within influencer culture.[25] The visual and textual affordances of blogging have been absorbed by platforms like Instagram, which have centralized an available audience and offer additional features for visibility. Blogging is also an uncommon practice in art worlds; it wasn't mentioned by any of the participants I interviewed.

In this sense we can see a lag in the advice given by arts organizations like the Design Trust. The drive toward influencer content is there, but the recommendations are outdated. Reaching backward, we can identify influencers as the proverbial canaries in the coal mine: the advice shared now among contemporary creative communities is anchored by strategies designed and finessed by influencers in the early aughts. Influencer creep therefore reorders intermediaries and expertise within art worlds. Artists seeking information about how to garner visibility and legitimacy on social media platforms are led to search beyond the art school, and under influencer creep, they work to source information and test visibility using strategies commonly used in content creation economies, like following and hiring algorithmic experts.

## Algorithmic Tests and Experiments

The artists I interviewed engaged in the kinds of algorithmic tests and experiments that were developed by content creators, but they tailored these to the requirements of art worlds. One experiment mirrored the kind of account hopping discussed in chapter 1. It involved testing algorithmic reach and audience engagement by toggling between a personal and a business account. Instagram business accounts are designed for commercial use and they include features like post scheduling, audience analytics, and shoppable links. Social media scholars Lee McGuigan and Emily Hund have shown how these kinds of commercial features of Instagram are part of the platform being optimized for "shoppability"—that is to say, fully integrated with the demands and needs of marketing firms and retail industries, particularly for Instagram's targeted advertising architecture.[26] After all, marketers fund Instagram through advertising dollars, and they demand these features and functions, including real-time performance data about their return on investment. The analytics data provided are designed for these advertisers, retailers, and brands—together they form an "immense bloc of organised power" influencing the processes of platformization that affect our social and cultural lives.[27] While some of my participants did find the additional Instagram business features to be beneficial, they were suspicious that Instagram owner Meta had surreptitious financial motives in pushing them toward commercially oriented accounts. A widely held line of algorithmic gossip was that Meta deliberately reduces free or organic algorithmic reach on business accounts in an attempt to pressure and cajole business owners into paying for targeted advertising.

Lucilla, a ceramicist, told me that she received a bump in visibility when she first set up her Instagram, which was then followed by a sharp decrease in audience engagement. "I used to have 200 to 250 likes on a post when I posted it. Recently, it's been 50. So I know it's the algorithm, because they want you to pay." Rose, who runs an art market with another person, believed that Instagram depressed content visibility because the company hoped to lure business owners into a consistent pattern of paying for targeted advertising. She felt that giving in just once sent a signal to Instagram that you were willing to pay and that the platform would no longer need to give you free access to an audience, instead keeping you dependent on their ad products. In our interview, Rose couched her claims with the caveat of "conspiracy theory" to address the speculative nature of what she was suggesting; she felt, however, that she could give evidence to prove her point based on her own significant experience with the platform. As she put it, "After we had ... paid Instagram advertising, our organic Instagram engagement massively fell, and it took months to rebuild it back up. And there are so many, what's the word, conspiracy theories about what Instagram does, and blah-blah-blah, but, genuinely, it fell off a cliff and it took us months to rebuild it."

Dani, a screen printer, conducted account-hopping visibility tests based on whether her Instagram account was registered for personal or business use by checking if content she posted from her business account appeared on her personal Instagram feed. Regularly, it wasn't there: "I would sign into Instagram from my personal account, and even though I follow my business account, nothing was showing." After switching her account to a personal one, Dani realized that some of the business account features she lost were actually essential for her growing screen-printing business—she needed its built-in platform shopping and commerce functions. So she switched back. Despite keeping her business account, she told me "anecdotally, we were getting more engagement" when using a personal account. Based on her daily experiences of posting and monitoring interactions, Dani was confident that she did not have the same access to her own audience that was afforded by using a personal account.

Instagram for business is not designed for small-scale, independent creative workers. Instead, platform analytics function to meet the needs and capabilities of top-tier brands operating at global scale. These brands can employ expensive third-party agencies to manage the complexity of their targeted social media marketing. As independent small business owners, artists did not find Instagram's audience analytics information to be useful. Lucilla, for example, compared Instagram analytics functions to the fast-moving complexity of a "board in the New York Stock Exchange." Artists found information provided about their audience patchy, shallow, and functionally useless, and they often decided to instigate their own investigations into who their buying audience actually was. Klara told me that she often searched for her customers on Instagram to check who they were. Fern also searched for those who bought her work: "Is that unethical?" she asked. "Probably, but where are they? It's just like, oh my God, Lauren. Lauren's bought something, who's Lauren? Immediately looking them up." In cultural and creative industries, artists often view their audiences as communities and even coproducers in a shared endeavor. They seek to understand and manage the complexity of their preferences, motivations, and relationships.

Influencer creep accelerates and widens the demands for sociality from art worlds. The platformization of creative industries increases access to audiences and with it artists' need to enact what social media scholar Nancy Baym calls "relational labour,"[28] a tightly managed push and pull of intimacy with those who connect with their work, while also striving to protect privacy and maintain boundaries. Relational pressures are further heightened under the normalization of authenticity and intimacy within influencer work, a pattern I will discuss more completely in the following chapters. Like influencers, artists now need to maintain a "perceived interconnectedness" with their audiences— integrating them into what digital anthropologist Crystal Abidin calls an impression of "exclusive, intimate exchange."[29] These exchanges are designed to maintain an illusion of closeness. Under the pressure of a drive toward "reciprocated intimacies" sharpened and developed by influencers, artists are motivated to connect with their audiences.[30] Chloe said that she did look at analytics data; however, she found the "actual identity of these people from messages and stuff." What Chloe refers to as the "actual identity" is the thick and complex information about preferences, interests, and specific details that cannot be provided by analytics tools designed for a bird's-eye view at huge scale. This information is useful as value in art worlds and it is inherently social; it is also based on highly integrated networks of cultural intermediaries, buyers, and sellers. The complexities of identity in networking and relationship building cannot be represented by social media platforms that are driven to offer higher and higher volumes of granular data—which is often overly generalized, inaccurate, and poorly communicated.

## "I Tried to Find Help but There's No Help on Instagram": Platform Dependency and Broken Trust

The adversarial relationship between influencers and platforms hinges on a deep lack of trust. Platforms set the terms of engagement, but they don't play fair—they provide incomplete or misleading information in a one-sided manner that Kelley Cotter has referred to as "black box gaslighting."[31] Artists also feel deeply suspicious about the information platforms provide to them. For example, they question the accuracy and value of paid targeted advertising. Many artists find that the targeted advertising they pay for to attract a wider audience is instead reaching their existing Instagram followers—people who had already voluntarily elected to see updates from them. Maye told me, "People who were already following me were saying that they were getting my adverts. And it's like, well that's not who should be getting my adverts, which is weird." Klara offered the same theory from an audience perspective: "I see, [from] people who I already follow, their ads all the time, while I don't that often see ads by people that I don't follow."

In these cases, artists felt duped into paying for access to an audience that they thought was rightfully theirs. As Fern put it, "[I have] literally just given Instagram, which otherwise is free, sixteen pounds. Why did I do that?" Instagram's affordances ostensibly allow creators to build a following, but they do not guarantee to account holders that these followers will be notified when they post something, or even that they will be shown the content that creators post. On the topic of account following, the Instagram terms of use are addressed to platform users—in other words, to those who are more likely to be following rather than accruing the followers. These terms claim that "your Instagram feed includes posts from accounts you follow," and speak of "suggested posts and ads from businesses that may be interesting and relevant to you." This means users will be shown content from accounts they are following, but not all of them.

Regarding the ways in which the feed is prioritized and ordered, Instagram says that its "technology uses a variety of ways, or signals, to determine the order of posts in your feed." These signals include users' activity (whether or not they have commented or liked a post), the wider popularity of the posts, and whether or not a user has historically interacted with the post creator. In other words, simply following an account is not a sufficient indicator that users want this account's content on their feed; nor are account holders owed access to any following they have built. Instagram's approach here is an example of what Caitlin Petre, Brooke Duffy, and Emily Hund call "platform paternalism," a phenomenon whereby platforms cast themselves as neutral actors who are simply looking out for the best interest of their users.[32] Although individuals have explicitly elected to follow an account for updates, the platform creates additional hurdles and requirements in the service of improving user experience. Because Instagram didn't actually send the artists' content to their core following, the artists themselves felt that Instagram was failing to meet the very basic premise of the following/follower feature.

Both artists' and influencers' relationships to platforms are underpinned by a deep anxiety and stress about the possibility of losing account access, a painstakingly built following, and the potential for wider visibility. Lucilla told me that Instagram had deleted her business account shortly before our interview. "They've changed some rules, some legal stuff," she told me. "And because it didn't have a personal account connected to me, [my business account] just disappeared. I tried to find help but there's no help on Instagram." Lucilla's observations echo widespread complaints from other influencers about the lack of support they receive from Instagram; platforms maintain complicated systems of governance that are often inscrutable to users.

Because of the central function of Instagram in selling directly to audiences and in addition to the problems of reaching professional intermediaries, the risks of losing access to the platform are acute. Chloe, an illustrator, put it this way: "Quite a few friends of mine have had their Instagram deleted for no apparent reason . . . so I feel like if you're going to put all your eggs in one basket, in that way it can be quite distressing if that happens." Chloe's statement directly echoes the points raised in Zoë Glatt's ethnography of the YouTube creator industry, where platform dependency, or putting all your eggs in one basket, represents a "deep-seated anxiety that a platform that appears to be a pillar of the social media ecology can disappear overnight."[33] Although artists are not platform-native creators, they have arguably become equally as platform-dependent for income generation as professional influencers are.

The atmosphere of anxiety about accidentally doing something wrong and jeopardizing one's position on social media—without explanation—represents a distinct layer of platform governance.[34] In this sense artists, like influencers, labor within what Taina Bucher frames as a permanent "threat of invisibility," where social media platforms maintain power through the capricious ways in which they decide what should and should not be seen.[35] Artists are always on edge. Lena, a knitwear designer, ended up not going through with the launch of a promotional campaign that she had worked hard (and paid significant up-front costs) to create because of an error message she received when she tried to post it on Instagram. "The campaign was great, but I had wanted to put in all the work to create imagery and new products and do it on time, which felt like a big achievement. I wanted to sponsor them because it was quite a structured thing, but it wouldn't work."

The risk of being in bad standing with Instagram could jeopardize the future of the account that artists work hard to grow. The tandem features of platform dependency and platform opacity prompt a highly affective self-governing response: artists avoid any circumstance that may affect their platform standing. This adds a new level of governmentality to art worlds, and potentially threatens a key part of artists' creative process—what art sociologist Hannah Wohl calls the "process of experimentation."[36]

Artists use small-scale experimentation to decide what works are worth following or abandoning, thereby engaging in processes that allow for low-stakes tests of concepts, materials, and themes. Experimentation helps artists to minimize risk within the creative process, assuring against "evaluative uncertainty," or the unpredictability of how their work will be received by highly subjective intermediaries like commissioning editors, critics, gallerists, and customers.[37] Wohl shows that experimentation is an individual, emotional process for artists, which often relies on personal, affective connections with works in progress. The pervasive and constant nature of influencer creep, however, opens this individual process up to a platformized audience, as artists must document works in progress and invite audiences to engage with them. Artists engage their followers by inviting feedback through employing polls and reading comments, as well as inspiration and test concepts with potential customers. In this way, Instagram offers a useful line to audiences and potential clients. However, the connection with audiences can never be organic. It is always algo-rithmically mediated, which has consequences for the kinds of work that can be done, as well as the kinds of work that the audi-ence will be afforded access to.

## Influencer Creep and Algorithmic Art Worlds

Artists increasingly rely on Instagram but they don't trust the plat-form, for the same reason influencers don't trust it. Instagram is changeable and capricious, and it offers little support for even its professional users. This chapter has traced the anxious and uncertain feelings that artists share with influencers, and it has examined the ways they manage these feelings using strategies embedded within influencer culture—sharing algorithmic gossip, following algorithmic lore, and conducting algorithmic tests.

Artists might copy influencer techniques because they are inspired by a popular influencer's approach, or because techniques are promoted by algorithmic experts, or maybe they simply figure strategies out through everyday trial and error. However this may be, influencer creep has taken hold. Artists share the very same algorith-mic gossip as influencers—for example, that Instagram "loves" images of faces. In art worlds, this theory has nudged some artists to create work that includes images of people in order to afford Instagram visibility and more directly to paint white people because they are perceived to be more algorithmically recognizable.

Sometimes algorithmic lore is more specific to artists' experi-ences of what works on Instagram. Following lore in this case encourages artists to make bold, colorful work to build quick and easy audience engagement. Driven by the need to maintain a steady content baseline, artists feel pressured to document their artistic process. They balance heavy cameras on their heads while they draw, or they engage in time-consuming practices like restaging their work methods to show the process of making from different angles. The pressure to build content creation into the heart of all parts of everyday and working life is rooted in the cultural shift, driven by influencer creep.

Instagram's architecture, alongside influencer culture, shapes art worlds. The decisions made by Instagram about what becomes algorithmically visible echo the decisions made by other art world intermediaries like galleries, curators, and art advisors about what is and isn't art. These decisions are necessary to make the messy and unpredictable world of art more efficient and orderly.[38] In an analysis of interdependent artistic production, sociologist Howard Becker highlights the way that the creative process is shaped by what artistic distribution systems are able to handle.[39] Art distributors must "deal with the stability of their own business" rather than selecting what artworks to distribute based purely on their merit.[40] Distributors—like Instagram in this case—promote artworks based on their preferences, design, and funding. Instagram is a technology funded by commercial advertisers; the platform is designed to net maximum attention and engagement, to attract a buying audience to sell back to advertisers.

Instagram is not designed to work for advertisers, not artists, and so it's understandable that artists feel at risk; however, it's very challenging to opt out. When the artists make work that falls outside viable distribution pathways, like Instagram in this case, they defeat their chances of being visible to artistic markets—the ways, as Becker puts it, of being "recognised and valued."[41] Of course, there are many successful artists who mainly work offline, and these people are less subject to influencer creep. However, avoiding the role of Instagram as distributor relies on other axes of privilege—for example, access to gallerists, agents, and other networks that are overwhelmingly closed to all but the most well-heeled and well-connected individuals.

So most working artists are required to technically optimize their work based on what works well within the visual, influencer-laden culture of Instagram. But they must also represent themselves as authentic—that is, relatable to a common audience, coherent, and real. In the next chapter, I trace the historic value of authenticity within influencer industries. I examine practices like the performance of everyday amateurism, comparison with what is ostensibly inauthentic, and deployment of real emotions to negotiate scandal. Just like I did with the technical optimization techniques in this chapter, I highlight authenticity practices as cultural strategies, which are finessed over time to negotiate multilayered pressures within platformized creative industries. Throughout the following chapter, I continue to show the ways that influencer creep shores up inequalities in creative industries, highlighting the fragility of the concept of authenticity and for whom it may or may not hold value.

# 3   *Making Soup, Eating Dino Nuggets*

## Authenticity within Influencer Cultures

In a video titled "U Totally Caught Me Making Soup," the American influencer Emma Chamberlain guides her followers through the process of making a basil, pea, and potato soup.[1] The video has a similar rhythm to the glossy YouTube cooking tutorials produced by Condé Nast, while deliberately evading their professional sheen. Chamberlain opens with establishing shots of her ingredients, starting with a close-up of sixteen wet, slimy English peas dimly filmed on an unpleasantly gleaming white plate. Then, two languishing basil leaves, a couple of unappetizing sweet potatoes precariously rolling toward a counter edge. Following the close-ups of the vegetables, Chamberlain fills a pan with water in a sink strewn with used dishes. There are dirty plates, knives, and forks, as well as a reusable cup for iced coffee with a built-in straw. We move on to a close-up of two pots of boiling water on a gas stove. The camera shakes around to the left, then to the right, panning upward toward the oven fan. We linger on a marble backsplash for a couple of seconds, the pans of water no longer in shot. Chamberlain's voiceover unconvincingly takes us through the process of making this soup: "I don't know what the fuck I'm doing when it comes to cooking. I still do not know how to properly dice an onion, etc., etc." Later, she stumbles over the word "in . . . edible, unedible, in . . . inedible." She admits to missing a timer: "the timer went off, and then I stopped it, and then I forgot to take things off the heat . . . who knows how long I boiled them." Chamberlain's video engages with two dynamics of influencer creep—an amateur aesthetic and a performance of emotional vulnerability. These stylistic practices have been developed and used by influencers to negotiate the contradictory demands at the heart of influencer culture. Content must be convincingly ordinary and *real*, and yet polished enough to be commercially viable.

These pressures are not new. Artists have long used the language of *authenticity* to attain a competitive edge in challenging economic conditions. Sociologist David Grazian, for example, wrote about the "economy" of authenticity for blues musicians in Chicago. Authenticity was often evoked as a performance to navigate competing demands between artistic autonomy and commerciality.[2] In *Creating Country Music: Fabricating Authenticity*, Richard A. Peterson articulates the music industry's attempts to "find the formulas" of "rustic authenticity" within country music.[3] Peterson traces the ways that authenticity is constantly renegotiated between commercial actors and audience preferences, all underscored by social and cultural factors such as class, race, and gender. Informed by these contextualizing works in the study of cultural and creative industries, I offer a focused examination of how two styles of authenticity—strategically built amateur aesthetics and a particular evocation of emotional vulnerability—have become developed under distinct economic and cultural conditions wrought by platformization, coupled with the unique political economic conditions of influencer industries.[4] Influencers have developed and sharpened these styles of authenticity in response to platform governance, commercial requirements, and audience demands. Under influencer creep this style has spilled outward, being taken up among other forms of creative entrepreneurship.

But what is authenticity? Cultural studies scholar Sarah Banet-Weiser argues that the concept of authenticity is central as an organizing principle in a highly commodified and branded world. Authenticity, she claims, is formed as "part of a relationship between individuals and commodity culture."[5] Banet-Weiser's insights are vital. What we define as *authentic* are personal values that develop under specific conditions of economic exchange. It is important to reflect on the ways that authenticity is established and how it accrues value. This chapter will follow the tensions presented by this version of authenticity—how it travels and how it functions. I will examine how this kind of authenticity is wielded strategically by content creators and how it shapes representation and participation within influencer economies.

The performances of authenticity examined here allow influencers to move between the demands to be creative and original while negotiating the institutional logics and rationalization demanded by social media platforms. For social media scholar Brooke Duffy, each stakeholder within the influencer economy offers their own yardstick of what being "real" is measured against. As she puts it, "conceptual imprecision enables bloggers to deploy [authenticity] in ways that resonate with their ever-shifting allegiances—to themselves, to their audiences, to their advertisers and to members of the public who celebrate them for wresting power from fashion's old guard."[6] Focusing on the complexities of authenticity also directs us to moments of breakage. Like authenticity itself, "fakeness" is constantly evolving, is forever in flux. Social media scholar Alice Marwick has drawn attention to the fragility of authenticity within a precarious working environment: "being authentic is a very tenuous definition that can be broken by almost anything."[7]

It would be a mistake to view social media content creation as an activity that can be measured as *more authentic* than "traditional" media production.[8] Instead, influencer creep includes a specific generic performance of authenticity that has been formed and sharpened within the conditions of contemporary social media culture. Creators are tapping into a recognizable generic convention using practices and conventions that have arisen owing to market and platform conditions. These authenticity strategies have become foundational to creative workers in art worlds and beyond as key tenets of influencer creep. With this in mind, then, it is important to understand the pressures that have contributed to the authenticity demands within the influencer economy before locating the ways that they have crept out into other areas of social life and culture.

## Amateurism in Authenticity

The intentional deployment of an amateur authenticity in content creation originated within one of the earliest examples of online content creation, fashion blogging. Fashion blogs were independently hosted and diary-like, only lightly peppered with images. Some of the first fashion blogs were published in the mid-1990s, but the phenomenon entered the popular cultural imagination in the late 2000s.[9] At this time, fashion bloggers were positioned as a welcome break from fashion magazine editors (such as those working for *Vogue*), who were seen as representative of a musty old establishment, entrenched within cultures of unreachable and out-of-touch fantasy fashion. In her prescient analysis of the fashion blogging economy in the early 2010s, Brooke Duffy emphasized the ways that bloggers embrace their "ordinary" roots in order to distance themselves from traditional media or mainstream beauty culture. Yet as Duffy points out, the most successful aspirants within this space often *did* have training, experience, and connections within fashion and marketing industries. Fashion bloggers engaged directly in discursive labor to position themselves as real, glossing over the time and monetary investment demanded within the blogging industry. This work obscured "important variations in professional experience and economic capital that characterize the fashion blogosphere."[10] Drawing from Duffy's observations, I argue that the contours of amateur presentation are nuanced and intentional, and authenticity is not a stable, immutable concept that exists unfiltered within social life.

Influencers often amp up their amateur credibility to reiterate their authenticity following a public association with mainstream media or with commercial interests. To explore these kinds of strategies, I return to the generic conventions of amateur authenticity as engaged in by YouTuber Emma Chamberlain, who, at the time of writing, has eleven million subscribers. Originally from Northern California, Chamberlain started making videos as a young teenager. She left high school in her junior year to move to Los Angeles, in order to create content full-time. Commentators have praised the unfiltered aesthetic of her YouTube channel. Tech journalist and creator culture expert Taylor Lorenz wrote in the *Atlantic* that Chamberlain was the most important YouTuber working in 2019. As she put it, Chamberlain "doesn't seem to care if she looks weird or if her camera is poised at an unflattering angle. . . . [She] posts lo-fi vlogs using default fonts, clashing color schemes, and lowercase titles that never overpromise."[11] The *New York Times* commented on Chamberlain's innovations within the form—for example, "adding text to the screen and pausing to point out the best parts."

As Chamberlain has moved into her twenties she has caught the attention of prominent intermediaries in high fashion. In 2022 alone, her diarized trip to Copenhagen was featured on *Vogue* magazine's YouTube channel, and later in the year she was shot by the Andy Warhol–founded magazine *Interview*. She was also invited to the high-fashion Met Gala in 2021, 2022, and 2023. The Met Gala, in particular, has a legitimizing quality that lends distinct cultural capital to invitees. Chamberlain also received widespread online attention when she gave a tour of her house to *Architectural Digest*. Her mid-twentieth-century chalet-style abode also drew fawning praise in the form of write-ups by *Vice*, *Buzzfeed*, and *People* magazine (in addition to the wider internet on Twitter and TikTok).

In light of her recent foray into the world of high fashion, Chamberlain has engaged with strategies to maintain her authentic identity as an independent content creator and influencer through a distinctly amateur style of self-presentation. Digital anthropologist Crystal Abidin has called attention to the strategic labor of "calibrated amateurism," which she defines as "crafting contrived authenticity that portrays the raw aesthetic of an amateur, whether or not they really are amateurs by status or practice."[12] Abidin traces the techniques that influencers use to provide a convincing snapshot of their everyday life. This "filler content" is ostensibly unconsciously crafted, more spontaneous, and thus more real than glamorous mainstream media. The concept of *filler content* allows people to understand individuals' direct and intentional engagement with amateur conventions—the inclusion of bloopers (mistakes made in speech or goofy outtakes) or the documentation of banal everyday events, such as a trip to the supermarket. Abidin points out that creating amateur content underscores influencers' positioning as "passion-driven, independent and unpaid."[13] Much of Emma Chamberlain's YouTube strategy is taken directly from the "calibrated amateurism" playbook; it's a carousel of filler content. She drives to grab iced coffee or go to the gym; she paints clumsy watercolors; she lounges in bed.

In these slice-of-life videos, Chamberlain muses on what she is up to and on life in general, interjecting her reflections with frequent bloopers and outtakes. Viewers can see a soundtrack of a muffled mic's clang against her dashboard as she adjusts her camera, she drops her keys, she struggles to park her car, or even when she (frequently) belches directly toward the camera. Playing with the affordances of different social media platforms and technologies—for example, manipulating image quality and sound—is a common strategy, one used to invoke ordinariness and relatability. Practices like Chamberlain's emerged out of a distinct creator culture developed from the earliest days of YouTube as a peer-to-peer video sharing platform. Social media scholars Jean Burgess and Josh Green trace these genre conventions back to domestic media production or "formerly private forms of 'vernacular creativity,'" which, through vlogging, became "part of public culture."[14] In negotiating criticisms of their work, influencers reach back to the conventions of camcorder culture—the private, the domestic, the nostalgic.

Chamberlain opens one 2022 YouTube video titled "It Will Be OK" with a dimly lit shot of herself in bed, as she shares with her viewers a recent experience of a panic attack.[15] After this, she chats to viewers in her car as we follow her to an outfit fitting for what she initially describes as a "dinner party." She qualifies this, though, by saying, "it's not like a dinner party where it's like friends or something, it's kind of more of an event," adding, "I'm a little anxious about going to a dinner party after my little emotional episode." Chamberlain hints at her glamorous plans, including a shot of a rack of clothes and a hot pink Yves Saint Laurent bag, but then the video moves on to an establishing shot of the upscale, organic (celebrity hotspot) Californian supermarket chain Erewhon. There are about 50 seconds of shaky camera shots of the inside of the market—the canned beans and legumes aisle, the oatmeal and chocolate aisle, a wall of greenish bananas (zooming in onto one bunch until it becomes a yellowish/kelly green blur), and finally a shot of Chamberlain's own company, Chamberlain Coffee, with bags carrying its logo sitting on the shelves. In this video, snapshots of a custom designer clothing fitting are afforded parity with grocery store B-Roll. The video ends with a close-up of the outfit Chamberlain wore at the event crumpled on the floor, including the hot pink Yves Saint Laurent bag. Lastly, we see a shot of Chamberlain scrolling on her phone, exhausted after the party, wrapped in a blanket. Influencers, the shot seems to want to indicate—they're just like us!

Chamberlain is particularly interesting, since she is often depicted as being different or unique, as distinct from other professional content creators because of her authenticity. For example, *Vogue Business* reported on beauty brand Lancôme's decision to hire Chamberlain as an ambassador.[16] The report reads: "Lancôme has an unexpected new ambassador. After years of partnering with A-list Hollywood actors, from Julia Roberts to Lupita Nyong'o and Penelope Cruz, the L'Oréal-owned beauty brand is turning to 21-year-old American YouTube star and fashion cool kid Emma Chamberlain to help it target Gen Z."

The article extols how their decision to work with Chamberlain spells a strong departure from their previous partners, who were the expected—that is, Hollywood stars. But is this partnership really so unexpected and groundbreaking? Partnerships between influencers and beauty corporations are not without precedent, not even for Lancôme. Influencer Michelle Phan was hired as the first YouTube Lancôme ambassador in 2010, which *Vogue Australia* similarly put down to her ability to mix the "the guerrilla fun and instant gratification of blogging with the polish and professionalism of a Lancôme partnered expert."[17] And the global director of Lancôme makeup, Lisa Elridge, first gained global attention as a beauty YouTuber, with two million subscribers on the platform. Instead of viewing the partnership between Lancôme and Emma Chamberlain as a novel moment that represented the brand's increased drive toward real authenticity (it isn't and, I would say, it can't), it is possible to reflect on this moment as proof of the apparent lure and discursive power of authenticity within contemporary capitalism.

Chamberlain's claims to authenticity sit squarely within the bounds of commerciality—she signals her "realness" through highly individualized reflections on her own personal challenges, deliberately distanced from any form of structural critique. Consider *Vogue*'s comments on Chamberlain's popularity and suitability for lucrative cosmetics partnerships: "Her secret sauce? Her authenticity and relatability; speaking to her community about everything from her glamorous red carpet moments to mental health and her skin issues."[18] As her content looks studiously inward (at her anxiety and acne), Chamberlain cautiously evades political or social topics of conversation and sticks to brand-safe signals of *being real*. She offers a successful interpretation of the requirements of authenticity in content creation, bolstered by a sharp editing skill and a direct invocation of amateur aesthetic. As a white, young, middle-class influencer, Chamberlain has an amateur authenticity that passes so successfully *because* of her race, hegemonic beauty, and class position.

The value of Chamberlain's whiteness is significant. Black content creators are subject to additional pressures to maintain a real but commercial reputation within online ecologies. Feminist media scholar Catherine Knight Steele has reflected on the durable existence of respectability politics for Black women within online spaces. In writing about self-presentation strategies online, Knight Steele argues that "Black women considered deviant and 'other' in American society have had extra practice in navigating their sense of self in stark contrast to societal expectations."[19] To this end, Black women in digital spaces are skilled at self-presentation and audience management, carefully anticipating how their content travels in order to manage specific situations, audiences, and goals. What is considered an acceptable performance of respectability varies based on social and cultural norms. As Mikaela Pitcan, Alice Marwick, and danah boyd note, most commercial stakeholders value a "vanilla self"—"repercussions for defying norms vary based on privilege" and are bound up with cultural hierarchies related to race, class, and gender.[20] While Chamberlain has achieved great success through a spectacular and artfully constructed incompetence, it is unlikely that *everyone* would garner such a fawning and lucrative reception for this style of content creation. For cultural theorists Sarah Banet-Weiser and Kat Higgins, the measurement of authenticity (and its inverse, fakeness) are bound up in an "economy of believability," whereby white women inherently "possess a conditional believability" that is weaponized in ways that position marginalized people, such as women of color, trans women, and sex workers, as "inherently unbelievable."[21] The quiet part here is arguably said out loud about Chamberlain in a write-up from British *Vogue*: "whether she's being genuine or just using her preternatural ability to sell anyone on anything in a way that *feels* genuine, I believe her."[22]

## The Limits of Authenticity

Performing amateurism convincingly can bring great success to influencers like Chamberlain. Yet while influencers set themselves apart as something new and fresh, established media intermediaries rushed to critique them as amateurs, or as wannabes who are even potentially *dangerous*. In an article about Fall Fashion Week in Milan in 2016, a group of *Vogue* editors took it in turns to take shots at the influencers present at the week's events.[23] Creative digital director Sally Singer wrote the following: "Note to bloggers who change head-to-toe, paid-to-wear outfits every hour: Please stop. Find another business. You are heralding the death of style." Chief critic Sarah Mower chimed in, calling bloggers "trolling" the streets of fashion week "desperate." Alessandra Codhinha, the fashion news editor, wrote:

> Am I allowed to admit that I did a little fist pump when Sally broached the blogger paradox? There's not much I can add here beyond how funny it is that we even still call them "bloggers," as so few of them even do that anymore. Rather than a celebration of any actual style, it seems to be all about turning up, looking ridiculous, posing, twitching in your seat as you check your social media feeds, fleeing, changing, repeating . . . It's all pretty

embarrassing—even more so when you consider what else is going on in the world. (Have you registered to vote yet? Don't forget the debate on Monday!)

In this article, these editors engage in speculation about the harm caused by nonprofessionals entering into existing, established institutions. The critiques here tap into the concerns raised by advertisers about content production for ostensibly accessible spaces like YouTube—namely, that that content is sophomoric, unfiltered, unpolished, and unmanageable. These critiques work to dissociate influencer work from skill, experience, intention, and craft. They position the influencer economy as commercially saturated and even unethical, deliberately distancing their own journalism from this commercial ecology (an interesting choice for advertiser-funded media, particularly for a glossy fashion magazine like *Vogue*). There is a fine line between an acceptable amateurism (which is commercially celebrated by brands such as Lancôme) and an amateurism that is unprofessional, unacceptable, overly commercial, and phony. Moreover, the way these editors discursively position content creators tells us something about the cultural imaginary around influencers, which is bound up with their concerns and fears. Through a vitriolic takedown of influencer amateurism, these editors may tellingly reveal some of the ways that content creation has threatened legacy media.

Rather than attempting to weigh which kind of content production is genuinely *more real* (for example, journalism as opposed to influencing), it is more important to follow the public imagination of authenticity and amateurism: what do these concepts do? Authenticity is given value when it is positioned against *something else*. Here we can consider the Instagram account Influencers in the

Wild (as of 2023, it has five million followers). The page solicits submissions of images drawing attention to the laborious nature of crafting authentic or spontaneous influencer content. One video shared on the page shows two girls perching on the Brooklyn Bridge for a photo shoot, later panning to the bridge behind them, and a trail of gridlocked traffic caused by their antics. Other images show "humorous" videos of waves crashing into women posing in the sea, ruining influencers' styled hair and makeup. Frequent posts depict women posing for pictures in bikinis in "inappropriate" venues such as ski hills, or dancing joyfully in public places while passersby look on in horror. The account chooses to take aim at the most feminized genres of influencer culture. Nearly all the images are of women, many of whom are engaged in highly gendered and stylized forms of content production. Influencers in the Wild collects and shares images depicting socially unacceptable forms of amateurism and authenticity to its five million followers. In so doing, it frequently takes a shot at spectacular and glamorous forms of femininity that have been associated with the working class.[24] These women are positioned as inexperienced and oblivious: they cause traffic jams, dance when no music is playing, and fall ungracefully into the ocean.

In some contexts, a performance of amateurism may beget a positive reputation for authenticity within influencer culture, but this style of content production requires tight management. Influencers in the Wild retraces the highly classed distinction between an appropriate style of feminized self-presentation (which hides its seemingly "natural" work) and glamour and excess, which is both out of control and risky. This is the kind of risk that commercial stakeholders are hoping to avoid within influencer culture and is deeply imbricated with moralistic concerns. Performing amateurism means individuals are always at risk of spilling over into being unacceptably incompetent and unprofessional—a fine line. In this sense, the trick is performing a convincing amateurism which ultimately stays within the bounds of commercial legibility.

## Emotional Authenticity

In November 2020, TikTok dance stars Charli and Dixie D'Amelio published a video titled "Dinner with the D'Amelios" to their family YouTube channel.[25] In the video they host beauty influencer James Charles at their Los Angeles home for a dinner catered by private chef Aaron May. Slouching around their dining table, the teenage sisters appear sullen, fidgety, and withdrawn. Dixie spits out an intricately prepared paella cooked by their private chef, makes barf noises, and asks if the chef has any "Dino Nuggets" instead. At the end of the video Charli discusses her follower count of ninety-five million, complaining that she has not hit a hundred million followers within a year of starting TikTok.

After the video's release, viewers (and other influencers, such as notorious online pot stirrer Trisha Paytas) commented that the sisters were spoiled and ungrateful. The backlash was written about in *Vanity Fair* with the heading "How TikTok Star Charli D'Amelio Lost 1 Million Followers Over a Paella Dinner"; in *Seventeen* magazine there was a similar article titled "Charli and Dixie D'Amelio are Being Called 'Ungrateful' Following Their Latest YouTube Video." Following the public criticisms leveled against her and her sister, Charli took to Instagram Live to apologize for her actions. In a stripped-back video filmed against a neutral background, she openly cries while citing the impact that these comments have had on her mental health. Breathing shakily, she wipes away tears as she tells her audience, "If this is the community that I am in, that I have put myself in, I don't know if I want to do this anymore." The apology video strikes many familiar chords of a recognizable cross-platform genre: authentic presentation with minimal makeup and poor lighting, tears, and an acknowledgement of personal turmoil and poor mental health. The video was included in a listicle published by the Vulture website: "The Best, Fakest, and Most Teary Influencer Apologies of 2020."

The second half of this chapter will take a closer look at the ways influencers use well-worn authenticity strategies to navigate the *risks* of influencer culture, engaging in a specific form of emotional labor. In many cases, influencers utilize authenticity work to navigate charges of fakeness that are nebulous and idiosyncratic. "Fakeness" scandals include the so-called "spoiled" or "ungrateful" behavior apparently shown by the D'Amelio sisters. They also include influencers being accused of cash grabs or of being paid too well, of ingratitude, of complaints, of overt and insincere sponsorships, and of engaging in (what is perceived to be) "too many" sponsorships. Pressure is compounded as young (often female), highly visible influencers are what feminist sociologist Angela McRobbie describes as "A1 girls": they are "ideal girls, subjects par excellence, and also subjects of excellence."[26] This particular brand of spectacular and luminous success often goes hand in hand with being positioned as a *role model*, a designation that is highly precarious. It can be withdrawn quickly by an expansive range of actions, behaviors, or speech acts that are often associated with commercial or celebrity culture.

Scarlett London, a UK-based influencer, found herself at the center of an authenticity scandal in 2018. London posted an image on Instagram ostensibly representing her morning routine as part of a paid partnership with the mouthwash Listerine. The Instagram image shows London sipping tea while perched on a bed (covered with a blanket featuring her own glamorous portrait) next to some strawberries and "pancakes" (on closer inspection one can see that these are folded corn tortillas). London's bedroom is adorned with pink, heart-shaped balloons, a billboard sign reading "good morning," and a bottle of Listerine inexplicably balanced on her nightstand. The post was surfaced by an individual who shared the post across Twitter and Reddit with the caption "fuck off is this anyone's normal morning. Instagram is a lie factory to make us all feel inadequate." His post was liked 89,000 times and London received a wave of criticism, abuse, and even death threats. Audiences gleefully tore the post apart. One Twitter user wrote, "You can refer to yourself as a poor, bullied 'young girl' all you like but if you're going to effectively sell products to your followers, your methods are going to come under criticism."

London responded to this onslaught by apologizing: "I personally don't think my content is harmful to young girls but I do agree Instagram can present a false expectation for people to live up to. And I am wholeheartedly sorry if I've ever made anyone feel inadequate through my content. My life mission is quite the opposite." For influencers, avoiding being seen as "fake" offers significant challenges when content production is deeply overlaid within a commercialized, advertiser-funded platform culture of visibility. If we take this context into account, we see that it makes sense, then, that instances of influencers strategically undertaking *authenticity work* surface frequently through the distinct conventions of the influencer apology video.

Creating apology content is encouraged by algorithmic experts, the professional purveyors of algorithmic lore. Lissette, a US-based "influencer coach, creator and speaker" with eighty thousand followers, jumped for joy in one Instagram video, accompanied by this on-screen text: "*client tells me a relatable personal story* . . . OMG this is a great content idea." In the video caption, Lissette goes into more detail about what kinds of personal reflection really make for the most effective social media posts: "the best content is made from those *inside thoughts* or insecurities that you are convinced are the only one thinking them. . . . I felt really embarrassed that xyz happened . . . I had this really big learning moment." Algorithmic experts encourage authenticity work alongside technical advice about algorithmic visibility, this being an example of the way that what algorithms want is often inextricably linked with the content that perceived audiences want. In both cases there is uncertainty: the audience and algorithm can both only be imagined.

The inward-looking generic conventions of the influencer apology video are now so recognizable that they have been parodied by the comedy sketch show (and liberal cultural litmus test) *Saturday Night Live*. In the 2021 sketch "Viral Apology Video,"[27] cast member Kyle Mooney and guest movie star Daniel Kaluuya play "viral YouTubers" who create a series of rambunctious prank videos that are interjected with earnest apologies for their bad behavior. The video skewers the perceived insincerity of influencer apologies—the viral YouTubers look somberly into the camera and claim to be "sorr" (shorthand for "sorry"), promising that they are "learning and growing as we speak"—while their bad behavior contradictorily escalates in their next viral videos, which are followed by increasingly mealymouthed apologies, and then more pranks, and so on. While the joke is the hypocrisy of the YouTubers, who in practice are doing the exact opposite of "learning and growing," the sketch also makes visible the structure and mise-en-scène of a typical YouTuber apology video. The prank videos in the sketch are of a typical YouTube style—fast-paced with sharp jump cuts and heavy use of zooms, graphics, and animations. On the other hand, the apology video is muted, set against a neutral domestic backdrop, with tears gushing down Mooney's face and forlorn strings playing the background.

Through the genre of the apology video, influencers have developed a blueprint for commercially viable authentic emotion that is at once contingent on and also shaped and made visible by social media platforms. Emotional authenticity is a genre, one that is deployed strategically. Sociologist Arlie Hochschild's *The Managed Heart* offers a compelling framework for understanding the ways that private feelings are used instrumentally within an organizational context: they have "commercial uses" that shape individuals' labor and value.[28] Within a commercial context, emotion becomes "part of what we sell to an employer for a day's wage,"[29] meaning emotions "take on the properties of a resource."[30] For Hochschild, these emotions are not only surface performances, in which individuals put on a particular emotion, but forms of deep acting whereby individuals induce or suppress feelings. Hochschild raises the concern that conditions of commercially managed feelings ultimately estrange workers from their own emotions. She asks, "when a worker abandons her work smile, what kind of tie remains between her smile and herself?"[31]

Hochschild focuses on the example of emotional labor performed by commercial flight attendants, tracing the pressures "to feel" placed on these employees back to management practices.

These management practices are developed in light of specific market conditions that lead airlines to squeeze their staff to provide a service that would differentiate their product from competitors. Flight attendants are therefore responsible for "selling the company" through an ability to *genuinely care* for their passengers within these interactions.[32] The emotionally positive and cheerful flight attendant is featured prominently in company advertisements, further promoting and entrenching a specific emotional state within this occupation. In a similar vein, social media platforms also promote an ideal influencer and an ideal emotional state, through their algorithmic recommendations and PR campaigns. Individuals prominently featured on the YouTube home page represent the ideal standard of behavior held by the company. The most visible content on platforms creates a standard for algorithmic lore, and the message about the kinds of content that will be promoted is reinforced through algorithmic gossip. Videos that are promoted and monetized on social media platforms like YouTube are what social media scholars Robyn Caplan and Tarleton Gillespie describe as an "elite set of the most popular and acceptable channels" that uphold "proprietary" values and are in "good standing" with the platform.[33]

The personal and individualized nature of influencer work mandates emotionally deep acting. These conventions ensure that emotions are used to meet a specific commercial end. Like other workplaces, platforms such as YouTube have developed rules and norms that make sure inappropriate emotions are managed by employees using a range of techniques, which for YouTube come under the guise of "advertiser-friendly content guidelines." Social media platforms do not employ influencers, yet the distributed effects of their "governance mechanisms" are keenly felt by content creators who must adhere to these guidelines to ensure their content remains eligible for monetization.³⁴ The following elements are classed as not advertiser friendly: "inappropriate language, violence, controversial issues, sensitive events, and incendiary and demeaning content." While this list might seem logical, in practice its consequences are far from straightforward. Caplan and Gillespie have pointed out that these guidelines are applied broadly by flawed and error-prone automated systems that struggle to parse important nuances or context within creator videos. This contributes to an atmosphere of anxiety, further confusion, and self-censorship. YouTubers who rely on revenue-sharing and YouTube visibility are scared to create content that may be determined to include such broad concepts as inappropriate language or controversial issues. In this sense, creators ostensibly must avoid anger and draw from their emotional reserves by managing their emotions through empathy, sincerity, and never placing blame. Influencers manage their feelings by a specific and strategic emotional authenticity that allows individuals a fixed framework that can be deployed to navigate their advertiser-unfriendly, uncommercial, and messy feelings.

The conventions employed within the apology video represent a formulaic response to stabilize messy emotions that are unacceptable for platform architecture and culture. Authenticity work in this context takes the guise of a stripped-back aesthetic. An influencer is either dressed in white or with a white setting to connote innocence. In makeup influencer James Charles's apology video "No More Lies," he appears against a white backdrop, simply dressed down in a black T-shirt.³⁵ Charles is notably makeup free, his skin pink and oily. This is a far cry from his usual high-glam, colorful, and stylized aesthetic. In the video "I'm Sorry," influencer Olivia

Jade acknowledges the marked change in presentation by saying "this video obviously looks really different."[36] The video is filmed in her bed in black and white, departing from her usually vivid and chaotic "daily vlogs" that document her daily errands and activities. In apology videos, influencers hope to underscore their ordinariness by showcasing an unusually amateur deployment of technology or shot composition. In "So Sorry," prank vlogger Logan Paul is poorly lit video and has audible background noise, eschewing his usually high-spec videos and slick production.[37]

And then there are the tears—tears gushing freely down influencers' faces or glistening in the light as they promise to gush forth. Influencers can open their videos crying, or start crying halfway through, or end the video because they can't stop crying. When audiences located racist tweets posted by white American influencer Laura Lee, she responded with an apology that was barely audible as she struggled to catch her breath through squeaky sobs. Sarah Banet-Weiser has pointed out the ways that "authenticity labour" on social media correspond with dominant ideals of fragile white femininity, underscored by "failure, pressure, depression, tears, vulnerability."[38] More directly, I argue that the apology video represents a strategy to communicate authenticity in a way that concretely responds to stringent limits on influencer behavior by platforms, commercial industry stakeholders, and audiences. The specific conventions of the influencer apology genre offer a stabilizing blueprint to help manage risks inherent within influencer work.

In this sense, reaching toward a recognizable emotion (in this case, grief or anxiety) can be seen as a strategic and stabilizing performance of an established genre, which is artfully constructed through the use of setting, style, and media technologies. A drive toward emotional authenticity can be tracked back to market conditions of risk, which loom large over influencer culture. Professional content creators rely on platform visibility, but they are subject to capricious algorithms and uneven platform governance that may promote or restrict their content with little reason or recourse. This book has shown how the symbiotic relationship between social media platforms and advertisers works as a destabilizing force for professional content creators. Caught up in the tidal flows of public relations concerns levied at platforms, influencers' content may also be suppressed without recourse (shadowbanned) or removed after being subject to human or automated moderation with little explanation. Content creators have discussed how the unpredictable nature of platform visibility has affected their mental health and sense of self. YouTube influencer Anthony Padilla summed up feelings of precarity in the following way: "I could put hundreds of hours of work into something and the views would be much lower than expected, and I would start to equate that with my sense of self-worth."[39]

For social media theorist Kelley Cotter, the atmosphere of opacity within platform cultures can "destabilize the very possibility of credible criticisms" of platform policies or code.[40] Platforms may release public statements that directly contradict the experiences of content creators, whom they may dismiss as "irrational or uninformed."[41] She refers to the way that platforms treat influencers as a form of gaslighting, a term taken from psychoanalysis that refers, as we have seen previously, to a form of manipulation that causes someone to question their reality and experience pervasive self-doubt. Along with other researchers within this space,[42] Cotter shows the ways that a lack of consistency, contact, and confirmation creates a broad atmosphere of anxiety that underpins the working conditions of influencers and, latterly, other working people through the phenomenon of influencer creep. The platformized instability and uncertainty outlined here contribute to what has been referred to as an "anticipatory anxiety" prior to sharing content and interacting with fans.[43] The anxiety here spirals off in a number of directions. Indeed, Brooke Duffy and Ursula Pruchniewska describe how a threat of *invisibility* (in which career sustainability is threatened) dovetails with a threat of *visibility*, in which a creator may be subject to "authenticity policing" and "more insidious forms public scrutiny," such as "hate speech, trolling and other acts of online misogyny."[44] The risks here are redoubled for women and marginalized people.

This culture of risk outlined above is neatly summed up by Emma Chamberlain in a 2023 interview with the *New York Times*:[45]

> I am a young gal. I spend a lot of time by myself, and I feel like a target. It's hard to feel safe. That's on a physical level. But on a psychological level, the internet is constantly witch-hunting. I understand why. Seeing somebody get burned at the stake sucks you in in a way that nothing else does. I don't blame people for having this interest, but I'm terrified because I am human and I'm not perfect and who knows what people could find about me.
>
> Feeling out of control in my identity has caused psychological harm. It's caused severe perfectionism. Everything I do, I must be perfect. I must treat everyone perfectly. I must show up to everything on time. This is all behavioral, by the way. I don't care about having perfect Instagram lips and a perfect Instagram body. It's this fear of not being a perfect-enough person because I feel like any moment, any mistake, could be the end. I've seen people get destroyed on the internet. It's a scary place to exist.

This statement captures the atmosphere of anxiety surrounding influencer culture. The opaque, obscure, and changeable platform conditions dovetail with an audience conditioned to test and police influencer behavior against an idealized authenticity and behavioral standards. In this sense, the influencer apology video forms an algorithmic negotiation strategy and direct stabilizing genre, whereby emotional labor is directly employed to mitigate conditions of risk. The mise-en-scène of the genre video is designed to remind audiences of influencers' ordinariness, the performance of grief directly evading anger or inappropriate emotions unsanctioned within commercial influencer culture.

Understanding how creators mitigate moments in which their brand value and source of income are at risk is instructive, since these strategies have directly crept into platform cultures. The conventions of authenticity stem directly from influencers' lack of control and from platforms' lack of response and care. They are designed to mitigate anticipatory anxiety about posting that stems from uncertainty about what platforms and audiences will tolerate. It is squarely within this context that the specific conventions of authentic performance can be understood as a generic strategy. In spaces of cultural production like art, media, and music, the concept of genre offers a playbook for production, promotion, and distribution for risk-averse media companies. This is important when media organizations place an extremely high price on *rationality* and on *ensuring* stability, looking to growth in market share.

Genres do offer an important common touchstone between different individuals and intermediaries, but it is important to recognize that they are not totally normative or completely fixed. Rather, they are based on mutable and socially constructed organizing principles. In other words, generic categories are created, classified, and agreed upon based on the interaction between producers and institutions, and within the context of production and distribution. For sociologist Anthony DiMaggio, "new genres require the matching of social constituencies with systems of production."[46] Keith Negus has similarly written about the concept of genre as a stabilizing strategy within creative industries. Focusing on the music recording industry, Negus argues that "cultural production involves working with recognizable codes, conventions and expectations."[47] For Negus, understanding cultural production involves paying attention to the actors who mediate between the structures of corporate ownership and who facilitate the everyday experiences of cultural workers. These meanings end up shaping generic conventions, and they contribute to the complex ways that these genres are assigned commercial value. Doing this helps us to trace the observable trends and conventions within influencer work back to the preferences of commercial actors (advertisers), but it also supports us in attending to the ways that they are refracted through cultural intermediaries (social media platforms, talent agents, and influencers themselves).

The spectacular performance of emotion within influencer culture is not received by audiences equally. As Sarah Ahmed points out, "emotions are bound up with the securing of social hierarchy: emotions become attributes of bodies as a way of transforming what is 'lower' or 'higher' into bodily traits."[48] In this sense, claims to emotion are verified based on racial hierarchies within society. We may examine how emotions are wielded to verify claims to authenticity in addition to tracking which of these claims *stick*. It is thus relevant to point out that there are very few prominent apologies by influencers who are not white; apologies by nonwhite influencers are markedly different. In January 2023, Colombian/

Nicaraguan Twitch streamer and YouTuber Jessica Fernandez posted a TikTok capturing a man at the gym staring at her and then approaching her to load her weights without her consent. As the man stared at her in the background, Fernandez quietly commented that the man was "feral" and added text to the video, saying "this is what women mean when they say staring at them like a piece of meat."

Fernandez's gym video was picked up by influencer Joey Swoll, a fitness creator and "CEO of GYM POSITIVITY" with 6.7 million followers on TikTok. Swoll's lucrative online brand centers on debunking videos made by women discussing men acting inappropriately at the gym. He publicly criticized Fernandez for her video, saying "an act of kindness or a glance does not make you a victim." Following the call-out by Swoll, Fernandez publicly apologized on Twitter, including the following statement: "With my 600k followers on TikTok and as an influencer I hold a lot of responsibility to use my platform in a way that spreads love and happiness which I did the exact opposite of that. I'm sorry to the men and women who deal with or have dealt with false/true allegations of SA or SH and if I made their situations feel belittled by mine. I apologize to my fans who have supported me and have been supporting me through this, I messed up and I'm going to just own this mistake."[49]

Here we may return to the economy of believability discussed earlier in this chapter. Fernandez received so many comments from Swoll's fans, which were themselves bolstered by attention from mainstream media, that she revisited her account of her own experience and withdrew it. Popular news media offered verification about Fernandez's need to apologize. The following are examples of headlines from the website EssentiallySports and the *Daily Mail*, respectively: "'How Damaging This Could Have Been for

Him': Influencer Finally Apologizes after Wrongly Calling A Man 'Feral' In Gym" and "'I Feel Sick to My Stomach with Guilt': Influencer Apologizes for Calling Man a 'Feral Weirdo' for Trying to Help Her at Gym in Viral TikTok Video." Fernandez turned her attention inward, letting others know that she was going to work on herself in the wake of this moment, stating, "This will be an ugly scar on my character for a long time until I can show that I am growing. I just hope people give me the chance to." To understand these statements further we can turn to the work of sociologist Eva Illouz, who has drawn attention to the value of the "failed self" within cultural life, whereby one is called to spectacularly present their individual issues to undertake a convincing performance of ordinariness.[50] Claims to authenticity involve discussing failed relationships, body image issues, and problems with confidence. Rather than being explained as structural issues, these are presented as wholly internal, "psychological obstacles" that cut through self-presentation.[51] This context affords a convincing claim to suffering and a verifiable, never-ending promise to *do better*.

## Conclusion

The conventions that influencers have pioneered to signal authenticity within influencer culture have shaped the practices and perception of authenticity for platform users, in addition to the way that authenticity is understood and measured. In this chapter I have shown the ways that influencers must skillfully negotiate a convincing performance of amateurism in its association with positive attributes like ordinariness. Yet going *too far* in their embrace of amateur aesthetics and performance can lead to challenges to their commercial salience and professional legitimacy. Similarly, we can examine the ways that authentic emotion is strategically used and highly mediated. Paying attention to the ways that influencers perform what is understood to be authentic emotion as a response to the regulation of their emotions by platforms and audiences can help us understand the ways that representations ripple throughout society and shape our understandings of what authenticity might be in the context of influencer creep. Tracking the conventions and measurements of these requirements in detail can help us in identifying how influencer culture has set the foundations for professional and amateur platform use more broadly.

The centrality of the value of authenticity (and its fragility) within popular culture is longstanding. For example, David Grazian acknowledges the value of authenticity within cultural economies while attending to its subjective and community-driven nature.[52] He shows how, for blues musicians, authenticity is often evoked as both a sense-making process and a performance in the face of competing (or even contradictory) demands, such as between artistic autonomy and commerciality. Indeed, for Grazian, attempts at (by definition, manufactured) authenticity can be located as *a style*, but authenticities are also mutable, based on changing social and cultural contexts. For blues musicians, assessments of authenticity cannot be pulled apart from the politics of race, where "Blackness connotes an extreme sense of authenticity," which plays into racial stereotypes and elides the significance of musical training and skill.[53] Indeed, this framing supports a critical understanding of the ways that pressures about what is real are not distributed equally. Anthropologist Forrest Stuart meaningfully draws attention to the ways that impoverished young Black men can view content creation on YouTube as "one of the few viable options for upward mobility and self-worth."[54] The distinct attention economies and sociocultural contexts of drill music have contributed specific authenticity demands. Stuart notes that "today's cultural producers . . . [prove] they're more authentic in their online persona than their competitors are. For those with limited resources, this means finding new and innovative ways to demonstrate they truly embody the negative stereotypes of their stigmatized social group."[55] The cultures within drill lead producers to validate their authenticity, "greatly increasing a young man's risk of exposure to violence."[56]

With these contextualizing theoretical tracks in mind, I have considered the specific authenticity demands that are laid bare within commercial influencer culture, arising from specific political economic and cultural conditions. Over time, and with the changing patterns in social media cultures, these demands will eventually alternate. For now, we can locate the specific kinds of authenticity that come under the banner of influencer creep, where authenticity is rooted in a strategic attempt at negotiating the manifold risks and uncertainties diffused within platform economies. The dimensions of authenticity rooted within influencer culture function to conceal the harsh realities and challenges that have been brought to the fore in platformized creative work. In the following chapter, we will examine the ways that the specific performance of authenticity has tracked forward. Art worlds have their own definitions and expectations of authenticity. I will now explore how authenticity for influencers and for artists overlap and come together, shaping cultures of creative entrepreneurship on social media and beyond.

# 4  *Linen, Looms, and Limestone Cottages*

### Being an "Authentic" Artist on Social Media

"Get ready with me while I tell you about how my small business is failing, while I try not to cry." This statement opens a TikTok video by Jodie, a London-based ceramicist. In the video she talks viewers through the meticulous process of building up her small ceramics business, involving expensive moves like moving into a new studio and purchasing a kiln. Jodie exposes her vulnerability; she laments the lack of expertise leading to some of her professional moves: "I'm not a business person—which I should be—I'm not very good with numbers and stuff." The video employs the framing of a standard influencer genre—the "get ready with me" (GRWM) video. GRWM videos employ a fixed narrative arc, initially situating the protagonist as unglamorous and as ordinary as possible before they transform themselves into someone "made up" and put together. As the TikTok opens, Jodie does not wear makeup, and her hair is messily scrunched or pinned back. She appears fresh-faced, sitting on the floor, carefully applying cosmetics throughout the video. Faithful to the amateur labor of influencer cultures,[1] Jodie keeps in bloopers and moments when she does her makeup wrong, even drawing attention to her mistakes by saying "I just got mascara everywhere." Jodie's video offers a prototypical example of authenticity work within influencer creep—a candid, strategic, yet personal response to the institutional vulnerability of creative work.

In the previous chapter, I outlined the multisited pressures for influencers to build and maintain authenticity in order to reconcile a paradoxical tension between creativity and commerce. Platform conditions, advertiser expectations, and audience cultures mean that influencer content must be commercially viable but also originate from an influencer's (ostensibly) genuine self. In response to these intertwined demands, influencers embrace a distinct performance of authenticity by engaging two generic conventions: amateurism and emotional vulnerability. The earlier examination of authenticity genres for influencers provides a foundation that allows us to map influencer creep—that is, the way that influencer strategies have been taken up outside professional content creation to underpin how anyone who makes creative work must navigate social media platforms. This chapter will examine how the conventions of authenticity, as developed and finessed by influencers, are taken up by craftspeople and visual artists. I investigate how influencer creep functions alongside the unique components of the "authenticity ideal" in creative industries, components that are specific to art worlds and that are distinct from the influencer authenticity framework.

I will first explore the foundational art world authenticity pressures before moving on to examine the ways that working conditions may have been altered by influencer culture. Secondly, I will show how creatives reach for the genre of authenticity as a stabilizing response to their political and economic conditions through two distinct genres of performance that are underwritten by influencer creep: amateurism and emotional vulnerability.

musee.roo
Bristol, United Kingdom

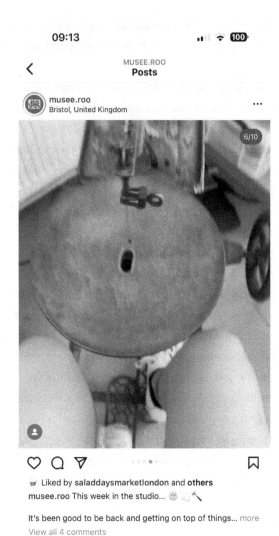

6/10

🏆 Liked by saladdaysmarketlondon and **others**
**musee.roo** This week in the studio... 😴 🔨 ⚒

It's been good to be back and getting on top of things... more
View all 4 comments

FIGURE 4. A still from a day-in-the-studio Instagram video by metalworker Roo. Courtesy of Musée Roo.

♡ ⚪ ▽                                    🔖

 Liked by saladdaysmarketlondon and others
musee.roo This week in the studio... 😊 🔦 🔧

It's been good to be back and getting on top of things... more
View all 4 comments

FIGURE 5. Golden treasures appear in a second still of Roo's day-in-the studio Instagram video. Courtesy of Musée Roo.

## The Politics of the "Really"

We can start with what I have termed the politics of the "really" for art worlds and influencers. In other words, what are the expectations for truth and verification in each market? We know that within influencer culture, audiences are concerned that the creator in question is *really* ordinary and relatable. Within art worlds, however, there are additional concerns that a particular artist *really* is an authentic creator. Observing a persistent fixation on authenticity and aura (the unique atmosphere of an object or text) in the worlds of art, philosopher Walter Benjamin argued that perceptions of authenticity in art are influenced by the conditions in which an object was made, the trajectories of ownership, and its "presence in time and space."[2] The importance of aura stems from what we know about an artist and how the artist's work was made, which recalls art's origins in ritual and ceremony. In the book *Art Worlds*, sociologist Howard Becker examines the symbiotic relationship between artistic reputation and the value of artistic works. "How do we know that artists have special gifts?" he asks. "By their works which produce special emotional experiences and reveal their exceptional skills."[3] He notes, however, that it is also important to understand that what we know about artists influences how we perceive their works. "We also know works by their makers whose abilities give works a warrant that they would not otherwise have"; and in this sense, we make an inference about the reputation of artists through "a quest for adequate evidence."[4] The volume of evidence that we have access to depends on the working life of the artist. Emerging or smaller-scale artists will not have a long canon of works ready to support an assessment of their skill or value. Therefore, artists themselves seek to add value to their work in order to make their creative processes, skill, and expertise visible.

Pierre-Michel Menger, a sociologist of creative work, shows the ways that artists demonstrate an authentic connection to their work—for example, through publicly documenting unfinished creative works.[5] In this vein, artists engage in strategies to show the evidence of their labor and skills as well as to justify the value of their work. To achieve these ends, they provide audiences with a window into their creative process—for example, hosting studio tours and engaging in artist talks, or including drafts, reworkings, materials, and contextual information within public exhibitions. This is also a part of the way that newer artists forge a reputation. Menger argues that—particularly when artworks are not attached to "great names"—"other guarantees are necessary to convince audiences that art, up even on its most radical and nihilistic expressions, is still matter of serious skill, knowledge and involvement."[6] Artists are compelled to verify their unique ability and expertise in a highly competitive market. The mandatory nature of social media use for creative workers has accelerated and deepened these existing pressures for artists to show their processes. Many creative workers I talked to publicly documented their artistic processes via social media platforms. Sociologist Karen Patel describes this practice as "staging the work," which allows artists to "provide evidence of their creative knowledge and skills and demonstrate [their] creative process as work comes together."[7] Evidencing the artistic process in this manner can be seen as an attempt to *reattach* context and aura, adding important contexts and associations that exist beyond the art object.

The Instagram profile of Ro Robertson, a multidisciplinary artist who produces sculpture, drawing, and performance art, is a good example of the attempts artists make to reattach context to online artworks. Their Instagram feed offers a mix of finished work interspersed with content that provides evidence of their process. In a close-up video with loud diegetic sound, Robertson brushes thick orange paint into the messy curves of a sculpture. There is a top-down shot of a large work in progress, including Robertson's feet tinged blue with paint. A further shot is captioned "Practicing!" and shows the setup of a performance practice: messy cables, microphones, paint, and dirt.

A further example can be found in the Instagram profile of Poppy Fuller, a weaver and textile artist based in the United Kingdom. The images published on Fuller's Instagram profile alternate between finished pieces and candid videos documenting her artistic process. Hands thread a machine, soundtracked by sparse, diegetic sounds. A wooden loom softly clatters as it is rearranged. Hands dye threads a spectrum of indigo blue as they are rinsed by a jet of water in a kitchen sink. In another post (outside the studio), we are shown clips from a day on which Fuller took a train, then a bus, to undertake historic natural dyes in the archives of a craft museum. Fuller explores the archives, the camera presumably resting on a surface to capture the shot. Hands thumb through a book of fabric samples, rustling through drawers with rolls of material covered in protective tissue paper.

Each of these pieces of content evinces distinct strains of labor involved in the artistic process. They click into place on an Instagram grid, building a convincing bricolage, representing the authenticity of the artistic process and the connection to craft. Communicating the skill, the training, and the labor involved in making is particularly important for an artistic practice that can be undertaken more efficiently by automated processes, mass-produced using machines. Many artists' practices hinge on the value proposition that there *is* an important difference between handmade and machine-made objects. Creative industries scholar Susan Luckman argues that the value of handmade goods is that they offer an opportunity for buyers to engage with the authentic in an "inauthentic world"; such objects offer a "connection to the maker through the skill and learning apparent in their production."[8] But more than this, documenting making by hand arguably offers evidence of the ways that the artistic process is laborious, particularly when we take into account the volume of content that artists realistically are required to produce to operate as a business, or what I called the *content baseline* in chapter 1 of this book.

Artists strategically use the affordances of social media to represent the ways that they are working under authentic artistic conditions. Interviewees cited the challenges of digitally conveying the complexities of their production processes and technical skills developed throughout their practice. Chloe, an illustrator, said: "I think people don't even really know how I make my work, which is crazy because I spend so much time doing [linoleum] cutting, which is so arduous." Dani, a print maker, made a similar point about her own Instagram profile: "the fact that we hand-print stuff means that it's different to digitally printing something. So there's a tactile quality, and just a different quality to the way it looks in real life. That is sometimes challenging to get across." Both Chloe and Dani feel compelled to present their work as digital images on Instagram, which flattens the material, touchable qualities of the pieces—the hallmarks of their creative labor.

Lena, a knitwear designer, told me that she creates content documenting her creative process to represent the technical skills and training that go into her work, particularly in order to justify its cost. As she put it, "It's impossible to show the quality of a garment online. But you can obviously show that your serious." I love this sentiment because it gets to the heart of a tension within creative labor: a social disbelief that what one really does is a job, really has value, is not frivolous; it is serious. Many self-presentation strategies used by both influencers and artists are born from a deep struggle over legitimization. And at a basic level, social media adds another venue that artists must use to communicate and maintain their own professional integrity.

## The Amateur Artist

The previous chapter outlined desirable and lucrative conventions of amateurism performed by high-profile social media creators, used to promote themselves and their work as ordinary, relatable, and real. Artists also evoked amateurism in this style to show they did not take themselves too seriously. They would include outtakes and bloopers in their social media presence or include "real people" (rather than models) within their images to mitigate an overtly serious or professional self-presentation online. Fern, a ceramicist, described her approach to presentation on her Instagram grid: "I try and make it a mixture of lovely lifestyle images and something silly. Something that I'm doing that's a bit, yes, that cuts a bit of an edge off that because, yes, I don't want it to seem like I live this constructed lifestyle." Similarly, Elsie, a textile artist and clothes maker, described avoiding posting professional photography or paid models on Instagram, even when she had such images available. "It sounds a bit lame," she said, "but I like the look of the grid when it's peppered in with other photos that have a nice composition or something. I don't just do model after model after model."

The use of amateur images borrows heavily from "casual photography," a term coined by artist and theorist Lev Manonvich.[9] For Manovich, casual photography mixes some unique Instagram conventions with the techniques developed in the "vernacular photography" of the twentieth century. While such techniques are not professional, strictly speaking, they are highly intentional. As Manovich puts it, casual photography "filters the visible world and the flows of human lives to select the moments and occasions worth documenting. In this sense casual photography is anything but casual."[10]

Embracing amateur aesthetics presents a challenge for creative workers who must also use their social media presence to successfully convey their technical expertise. Artists are unable to embrace a *spectacle of technical incompetence* in the style of high-profile creators.[11] Unable to perform amateurism related to their honed craft skills (essential to their professional success), they instead put forth a great deal of effort to distance themselves from associations with work and entrepreneurialism, specifically downplaying their *business expertise*. I found this distancing strategy to be particularly interesting, as all the people I interviewed for this chapter make their living from their artistic practice; they run successful small businesses. Yet when I asked artists about their marketing strategy, I received a near-standard response every time: they didn't have one. After probing further, however, it ultimately became clear that the artists I interviewed did have a considered and tactical approach to marketing activities, which fit into an overarching business plan. To take one example, Elsie characterized her marketing strategy as "nonexistent" at the start of our interview, but later described a time-intensive and thoughtful approach to increasing her online visibility, planning her Instagram posts in advance every week, and even gifting some of her textiles to influencers in advertorial partnerships.

Fern used some technical marketing language in our interview, but immediately shrugged it off: "I don't even know where I've learned this word 'conversion.' But is a 10 percent conversion good? [I] find myself perpetually [thinking], 'Oh you idiot, you're so naïve if you thought this would work, or that would work, or that sort of thing.'" As our interview closed, she joked about how talking to me had helped her understand the ways that she did, in fact, have a marketing strategy. She quipped: "So I *do* do some marketing—great!" Fern also shrouded her embrace of marketing in *disgust*, expressing how repelled she was by the very idea of engaging in marketing: "My marketing strategy . . . I've found the thought of it is such a sickening thing." I was surprised by the force of this reaction, but Fern was not the only one who was repulsed by the idea of promotion. Aoife, an illustrator, said, "That idea, of having a strategy for marketing, makes me recoil a bit." These reactions reveal how individuals see themselves as creators who have to engage in creative economies in order to make money to live. There is a strong emotional connection to the ideal of artistic practice and craft. The artists I interviewed described themselves as being reluctantly shunted into marketing, particularly on social media. The idea of putting themselves *out there* was very emotionally fraught.

It is important to recall Alice Marwick's point that authenticity is always invoked in opposition to *something* else.[12] Similarly, Brooke Duffy observes that the fashion bloggers she studied claimed authenticity by "distinguishing themselves from the imagined archetype of the blogger/model/jetsetter."[13] Following Marwick and Duffy, we can see that authenticity is often in opposition to an imagined *other* in practice—namely, someone who is inauthentic and overtly commercial. Chloe situated her own practice in direct opposition to the activities of individuals that she described as "Instagram artists." For Chloe, these individuals had a totally different motivation to work: "their whole practice is all about Instagram and creating work for Instagram, and engaging with an audience on Instagram."

Chloe believed what kept her apart from these individuals was her lack of intentional engagement with social media platforms. Although she had fifty thousand followers on Instagram at the time of the interview (she was one of the most successful artists I interviewed), she told me was not explicitly *trying* to accrue followers, depicting her social media use as haphazard or even lazy: "I'll just throw something up." Chloe represented her artworks as more important than the strategic aim of visibility; she felt she was being faithful to her practice rather than courting social media popularity. The discourse of *the really* becomes synonymous with emotional authenticity; artists only post content if it is reconciled with their true inner desires. This recalls an organizing principle of influencer culture—namely, that doing something with commercial goals could be offset by a genuine emotional intent. As social media scholars Thomas Poell, David Nieborg, and Brooke Duffy write, "Instagram influencers use a common refrain to reconcile authenticity and self-promotion, namely that they only hype a product or service if they *really love it*."[14] If engaging in social media is consistent with one's genuine inner life, then to do so can be acceptable. Participants told me that they simply followed their gut when it came to marketing their work online. For example, Lucilla, also a ceramicist, described use of social media as "intuitive," and Maye said, "I don't think I have a current marketing strategy. I just go with the flow at the moment."

Others doubled down on their own emotional fidelity and consistency by comparing their social media use favorably (as more authentic) to what is undertaken by their peers. Lucilla ruefully lamented that her friends' use of Instagram was *pure marketing*. For her, these individuals had jeopardized their authenticity and had even become ghoulish. "I can see what Instagram has done to them," she told me. "And it can turn them into people I wouldn't recognize in real life. It's almost like some of their posts make me feel like, gosh, this is so not you. Why are you doing this? They sound different. . . . It's what they've been told to do by the marketing people." Artists often distance their own practice from a specter of intentional and strategic social media use. Lena characterized the contradictions in this approach more directly: "It's like this weird nonmarketing marketing, where you're like, 'I don't want to be seen to be marketing.'"

## Representing an Authentic Artist Backstage

Social media scholars have drawn from the sociological writing of Erving Goffman to understand the strategies and techniques that social actors use in online self-presentation. Through the concept of "impression management" Goffman shows the ways that social actors are understood as "a team of performers who co-operate to present to an audience a given definition of the situation."[15] In this sense, individuals have "one informal or backstage language of behaviour, and another language of behaviour for occasions where a performance is being presented."[16] The backstage of social life is implicitly less curated and more authentic, and it includes behaviors like "smoking, rough informal dress, 'sloppy' sitting and standing posture, use of dialect or sub-standard speech, mumbling and shouting."[17] The characterizations of the backstage articulated by Goffman have been updated by digital anthropologist Crystal Abidin in her application of the concept of impression management to the influencer economy.[18] Abidin shows how influencers deliberately offset the more glamorous aspects of their lives by including monotonous footage of housework or trips to the grocery store as "filler content" to prove an identity as amateur, uncommercial, and authentic. While the backstage performance must corroborate the ordinariness of influencers' lives, it is also required to be glamorous and aspirational. The management of the backstage shows the way that professional content creators must also depict what Brooke Duffy and Emily Hund call "a well-organized, inspirational working environment"—that is, a stylish, glamorous, convincing representation of digital creative labor.[19]

I think it's useful to connect this writing on digital impression management techniques with sociological writing on the way that artists curate their artistic identity. Offline, this has tended to take place in spaces like the artist studio. Karen Patel has written about the studio as a space for the "development and display of aesthetic expertise."[20] In her work, Patel shows how artists represent their studio space to confirm their professional reputation and showcase their technical skills. Similarly, Alison Bain has written about how the public display of studio spaces can work to "establish the individual's reputation as a serious artist."[21] The artists and creative workers I study did include representations of their studio space in their social media presentation. However, the demand to represent their working studio merely scratches the surface of the requirement to present a *holistic* backstage identity tied to one's deeply personal private life. Influencer creep means a wider calling toward the *authentic backstage* that is connected to the self. The pressures to consistently post and promote content mandate that artists push themselves to document highly personal snapshots from behind the scenes of their creative lives. It is in light of these pressures that we can investigate how creative workers directly invoke the backstage strategies developed by professional content creators as an illustrative example of influencer creep.

Here we can return to the politics of the really. Creative workers feel a pressure to build a convincing picture of their real identity as an artist through the affordances of Instagram, using content creation on Instagram to attach aura and connotations of authenticity to their work. To many, this means representing the material context of their domestic lives and their homes. A promotional video posted to Instagram by Swedish hand weaver Estelle Bourdet is one example of the ways that artists can fuse a verifiable performance of skill with a kind of magic dust of nostalgic authenticity.[22] The video opens with a close-up of bookshelves full of historical and artistic reference books, spilling over with piles of textiles. These shots show the research and expertise that go into Bourdet's work, denoting the ways that she is connected to the historical and technical aspects of her craft. The video then documents Bourdet using her hand loom, close-ups of multicolored threads, and the soft click-clacking of her practice. The video is scored by plinky-plonky, wistful music, emphasizing the romance of weaving. In the voice-over, she describes growing up in the mountains in Switzerland and Sweden, which is conveyed through three grainy pictures of herself and her parents skiing, hiking, and biking in crisp, alpine surroundings. "I've been collecting textiles and yarns since a young age," she says. "I think I was drawn to hand weaving because I found something there that allowed me to merge and assemble all kinds of memories with these collected

FIGURE 6. Chickens peck around a colorful clothes-
line in this photo from weaver Estelle Bourdet's Instagram. Courtesy of Estelle Bourdet.

estellebourdet

203 likes
estellebourdet nov emb er
9 November 2022

estellebourdet

FIGURE 7. A wooden cabin appears in a misty forest
in this photo from weaver Estelle Bourdet's Instagram.
Courtesy of Estelle Bourdet.

materials." The well-worn family photographs, long-collected fabrics, and personal narratives evoke the scrapbook, a form of vernacular or everyday, domestic, family creativity. This video borrows heavily from strategies of private communication, arguably rejecting the commercial or the institutional. Bourdet draws together the video in the voice-over, citing her connections to the past but also invoking the innovation inherent in her approach: "Craftsmanship is to me a reverence to time and to knowledge . . . . But it's also a way of creating new ideas and new ways of living."

The video evokes another representation of craft by one of my interviewees, Mary, a weaver who works by hand. In our interview, Mary told me that she had recently renovated her rural home, creating space for a purpose-built workshop designed to host talks and courses. "We've just got to a point where we're really presentable now . . . and it's so much easier," she said. "[It's] so much easier to take a photo. It's so much easier to share or to invite people in." Her home has been featured in numerous craft magazines and films, and it is frequently represented as an aspirational example of living an artistic life with a young family. "We've got a few films about us," she claimed, "[and] the response I get from people about them and about all of that is, 'Oh, I want a little bit of your life' or, 'Oh, your life looks so perfect.'" Mary also materially benefited from the fact that her artistic process (which involved hand weaving with homegrown willow) is visually interesting. She told me that professional photographers regularly volunteered to visit her home and photograph her process for free: "It's the easiest craft on the planet to represent because it's so photogenic."

The presentation of the social media backstage can accrue value for certain creative workers—Estele Bourdet and Mary both present as white, and both of them are based in Western Europe. It is relevant to note that weaving is a highly gendered craft. The hand loom is a small portable machine designed to be used in the home (the private sphere) rather than in the masculine public space of the factory. It also has strong connotations of tradition and kinship. As Karen Patel puts it, "handloom weaving is associated with the past, rather than the future."[23] Bearing this in mind, we may examine *what* kind of domestic life is being fetishized in the Instagram videos documenting the beautiful homes and artistic processes of Estelle Bourdet and Mary. The social media presence of both artists celebrates their ability to choose to return to the glacial-paced practice of hand weaving. Mary's perfect life is aesthetically beautiful, but the perfection lies in the way she can negate the institutional inequalities experienced by women related to domestic responsibility. She has built a business in which she can stay at home, employ her husband, and flexibly manage her own childcare on-site. Of course, this dream is not available to all. As feminist scholar Michelle White writes, "women's geographic, cultural, gender, racial and class experiences are elided by claims that revived versions of domesticity are inherently creative and liberating."[24]

We should also note that the beautiful digital presentation of artisanal hand weaving here also reveals tensions between the production of craft in Europe and in the Global South. The European weavers in this chapter describe deliberately choosing hand weaving because of its artisanal allure. However, Annapura Mamidipudi recognizes, "in the Global South, [weaving] is production technology that at best offers a precarious livelihood."[25] Anthropologist Jeffery H. Cohen writes about government interventions within the artisan weaving communities in Oaxaca, Mexico, showing that interventions often encourage a population to "homogenize [their] livelihoods," which often "deny local economic variability" and "discourage diversity in production strategies."[26] Weaving is one of the only viable craft careers available in Oaxaca, and the ability to build a personal self-brand and a dreamy domestic life is functionally prevented by commercial and government intermediaries.

While it is apparently a choice to include more of one's personal life in social media representation, the impact of influencer creep means that it is invariably a choice that holds the promise of more social media engagement and greater financial reward and career sustainability. There is labor involved in developing and sustaining boundaries; successfully doing so allows audiences to feel close to the individual posting content while simultaneously minimizing their personal vulnerability.[27] But these boundaries are required to be elastic. Mary told me she uploads to Instagram "when we need cash" but often feels overwhelmed by the pressures this imposes: "If you promise a little bit of something, then suddenly people are like, 'I want it, I want it, I want it,' and you're not quite prepared to deliver." In this sense, platform economies fuse together the gaps between artists' practice and their personal lives, leaving artists to redraw and navigate boundaries related to their work hours, their everyday lives, and their personal privacy.

Of course, not all artists had access to an aspirational backstage. There are deepened and renewed challenges in patchworking together an authentic artistic identity when they do not have a linen-clad family located in a hand-built cottage-cum-studio within acres of pastoral countryside. As Fern put it, there is a "reluctance to show that you are in Leicester on a ring road surrounded by pollution and rubbish. The reality of where we are all situated and the working standards [in] the kind of studio and building that we work within." It is in this sense that artists' experiences of social media become uneven. Communicating an aspirational identity demands resources and start-up costs that require financial, cultural, and social capital. Pressures to convincingly portray a convincing and authentic depiction of the ideal type of artist shore up intersecting inequalities in art worlds.[28] The ideal artist prioritizes total commitment to their artistic endeavors, focuses on a highly developed single skill, and requires networking abilities and self-confidence.[29] These requirements become unsustainable in the face of caring responsibilities, a need to take on odd jobs to support oneself, and a lack of existing "networks."[30] Access to space as an artist—most importantly a studio—is also entwined with classed and geographic barriers.[31] Charges of pervasive inequality are true of creative industries more broadly, but particularly of cultural work and art worlds. Recent work has shown that parental wealth is an important driver of "class origins earnings gaps" in elite cultural work, shielding the "economically privileged" from precarity and occupational uncertainties.[32]

## Emotional Authenticity—beyond the Influencer Apology Video

The previous chapter showed how influencers strategically use emotional vulnerability in influencer content. Authentic emotions are deployed to negotiate the risks of influencer culture, particularly against charges of insincerity or fakeness associated with commerciality. In a similar vein, artists described the positive reaction they receive from audiences when they display public emotion. Artists, too, describe receiving the highest Instagram engagement when they discuss emotive topics like anxiety, grief, or unemployment. Dani told me that "personal stuff does well." "I had a lot of interaction on a post that said we were closing the shop early because we thought it was going to be the last day that was sunny," she said. "And I was like, that's quite ironic really." Similarly, Rose, who runs art markets, told me that Instagram "rewards you for being quite emotionally slutty." Rose felt an ambient pressure to perform for followers: "You feel like you get so caught up on it, having to turn up every day and give this really lengthy, emotional speech about why you're doing what you doing and why you love it so much and the downs and the ups and the highs and the lows. And I found it, in the end, very emotionally draining." The focus on the lows here is key. As Sarah Banet-Weiser points out, authenticity labor requires maintaining commercial professionalism in the face of "failure, pressure, depression, tears, vulnerability."[33]

Lily, who curates found art objects, offers a compelling example of both the promises and the limits of authenticity labor. She described a highly successful Instagram post where she discussed her experiences of being laid off and how these experiences led to the development of her business: "I just kind of said, 'I don't really regret taking a severance package, I'm still excited about this.'" Her upbeat and, in her own words, "inspirational" post about being laid off from her job was then picked up by a women's style magazine, leading to her inclusion in a list of "pandemic entrepreneurs" and the promotion of her business to their readers. In her interview with me, Lily described the pressure of keeping up with her more successful posts, consistently performing convincing emotion in a way that would get attention: "I have to constantly think about how to make things go viral, because that seems to be how I get more followers. I have to [do something different from] what I've done before: how am I going to make it pretty special?" Under the banner of influencer creep, Lily must be consistent. Displaying pockets or hints of emotion is never enough; she and other individuals are required to offer up their affect convincingly and frequently. Not only do platform logics and cultures compel users to include themselves in their content; many feel pressure to perform spectacular, yet consistent, affect. There is no acceptable limit or moment when authenticity is reached because the risks of inauthenticity in capitalism can never be left alone. This is true both in the advertiser-funded space of influencer culture and for the professional artists I talked to for this book.

Perhaps because of the commercial value of content that displays emotion, some creative workers discussed skepticism about how sharing experiences of mental health could be perceived, particularly raising concerns about coming across as fake. For example, Fern explained her hesitation about discussing her experiences of mental health. As she put it, "Mental health issues are really important and have been really important to how [my practice] came about. But then it's so hard not to take on board reactions when I see other people doing that, and I don't like it, or I don't think it's genuine, or I think there's something about it that doesn't resonate." Fern's concerns that discussions of mental health may not be perceived as genuine recall the way that authenticity within influencer cultures is tested by audiences. It is always measured, appraised, and valued within a wider economic, social, and cultural context.

## Conclusion

I don't know how to be authentic whilst having that marketing voice, or engaging with my audience. I haven't figured that out yet, what my voice sounds like online. I see other people doing it really well, and I'm not sure how much of myself I want to put publicly on the internet for everyone to see. I really value my own privacy, and there's that contradiction of putting a lot of yourself into a public profile. (Aoife, illustrator)

Aoife's sentiment neatly sums up the ways that influencer creep requires individuals to share more and more of their authentic selves on social media platforms. It also captures the pervasive uncertainty among the female and nonbinary artists I interviewed. They were consistently rethinking, reframing, and readjusting the ways they engaged with platforms in order to perform convincingly as aspirational and commercially viable creative workers, while also conveying a convincing emotional performance that comes from within their genuine selves. In this way, undertaking this mandated performance of influencer-driven authenticity represents renewed pressures for artistic and creative workers. Artists are required to document their authentic artistic process while also performing an authentic artistic identity by using influencer-built strategies like representing their backstage studio environments, technical skills, lifestyles, and emotional states.

Influencers often include a heartfelt and intense reflection on their own mental health within social media content. While influencer creep creates an individualized and persistent version of this pressure, the strategic performance of emotion has a long history within celebrity industries. As media scholars Heather Nunn and Anita Biressi have observed, celebrities often publicly discuss a "tragedy or serious dysfunction" following a scandal. This is a form of emotional labor that is used as a "means of attempted self-validation and often rehabilitation of the damaged celebrity persona."[34] Under influencer creep, individuals' content reflects experiences of stress and anxiety, fitting neatly within a feminized, neoliberal "self-help culture."[35] While these conditions are debilitating and serious, online reflections on mental health can be seen as "socially acceptable," at least as they are experienced by white, middle-class social actors. This is especially true of young, white, middle-class women, who experience intense media and societal scrutiny of their levels of "confidence."[36] Anxiety is normalized, perhaps even idealized, when experienced by white, middle-class women who have the luxury of time and the resources to treat their anxieties. The vulnerability and amateur quality within influencer genres trade on a performed binary opposition to representations of confidence, opulence, wealth, and glamour. Discussing anxiety is useful because it is humanizing and vulnerable. Such behavior can be at once pathologized and normalized. In other words, it is authentic.

In the previous chapter and this one, I have laid out the demands and value of a performance of authenticity for influencers and beyond. Building on this recognition of the promises and the limits of authenticity, the final two chapters of this book explore a complementary (and at times competing) component of influencer creep—self-branding and brand safety. In the following chapter I define self-branding in the context of influencer creep, with an overview of the ways influencers have pioneered demonstrations of consistency and commercial salience within the context of highly commercial influencer culture. Through this lens, I examine the ways that individuals navigate the commercial contexts and contradictions of social media platforms using strategies that have been developed, sharpened, and refined within influencer culture.

# 5  *No Historic Nudes Allowed*

Influencer Self-Branding and Brand Safety

Michelle Phan is a Vietnamese American YouTuber who began her YouTube channel in 2007, just one year after the platform was purchased by Google. Her work originated an emotionally driven direct-to-camera style of makeup application mixed with storytelling, forging the generic origins of the beauty vlog. Phan and her channel were foundational to the development of the commercial, feminized sides of YouTube. Phan's success is underscored by her ability to successfully self-brand—her ability to perform a streamlined version of herself, drawn from platform affordances and familiar cultural motifs.[1] In her videos, Phan performs in a way that is at once distinct and *consistent*—underpinned by ordinariness, a lack of professional training, and proclamations of genuine passion.

Phan's personal branding strategies are slower and more cautious than the unabashed style of near-constant self-promotion described by scholars of early web industries.[2] She does not boast or attempt to sell herself. An incredulous journalist reports that Phan assured her "I'm very normal" upward of seven times during an interview for *Elle* magazine.[3] Phan's videos are set in domestic space and often filmed in her bedroom; she tells viewers that when she first started out, her apartment was so small that she had to shoot her videos while sitting on the toilet. This content deliberately rejects glamour-seeking strategies of early fashion bloggers, whom fashion scholar Minh-Ha T. Pham described as coveting front-row seats in fashion weeks and seeking legitimizing relationships with designers, luxury brands, and "cultural, informational and financial capital."[4] Instead, Phan's chosen setting includes pillow-strewn, unmade beds and breaks in the action, during which we accompany her to her tea kettle. In her videos, Phan frames herself as an introverted nerd interested in drawing Disney princesses and superheroes, an early adopter of web technologies like Xanga and Blogger. In one video, she describes the painful loss of a childhood friend because she moved schools so frequently before reassuring herself, "it's OK, you guys are now my friends."[5]

Phan's proto-influencer strategies dovetail with a drive toward authenticity discussed throughout this book, her self-presentation that can be understood most effectively through the concept of the self-brand. Sarah Banet-Weiser notes that self-branding entails the "making and selling of immaterial things—feelings and affects, personalities and values—rather than actual goods."[6] Similarly, Alison Hearn argues that self-branding strategies involve "cultural meanings and images drawn from the narrative and visual codes of the mainstream cultural industries."[7] Successful self-branding means putting together a number of familiar yet niche personal attributes to build a consistent and commercially friendly online presence. Discussing self-branding for influencer economies, Brooke Duffy and Emily Hund highlight "narratives of passion and creative expression,"[8] which disavow time and financial investment (and earnings) and cement discourses of meritocracy and equality. Self-brands must be "consistent yet distinct."[9] In this vein, Phan skilfully mixes a number of touchstones: a confident command of beauty technologies, shy geekiness, an emphasis on feeling and intuition, and overwrought emotional sincerity. Her key business decisions each have an affective aura of happenstance and coincidence. She tells viewers that she decided to make her first video because she was bored; her intuition later told her to move to Los Angeles, then to focus on art school, and then to travel to Europe and Asia.

Phan returns to the central dimension of her personal story again and again in videos and interviews: her mother's disappointment that she chose art school over a more stable career like medicine; the fact that she was given her first-ever laptop when she started her art degree in college; the moment when she was rejected for a beauty advisor position in a department store. These moments offer opportunities for plunder and pastiche; Phan brings together cultural touchstones to borrow the values and meanings they evoke. Her narrative fragments are woven together to build the story of someone who has grown in popularity without money, connections, and relevant professional training. She frequently communicates surprise at the success of her first YouTube channel, launched with a video titled "Natural Looking Makeup," which attracted forty thousand views in a week. She compares herself to Bob Ross, the famous TV art instructor who, as Phan points out, art critics say "isn't a good painter"; this is exactly what critics do when they assess her makeup skills. As she told *Allure* magazine, "It's true. I'm not a professional makeup artist. I'm just showing people how to do their makeup."[10]

Phan has been making content for over fifteen years and, like many influencers, the value of her brand has waxed and waned over time.[11] The elasticity of her claims to relatability were tested as she grew more and more successful in the mid-2010s. In 2015, she launched a makeup brand with L'Oréal called Em, which was reviewed badly. In the same year she was featured in the *Forbes* 30 Under 30, and her company Ipsy was valued at five million dollars. Then she abruptly stopped posting videos on YouTube, causing her audience to speculate about what tragic accident had befallen her, or even whether she was dead. Phan's break from YouTube and her return two years later are now central aspects of her personal story.

Her return was marked with quietly posting a video on YouTube titled "Why I Left." The video involves dreamlike animations of clouds and flowers, underscored by soft music. Taking a leaf from the authenticity playbook, Phan offers an emotional narrative about the feelings of depression that led her to take a break from YouTube, which she traced to the success of her business. As she puts it, "Once I was a girl with dreams who eventually became a product . . . smiling, selling and selling."[12] In the video, Phan muses on the emptiness of modern life. She takes a sabbatical journey to Switzerland, travelling to a compound free from Wi-Fi or distractions. This trip is evocative of the one taken by Julia Roberts's character Elizabeth Gilbert in the 2010 film *Eat Pray Love*. Like Gilbert, Phan rejects the capitalist demands of modern life and finds meaning through going on vacation to locales ostensibly less poisoned by postmodernity than the United States. Nature, Phan said, "nurtured [her] broken spirit back to health," away from the "polluting" effects of technology and commerce. Her inspiration to come back arose during further travel in Egypt, where she saw the pyramids: "we don't remember the people who built the pyramids, but they're still here."[13]

When this video was posted in 2017, some audiences deemed it to be a radical break from Phan's hard-won self-brand, even describing it as a move to transform her life and risk her success. Phan reiterates this message in interviews and op-eds, describing her desire to "start over" and not "[dwell] on the past."[14] *New York Magazine*'s "The Cut" wrote that "Phan's almost as famous for leaving the Internet as she is for making a career on it."[15] In practice, however, "Why I Left" is an example of a continuation of Phan's core brand values: ordinariness, passion, and intuition. And through this lens, this moment actually offers a master class in crafting branded consistency. Phan's return video reiterates her long-spun personal narrative of passionate everydayness, describing why she originally started videos and showing a firm rejection of commercial and financial measures of success, underscoring her relatability. Scenes in the video feature images of faceless suits sliding contracts across long conference tables, apparently pressuring her to attach her name to products that she might not believe in. She describes staying busy to "numb the pain," becoming further detached from her friends and family. She was prompted to leave the platform when she observed her joie de vivre in one of her old YouTube videos: "I'd forgotten how genuine and full of life I once was."[16] Rather than being a break with her online identity, "Why I Left" takes her squarely back to the central conventions of her channel and away from her association with businesses or brands like L'Oréal. Her message at the end of "Why I Left" nearly completely matches that of another video titled "Draw My Life,"[17] which she posted four years prior. The 2013 video closes with a message communicating the possibilities of makeup with one of self-empowerment: "I just wanted to show every girl out there how beautiful she was and how makeup can be their own superhero costume. . . . We all have a story to tell and we are all part of something beautiful."[18] In "Why I Left," she says, "Back then, I was just showing you how to look more beautiful. Now I want to show you how to feel more beautiful."[19]

This chapter thus outlines the contours of a new shift in the conditions of self-branding under influencer creep, which involves editing a version of oneself in the direction of a consistent identity, with an orientation toward brand safety and commercial suitability. Online presence is now indelibly tied to a small number of platformized locations—where individuals become subject to specific, platform-decided conditions for participation, visibility, and invisibility. In an atmosphere of risk and anxiety, influencers have responded with strategies like using platform features, tools, and language. They can skilfully pastiche and communicate an acceptable version of themselves to their audiences and their commercial partners. In this chapter, I open with a historical review of self-branding, showing the ways that individuals must edit their online self, seeking to maintain consistency. I bring this into conversation with brand safety, reviewing the ways in which layers of pressure from platforms and brands mandate an orientation toward commercial suitability.

## A Brief History of Self-Branding

Contemporary self-branding strategies originated, or at least were accelerated, during the rise of flexible, casualized freelance work that was bought about by the rise of neoliberalism and the concomitant global, instant communication technologies, a form of work that has been compounded by domino-like global financial turbulence as well as recessions since the 1980s. Since that time, the concept of a "job for life" has all but ceased to exist, encouraging workers to labor toward personal improvement and mandating them to constantly *stay ready* for the job market.[20] According to sociologist Ulrich Beck, we now live in an insecure "risk society": the narrowing influence of religion, tradition, and community have spiked an atmosphere of anxiety. Risk society informs how we navigate the "openness, uncertainties and the obstructions of a self-created future."[21] Self-branding can be understood as technique of resilience and self-management crafted as a response to these uncertain conditions. While self-branding is highly emotional (because it is tied to the self), it is ultimately a competitive strategy characterized by a nearly constant striving for market share against contemporary society. Self-branding helps us to maintain an illusion of control—that is, the comforting belief that if people work and upskill enough, they can navigate systems of risk, anxiety, and precarity. This context is precisely what makes Michelle Phan's brand so compelling. Her success originates from her navigation of challenges. By successfully representing an essential self through YouTube, she has been able to move on from difficulties in her early life—the loneliness and isolation, the parental disappointment, the dropping out of school, the job searching in the wake of the 2008 recession. The humanizing form of her narratives allows her to nimbly spin a performance of the self that is (when necessary) both special and ordinary.

Self-branding strategies accelerated in the Web 2.0 era for cultural and technical reasons. Culturally, the fast-paced, entrepreneurial start-up culture in Silicon Valley (where online technologies were being developed) helped to sharpen and embed social promotional practices, normalizing a way of "thinking about the self as a saleable commodity that can tempt a potential employer."[22] Start-up culture prioritized norms of self-improvement and hustle within a blurred social and professional context underpinned by unending mandatory self-promotion and networking. The "meat space" (or in-person) conditions for access into this culture were exacerbated by pressures toward participating in "always on" digital social technologies. Technological pressure came in the guise of newly invented blogs and personal webpages, and this allowed for creative spaces for individuals to put together their own personal values in engaging and consistent ways. As Alice Marwick notes, blogs and personal webpages offered up the conditions for everyday workers to utilize "a set of marketing strategies applied to the individual,"[23] piecing together their desired identity through a pastiche of images and text. These technological developments were deeply embedded in the fast-paced, entrepreneurial start-up culture that was characteristic of Silicon Valley. It became a cultural norm to "[think] about the self as a saleable commodity that can tempt a potential employer."[24] Arguably, this specific version of self-branding brought with it the threat of what was called *context collapse*, a kind of erasure of ability to curate and perform specific versions of oneself dependent on who the audience is. Visibility was now available for potentially anyone, creating a "moral" pressure to perform one streamlined version of the online self that was both consistent and "constantly improving."[25]

The techniques and tools of self-branding became latterly shifted away from distributed blogs and websites toward the streamlined technical affordances wrought by platformization—a process defined as the "penetration of economic and infrastructural extensions of online platforms into the web."[26] The logic of platformization tightened the opportunities for individualization. As Thomas Poell, David Nieborg and Brooke Duffy note, social media platforms "do not foreground pages and collectives, but profiles and personalities."[27] Not only are social media oriented around opportunities for crafting and promoting an individual presence; they offer visibility structures that communicate the importance, relevance, and reputation of each of these individuals in fixed, standardized ways.

## Influencer Creep, Brand Safety, and Self-Branding

Neoliberal economies, digital self-promotion, and platformization all provide important inroads to the development of contemporary cultures of self-branding; however, these have become further transfigured in very specific ways within influencer culture. Practically, brand safety is a positive reproduction of a brand's ideals, an avoidance of controversy, and a circumvention of sex, violence, and profanity.[28] The term is not new; brands have long wanted to be understood as "noncontroversial, light and nonpolitical," since this sustains a "buying mood."[29] To investigate why brand safety is so important to self-branding cultures within influencer creep, we must first explore how advertisers leverage influence within social media economies both *to platforms* and *directly to influencers.*

To start, let's consider the ways that advertisers govern platforms. Just like radio, television, and print media, commercial social media platforms are reliant on income raised from targeted advertising. Once, a peer reviewer in a journal chastised me for calling Google an advertising company. I kind of understand this response; Google makes so many products that support our social, work, and everyday lives that it might not *feel* like this is all in service of fueling an engine that is designed to attract and distribute advertising. But in 2023, sixty-five billion dollars of Google's revenue came from ads (with a measly ten billion dollars from other services). Advertisers keep the light on, and the need to appease them has shaped platformized production. All monopoly platforms curate their policies and requirements based on advertiser demands.

Advertisers haven't always been happy to give billions of their spending dollars to new technologies. Google and its video sharing platform, YouTube, were originally considered a risky "Wild West." When YouTube was founded in 2005, user-generated content had a bad reputation as "grainy and unprofessional."[30] The platform was seen as a haven for sophomoric, low-quality videos of skateboarding dogs. To remedy this perception—that is, in order to become profitable—the platform launched the YouTube Partner Program (YPP) in 2007. The platform initially handpicked YouTubers to be partners but scaled this up quickly, allowing anyone with one thousand subscribers to join. The premise was simple: if a creator made the kinds of content that advertisers would be comfortable with, they would be rewarded with 55 percent of the money that advertisers decided to spend on that content. Media industries scholar Ramon Labato suggests the YPP was designed to reward "popular channels that align with specific consumer 'verticals'" with a "clear link to consumer markets."[31] Similarly, Jean Burgess and Josh Green describe the Partner Program as an endeavor to use "selective monetization" to "'manage' the community and institute more social norms that are palatable to the public and the advertisers."[32] The YPP became both carrot and stick, designed to incentivize and discipline creators to produce commercially viable content that would meet advertiser requirements.

Despite the success of the YPP, advertisers were not satisfied with the platform's assurances that the content they placed their ads next to was of decent quality. They were also used to the close relationships they had with commercial broadcasters, where they were able to directly influence high-level production decisions and "control the environment in which their ad was placed."[33] Advertisers wanted to know that they had a seat at the table. The 2017 YouTube Adpocalypse offers evidence about the extent of advertiser influence on the way YouTube operates: a moment in which advertisers swiftly, and publicly, distanced themselves financially and morally from the platform. This event was spurred by press investigations into YouTube advertising, which found that top-tier brands were appearing next to videos promoting extremist views and hate speech. The timing of this investigation was made worse by the actions of one of the most heavily subscribed YouTubers on the platform, Felix Kjelberg, who, in a now notorious video, used a micro-payment app to pay two kids to hold up a sign with a violent, antisemitic threat on it.[34]

In response, YouTube rapidly scrambled to reassure advertisers that they had the situation under control, announcing changes in content moderation and restricting Partner Program eligibility. Now, a focus on advertisers underpins YouTube's attempts at guiding cultural production; YouTube explicitly directs creators toward advertiser-friendliness, advising them how content can be made suitable for brands. For example, in one video on the Creator Insider channel about how monetization policies work, a YouTube employee says, "We are always looking to improve our policies in ways that make advertisers comfortable and creators happy."[35] Advertisers and creators are afforded parity as stakeholders that YouTube must manage, a departure from YouTube's early raconteur-ish "broadcast yourself" motto. The platform produces videos designed to encourage creators to bear advertiser perspectives in mind, to "put themselves in advertisers' shoes" when producing content, and to consider whether a brand would be happy.[36] Since 2018, influencers hoping to monetize their content must go beyond YouTube's baseline community guidelines and adhere to a stricter tier of advertiser-friendly content guidelines. Additional rules include restrictions on profanity, sexualized themes, "shocking" content, use of (even regulated, legal) drugs, "controversial issues," and "sensitive events." Meta has emulated YouTube's approach and maintains content monetization policies for Instagram and Facebook, which are designed for advertisers to "make Meta safe for brands and for people." These include a similar set of proscribed behaviors to YouTube's—for example, "debated social issues," sexual or suggestive content, and strong language. Meta also warns influencers to be mindful of who they associate with: "monetized creators . . . may lose the ability to monetize if an entity connected to [them] has violated these policies."[37]

An investigation into YouTube's advertiser-friendly content guidelines by platform governance scholar Susanne Kopf shows that the platform employs "vagueness extensively" to allow "room for manoeuvre" to afford broad decisions and create challenges for those seeking to challenge judgements.[38] Take, for example, the category of "sensitive events," which includes "civil emergencies, health emergencies, terrorism and related activities, conflicts or mass acts of violence." To explain this policy on the creator-facing YouTube channel Creator Insider, YouTube policy manager John gives an example of the 2016 mass shooting at a gay nightclub in Orlando, Florida. He recognizes that "a lot of LBTQ+ creators were uploading videos expressing how sad they were at this event"; however, it remains the case that discussion of this event was "just not safe to run ads next to in general."[39] Since marginalized communities are disproportionately victims of such "newsworthy events," this policy affects the experiences of individuals who want to discuss the harmful impact of a violent event on their communities. Social media scholars Brooke Duffy and Colten Meisner show that moderation and algorithmic punishment are often lopsidedly applied to marginalized creators posting about "social justice issues."[40] While some may believe these algorithmic inequalities are mistakes or "glitches," policies and discussion show that this kind of application is intentional. As John says in the YouTube video, "There's just some stuff that advertisers don't want to be connected to."[41]

Creators also must also adhere to YouTube's creator responsibility and monetization policies, which include calls to a broad standard of general behavior: "be respectful of your viewers, your fellow creators and our advertisers—both on and off YouTube." These policies apply to anyone who is accepted into the YouTube Partner Program. Creators' behavior is expected to holistically match advertiser expectations both on and off the platform. The stakes for this clause are higher than demonetization; in fact, YouTube states it will terminate disobedient creators' accounts, as well as any new accounts they create going forward.

The creator responsibility policy is evocative of the morals clause, first introduced in the early 1920s to "safeguard" organizations like Hollywood studios and sports teams against the bad behavior of celebrities. One of the earliest morals clauses was used by the New York Yankees baseball team to manage the behavior of Babe Ruth, who was garnering a reputation as a "glutton, womanizer, spendthrift, heavy drinker and smoker."[42] Morals clauses usually cover illegal behavior in addition to "immoral conduct," a flexible and changeable concept that relies on setting the "prevailing public sentiment of the day as [a] behavioural benchmark."[43] Morals clauses in traditional entertainment industries are contractually specific and heavily negotiated by a team of managers and lawyers. Platforms, on the other hand, do not afford negotiation; indeed, the relationship between the platform and influencer is not one of employment. Creators are automatically and sweepingly subject to one-size-fits-all rules, placed at the mercy of YouTube's intentionally vague assessments, with little recourse. These rules add an extra layer of threat, making creators concerned about erring and jeopardizing their livelihood. Marginalized creators are often disproportionately affected by the kinds of automated judgments made by platforms regarding brand safety.

Social media platforms sometimes say that safety is a broad church, something they prioritize to help everyone on the platform. For example, Meta advertises their brand safety page using the strapline "Facebook is committed to creating a safer, more welcoming community across all platforms for creators, brands and individuals."[44] But digging a little deeper, we can see that in practice advertisers are prioritized; indeed, they are the architects of platform policy. For example, on their policy pages Meta reveals that their community standards are dictated by the Global Alliance for Responsible Media (GARM), which is a coalition made up of global advertisers including Johnson & Johnson, McDonalds, Mondelez, Nestlé, and Pepsi. Through this coalition, advertisers have directly shaped the community standards that all individuals using Meta's products must be subject to, likely with very little input from influencers. YouTube puts it plainly: their responsibility is to advertisers first. Their policy pages note that "the success of your channel and the YouTube Partner Program is dependent upon the willingness of advertisers to associate their brands with YouTube content."[45] Influencers must anticipate what is commercially safe and behave themselves accordingly; if they do not, they may be responsible for the collapse of the whole YPP.

## Brand Safety and Influencer Culture

Although platforms are a newer form of media engine, they offer a mostly recognizable corporate landscape to marketing professionals. Influencers, however, are still considered uncharted territory— or risky wild cards. Former Unilever CMO Keith Weed made waves at the Cannes Marketing Festival in France when he delivered a speech calling for the "cleanup of the influencer ecosystem."[46] Brands are also concerned about the activities of influencers that they directly contract for sponsorships. Industry watchdog Influencer Marketing Hub, for example, found that 67 percent of brands were worried about influencers acting "in a way deemed inappropriate" by the brands they represent.[47] Brands are worried about an influencer they have partnered with causing a scandal. This might mean their brand suffers reputational damage, but they also worry, and perhaps even more importantly, about the danger that their advertising dollars could go to waste. In a think piece published in *Forbes* magazine, "industry leader" Danielle Wiley writes, "Once an influencer's reputation is tarnished, the value of the partnership is decreased."[48]

To mitigate against brand safety concerns, it is common industry practice for advertisers to conduct a risk assessment and extensive background checks on influencers that they hope to work with. In an illuminating piece, Cedric Dorudain, chief digital officer at L'Oréal, explains the detailed and time-intensive background checks his company conducts on prospective influencers. Dourdain states that L'Oréal hand checks influencers for the kinds of content that they have posted in the past—and will reject influencers who they believe engage in too much sponsored content or who have ever "had any [brand safety] concerns like nude pictures."[49] This level of scrutiny is, of course, highly gendered and dovetails with a wider trend toward the "sex-negative" forms of governance undertaken within the social media ecology, whereby platform and brand characterizations of sexually suggestive elements have been "opaque, inconsistent, arbitrary and puritan" in ways that more acutely affect the work of marginalized creators.[50] Brands and platforms draw together their own subjective understanding of brand safety in "sexist assemblages," which arise from social morals and norms.[51] I've suggested throughout this book that the commercial enclaves of influencer culture are feminized spaces; the risks within them are related to feminine excess. L'Oréal is concerned about influencers being spectacularly commercial, being connected to too many brands, which may impact assessments of authenticity. But it is also worried about influencers behaving in ways that are overtly sexual.

Influencers' working conditions are characterized by multiple layers of pressure to ensure brand safety, which is highly dependent on an assemblage of stakeholders' assessments of tolerance and risk. Brand safety is subjective and contextual. Drives toward brand safety are particularly salient within the individualized influencer economy because of its lack of historical hallmarks of reputation or established career trajectory. In an advertiser-funded ecology, it is advertisers who construct the foundations of branded acceptability in the influencer economy, thus shaping both the hard and soft governance of behavior for influencers, and latterly even for anyone creating content on social media platforms.

## Algorithms and Automating Brand Safety

Brand concerns have given rise to a valuable market of start-ups selling "brand safety tools" which claim to help marketers choose suitable influencers for partnerships and sponsorships. Tools laud many features—for example, that they can predict whether an influencer's behavior is brand safe, or if they will be likely to cause a scandal or be canceled. As part of my research into influencer economies I negotiated access to an influencer brand safety software tool I will call Clip, which boasted clients like Google, EA Games, and Lego. This tool has now been shut down; its technology was sold to another software provider that is still on the market. Spoiler alert: this tool functioned poorly, and some of its features operated in ways that may discriminate against marginalized creators.

In my research, I found this tool was likely running influencer videos through an audio processing software to identify how many times the influencer used profanity or vulgar language. This technology sifts through any influencer's spoken words, picking out instances of profanity to feed into a "family friendliness" score, which subsequently fed into an overall safety score—a value out of ten given to represent and rank an influencer's brand-friendliness. The severity of the influencer's language was categorized using a simple traffic light system: "Piss," "crap," and "damn" were coded green. Orange words included "ass," "dick," and "vagina." Severe swearwords like "fuck" and "shit" were coded in red, and importantly, so were racial slurs such as the N-word. The implied parity between these words is jarring from a functional perspective, even without a consideration of the ethical issues that I will go on to discuss. A consumer backlash caused by an influencer exclaiming "fuck" is unlikely to equal that of the (direct or indirect) use of a racist slur. The tool didn't offer a guide to the values informing its confusing judgments. You might wonder, what makes "tit" orange and "boob" green? What contributes to the medically correct term "vagina" being coded orange, the same categorization as "whore" and "ass"?

The intricacies of these categorizations are funny, but they matter because they affect the livelihoods of influencers, who do not have access to information on how words are categorized and why. These categorizations are used to rank influencers for brands, since the latter use these rankings to distribute income and opportunities. Even if an influencer decides to take a deep dive into how they were being categorized by *one* brand safety tool, this would just be one tool out of a huge number of automated tools in a market that was worth 21.1 billion dollars in 2024. Each new software start-up develops their own metrics and algorithmic recipes designed to categorize and present influencers to prospective brand partners.

We could now focus in on the word "queer," which is coded as green profanity—on a par with "boob," "butt," and "fart." While "queer" does have roots as a homophobic slur, it is a term used widely in activism and LGBTQ+ communities, often drawing from deconstructivist theory to recognize that sexualities are "unstable, fluid and constructed."[52] So, one may identify as queer, partake in queer activism, or discuss queer theory. In many of these contexts, "queer" can be an everyday or academic identifier, and the word is used by YouTubers to align content with LGBTQ+ communities and audience. My research into influencer management software revealed that several high-profile LGBTQ+ influencers were identified by Clip for their use of "queer" as a "naughty word"; these included A-list YouTuber Tyler Oakley, who the tool said had used the word thirty-nine times. Oakley's work features celebrities who have long attracted advertising partnerships—for example, Olympic skier Gus Kenworthy, the face of Head and Shoulders shampoo. The classification of "queer" as non-family-friendly lowers creators' safety score, reducing their visibility in tools' search functions.

"Queer" being categorized as not family-friendly could be read as a glitch, or an error; but in reality, LGBTQ+ creators have long been penalized owing to concerns about queer content. Maybe, then, the technology is working exactly as it should. Brand safety is often tied to the vague yet powerful notion of "public morals." These change over time. We know, for example, that advertisers' attitudes to media concerning lesbian, gay, bisexual, and transgender themes have been somewhat transformed over the past thirty years. In the 1970s, publications like the *New York Times* refused advertising that mentioned "gay" or "homosexual." Indeed, especially the AIDS crisis of the 1980s, which largely affected gay men and trans communities, led to what media theorist Katherine Sender describes as a "near-total moratorium on open appeals to gay consumers."[53] This hesitance to address LGBTQ+ consumers dovetailed with widespread protests from Christian and conservative advocacy groups, who were able to "successfully pressure the industry," ultimately leading to "elimination of [the topic] from televisions' exchange of ideas."[54] The 1990s and 2000s brought with them a change in public attitudes, and with it an exponential rise in the representation of LBGTQ+ themes in mainstream media, as advertisers recognized the consumption value of gay audiences. Yet despite an increase in representation, advertisers continue to have anxieties about mediated depictions of queer sexuality to this day, leading to representations of the ideal consumer as "gender-conforming and sexually discreet . . . to offer the most 'positive' image of gays to both readers and advertisers."[55]

In the present day, the conflation of "queer" content with brand risk in influencer software is just one among a sea of contemporary moments revealing brand avoidance of LGBTQ+ content. We could, for example, think about a prominent moment in 2017 when influencers started to notice that YouTube's restricted "family-friendly" mode was blocking content made by LGBTQ+ creators featuring words such as "gay," "lesbian," and "bisexual." Under this "safe" mode, used by schools and libraries, a wide range of ostensibly banal content was rendered unviewable—for example, a lesbian couple's wedding vows or creators offering queer dating advice. By YouTube's own guidelines, restricted mode is intended to block only "sexually suggestive content, violence, inappropriate language, promotion of drugs and regulated substances, and controversial or sensitive subjects and events."

YouTube initially refused to take complaints seriously, tweeting out a statement that only "mature" content was being hidden. But YouTube creators responded by becoming de facto detectives, flipping the restricted mode on their channels and evincing a wide range of videos that were not visible through screengrabs. Tyler Oakley responded to YouTube's statement, showing images of blocked educational content videos, including one titled "8 Black LGBTQ+ Trailblazers Who Inspire Me."[56] Queer creator Kristin Russo reported in *Autostraddle* magazine that over 150 advice videos that she had made were blocked under the so-called restricted mode. Russo shared her own perception of why flagging queer content as "inappropriate" or "mature" was concerning—"these are words that we hear thrown around by right-wing politicians and conservative religious leaders who seek to censor, limit or otherwise oppress queer and trans people."[57] The leaders that Russo refers to here are the very same ones who have historically sought to pressure advertisers to avoid advertising using queer themes or queer media. Whether they have a direct line to YouTube or not, these individuals have been influential within the historical culture of advertiser-funded media.

After the hashtag #YouTubeIsOverParty started trending on Twitter, garnering a slew of press attention, YouTube eventually acknowledged the issue. YouTube blamed its algorithms. They posted the following statement on their blog: "our system sometimes makes mistakes in understanding context and nuances." This is a common move, fetishizing algorithms for their "objectivity," painting them as "formulaic with an identified function or role that determines the steps and the processes that are employed."[58] Of course, YouTube isn't alone in introducing algorithmic moderation to manage datasets (often groups of people) viewed as unruly, messy, or risky. By using algorithmic influencer management tools, brands hope to make the glut of user-generated content produced by influencers manageable and monetizable. In so doing, however, they reify existing social inequalities. This is because algorithms are, as sociologist Virginia Eubanks puts it, "embedded in old systems of power and privilege."[59] They classify individuals while giving little insight into their processes or how to address instances of misclassification. Indeed, it is no coincidence that influencer management tools draw from colonial discourse in framing influencer ecologies as a Wild West that has to be stabilized and managed. As sociologist Ruha Benjamin points out, such technological solutions often "hide, speed up or even deepen discrimination."[60] Long social histories of discriminatory decision-making are baked into engineering practices, training datasets, and content moderation decisions by machines and humans.

The public reckoning wrought by #YouTubeIsOverParty in 2017 shows how platforms like YouTube are required to very carefully manage the needs and demands of two distinct stakeholder groups—influencers and advertisers. While YouTube initially sought to dismiss concerns raised by creators, press coverage of the public backlash forced them to apologize; they thereafter claimed they had "fixed" the moderation of "restricted mode." The glitch *could* have been algorithmic, but #YouTubeIsOverParty fits with a long-standing over-sexualization of otherwise banal, everyday gay content. Although it has more recently been socially judged "brand safe" to include LGBTQ+ themes within media and promotional content, queer content that is related to sex could still be viewed by advertisers as "incompatible with . . . advertising."[61] If the problems did lie with YouTube's automated systems, the conflation of queer culture with sexual risk likely becomes encoded through a long-standing (human) association. And indeed, advertisers are not trying to hide the fact that they cast a wide net when it comes to what they would like to avoid. Telecommunications company AT&T told the BBC, "Until Google can protect our brand from offensive content of any kind, we are removing all advertising from YouTube."[62] But we know that what is deemed to be offensive is socially, culturally, and politically diverse. Despite the socially progressive wins of the 1990s, societies continue to be embroiled in ongoing culture wars, involving topics like immigration, racism, abortion access, transphobia, and sex-negative stigma.

So, we may ask, what version of public morals are brands like AT&T following? And how are these branded concerns taken up and translated into policy by social media platforms like YouTube, Instagram, TikTok, and others? We know, for example, that LGBTQ+ influencers report being over-moderated and judged as advertiser-unfriendly; a third of content featuring the words "gay," "lesbian," or "LGBTQ" has been restricted by YouTube's AI moderation.[63] For a long time, queer and trans people have been a "variable in risk assessment formulas."[64] In the contemporary moment, it is overwhelmingly transgender influencers who find themselves at the mercy of cultural clashes and moral panics, squarely in the crosshairs of judgments of branded risk and safety.

To take one example, in 2023 transgender actress and influencer Dylan Mulvaney posted a sponsored TikTok video sipping a tallboy can of Bud Light with her face on it, offering a $15,000 giveaway promoting the brand. Mulvaney's ad caught the attention of some of the most conspicuous figures on the American right, including country singer Kid Rock, who responded to this event with a video of himself shooting a stack of Bud Light cases with an assault rifle. Right-wing activists called for a boycott of Budweiser, knocking the beer off its spot as the top-selling beer in the United States.[65] At the same time, Mulvaney received press attention of all stripes, and an extraordinary level of targeted abuse, including stalking and harassment. As she put it in another video, "What transpired from that [initial] video was more bullying and transphobia than I could have ever imagined."[66] It is important to note that the backlash here was not about the *content* of Mulvaney's influencer work, but about the fact that Bud Light had worked with a transgender influencer. But the consequences were individually felt by Mulvaney, who received extraordinary levels of negative press attention and targeted online abuse.

## Who Is Safe?

Who is brand safety for? Working with Budweiser certainly did not make Dylan Mulvaney safe. The brand refused to support her publicly, and Mulvaney has reported that Budweiser did not reach out privately. Instead, they shifted their marketing strategy to "refocus on sport," launching a major campaign depicting (mostly) men getting ready to drink Bud in bars or tailgating on NFL game days.[67]

Rather than affirm any commitment to LGBTQ+ causes, Budweiser sidestepped controversy. As the brand's North American CEO, Brendan Whitworth, said in a blog post, "We never intended to be part of a discussion that divides people."[68] And that's it. Platformized and influencer-oriented brand safety efforts contribute to a culture of risk avoidance within influencer cultures, and they arguably shape commercially oriented self-branding that becomes a throughline of influencer creep.

Dylan Mulvaney's is one of a number of highly publicized examples that reveal the swift economic and cultural consequences when brands determine whether influencers they work with represent a risk. We can also consider the case of Monroe Bergdorf, a Black, transgender influencer and activist from the United Kingdom. Bergdorf was hired in 2017 as L'Oréal's first transgender model. Shortly after, she posted comments on her own Facebook page decrying the neo-Nazi rallies held in Charlottesville, Virginia, with comments on the "racial violence of white people." L'Oréal quickly released a statement suggesting that Bergdorf's comments were "at odds" with their values to "champion diversity" and publicly dropped her, exposing her to a level of press attention and criticism that she has described as "extremely traumatic."[69] Clearly, L'Oréal got more than they bargained for when it came to hiring for "diversity." Indeed, Bergdorf's experiences recall Minh-Ha T. Pham's writing on Asian fashion bloggers working in Western contexts in the 2010s. According to Pham, bloggers were aware of the value of their otherness for brands but were equally aware of the limits of being too much, or in this case too Asian. Pham showed how these individuals dodged (rather than refuted) any discussion of race. They were required to "strategically recast their racial difference as an element of style and social distinction."[70] They were offering "something for everyone but offending no one."[71]

Three years after being so publicly dropped, Bergdorf was rehired by L'Oréal. The brand's new president, Delphine Vigure, personally apologized, gave Bergdorf a spot on their newly established UK diversity and inclusion advisory board, and donated an undisclosed sum to two social justice charities. The rehiring neatly coincided with the worldwide protests over the killing of George Floyd in 2020 and a cultural demand for brands to "respond to racial injustice in ways that seem sincere and . . . substantial."[72] Brands like L'Oréal became aware that audiences were monitoring their actions, and their public interaction with Bergdorf just a couple of years earlier served as an uncomfortable record of a moment in which they had very publicly punished a Black woman speaking out about antiracism. This kind of contradictory behavior made L'Oréal vulnerable to critiques of "performative wokeness."[73] To resolve this issue, they scrambled to work with Bergdorf in order to address and neutralize potential criticisms from audiences for being "inauthentic" in their support for the Black Lives Matter movement.[74] In this sense, we can see that brand safety closely tracked alongside public tolerance and morals. L'Oréal identified a renewed appetite for branded verbalization of antiracism, and a renewed risk of alienating customers outside Black and LGBTQ+ communities. Reflecting on the examples of brands engaging and then publicly dropping Dylan Mulvaney and Monroe Bergdorf, we can define brand safety concerns as following their audience's *tolerance* for discriminatory behaviors rather than a pursuit of the protection of the influencers that brands contract and work with.

## Self-Branding and Brand Safety in Influencer Creep

This chapter has mapped out the strategies used by influencers to self-brand: drawing together a pithy collection of attributes, behaviors, and values into one neat identity, and then sticking with this identity at all costs. When this self-brand is challenged or compromised, there is a very real price to pay. Michelle Phan, a founding figure of influencer culture, dramatically left YouTube in order to preserve her claimed identity as ordinary, passionate, and intuitive. While critics suggested she was throwing her business away by leaving the platform, we can instead view this move as protective, salvaging the value of her brand by communicating a commitment to the values that were central to her business. In the second half of this chapter, I showed how these kinds of influencer-created self-branding strategies are underscored with a mandate to be brand-safe for commercial partners. Brand safety pressures come both from social media platforms as they mediate the expectations of advertisers and from advertisers directly as they surveil and monitor influencer behavior. Social media platforms compel influencers to behave in "moral" ways when creating platform content, and they do so beyond the platform into their everyday lives.

To really understand how brand safety is established within influencer creep we could ask: what is brand-unsafe? The brand-unsafe content, themes, and moments we have explored in these pages have included (but are, of course, not limited to) influencers behaving in racist or antisemitic ways, instructional or terrorist-themed content, community grief over newsworthy events like public shootings, using the word "queer," partnering with too many brands, posting a nude, speaking out about antiracism, making educational content about coming out, covering queer historical figures, and simply being a transgender woman. Reviewing this sprawling list, we may ask again—brand safety means keeping whom safe and from what? Self-branding hinges on influencers garnering an independent understanding of "positive moral values."[75] Labor toward commercially conditioned brand safety does not end even when brands hire influencers; brands continuously monitor and surveil behavior, and are poised and ready to withdraw their support. In this sense brand safety only goes one way: influencers are expected to keep brands safe but brands will not keep influencers safe.

Successfully becoming an influencer means mastering self-surveillance and self-conditioning in the direction of commercially saleable values. Owing to their platform-first flavor of cultural production, influencers experience the stakes of platformized cultural shifts first. Their experiences and strategies can show us the ways that commercial platform culture has reshaped self-branding as rigid, inflexible, and stale. As platforms keep reputation and surveillance firmly bounded and centrally anchored, influencers must navigate the ever-humming risk of being designated "brand-unsafe" as determined within a double layer of branded surveillance. They navigate advertiser-architected platform policy, nestled within a wider net of advertorial monitoring and attempts at rationalization.

In the next chapter, I trace the strategies of consistency and style forward to show how creative workers outside influencer cultures have also navigated their platformized life within the push and pull of creativity and brand safety, specifically examining strategies used to navigate the challenges and fragility of successfully performing a consistent and brand-safe online identity. I show how the pursuit of platform-driven brand safety affects artistic production, and how an avoidance of risk born within influencer culture has changed art worlds and artistic production. Under influencer creep, self-branding unites with brand safety to diminish the (scant) opportunities for flexibility and play within creative work. Art becomes restricted by the deep penetration of brands into the platforms that enable creative culture, in addition to the cultural influence of brand surveillance.

# 6  *When Naked Becomes Nude*

Artist Self-Branding and Brand Safety

How do artists help audiences understand their artworks? Historically, the official artist bio has served this purpose, giving artists the chance to add textual context to art. However, these professional resources offer limited room for more than a few personal or biographical details. Now, and in line with influencer creep, Instagram allows artists to communicate a consistent and, importantly, personal online self-brand.

Jen Stark is a self-brander par excellence. She is an American artist based in Los Angeles who creates brightly colored abstract structures and sculptures. By any art world measure, she's successful: she has exhibited her art in galleries all over the world; her work is held in the Smithsonian; and it has been collected by celebrities like pop star Demi Lovato. Stark has successfully deepened her professional narratives through the skillful use of influencer strategies; she has a strong Instagram presence with over two hundred thousand followers. She regularly updates her Instagram grid with work-in-progress posts to show her career progress and gallery connections. She also allows intentional space for windows of personality to peek through. On Instagram we can see her throw a paintbrush into the air while she cartwheels and scrambles atop the freshly adorned wall. These moments communicate authenticity, energy, and playfulness, important values that also flow through her practice.

Stark communicates the aesthetic consistency of her art on Instagram by also showing the colorful palette of her everyday life. Her Instagram Stories offer snapshots of a breakfast table with a sunny egg yolk, a shining glass of orange juice, and brightly colored tropical fruits and sunflowers. In another post we see an image of an azure swimming pool against a cobalt blue sky, accented with fluttering, cloud-white flags. Stark's personal style matches her artworks. She wears fun overalls in peachy pastel shades, Lycra tops in neon pinks and yellows, patchwork tunics in loud geometric patterns. Images of her home and studio are similarly adorned with colorful accessories, brightly colored plant pots, strings of rainbow yarn, balancing towers of kaleidoscopic sculptures, a cute dog often wrapped in rainbow blankets. Stark showcases elements of her personal life that reflect and shore up the symbolism within her art work. The fun, trippy, and spiritual elements of her practice are underscored by fanned tarot cards, a Phish concert, a bike adorned with ribbons and flowers that has been ridden across the muddy flatlands of the US art and music festival Burning Man.

Stark's Instagram presence sometimes borrows from influencer genres directly. One video opens with an interviewer, invisible behind the camera, who approaches random individuals on the street to ask them a question: "do you make art?" These individuals hurry along a busy sidewalk, clutching coffees and shopping bags, shaking their heads in confusion. After approaching two sets of seemingly arbitrary pedestrians, our interviewer then hails Stark, asking her the same question. In an apparent moment of authentic spontaneity, she responds peppily, "Yes I do! I actually

FIGURE 8. In Instagram images, artist Jen Stark matches colorful outfits and mise-en-scène with her vibrant artworks. Image courtesy of Jen Stark. Photo credit: Rudy Duboue.

made this mural right here," and she points to a drippy, multi-colored work splashed across a large wall behind her. The video mirrors a genre of "vox pop" influencer content common to Instagram or TikTok, where an influencer approaches people on the street to ask them temperature-taking questions—for example, how much rent they pay or what they think of contemporary social issues. Usually this is a setup, and the interviewer will shortly be taken for a tour of the person's home in order to show the audience, for example, what a three-thousand-dollar-a-month studio in New York looks like. As is customary within this influencer genre format, Stark introduces herself and invites the interviewer to come along for a personal studio tour, where she shows her latest work and talks more about her creative practice.

## Histories of Artistic Self-Branding

Stark draws from the technical and cultural affordances of Instagram to attach further meaning to her practice. But, we should ask, is this kind of self-branding new for artists under influencer creep? To be sure, artists have created some of the earliest blueprints for these practices. American artist Andy Warhol, for example, was famous for framing himself as a brand with a "clear commercial mission of commodification and distribution."[1] Warhol intentionally played with celebrity and fame, publicly seeking notoriety, shamelessly befriending film stars, and coproducing the brand narratives of the rich and famous through his magazine *Interview*. Warhol's work rested on a spectacular (and lucrative) critique of the relationship between fame, art, and art world value. He developed a postmodern style of branded persona, affording the consistency demanded by the art world while opening up space for novelty and experimentation within his practice. He joined up artistic style with a streamlined performance of the self.

The richest living British artist, Damien Hirst, is known for being one of the Young British Artists (YBA) who dominated international art scenes in the 1990s. He approaches the style and language of branding and trademarking from a different direction, drawing from the fields of medicine and pharmaceuticals. Still, this approach to branding allows Hirst to cohere wide-ranging and diverse works. He built his brand on what cultural theorist Celia Lury terms the "relations between things, with assemblages and re-assemblages, appropriations and incorporations."[2] By embracing branding, Hirst digs into consistency. He can frame his most notable series, the "spot paintings," as a methodical science experiment, which allows them to be placed in line with his sculptural works that focus on scientific discovery and experimentation. Strategically developing the Damien Hirst brand also folds a wide range of activities into Hirst's artistic practice—for example, his Shoreditch restaurant Pharmacy (1998–2003), where guests sat on aspirin-shaped bar stools and the waitstaff wore Prada surgical gowns.

Andy Warhol and Damien Hirst were art world branding pioneers. While their promotional strategies were seen as unique and spectacular in their time, now they are akin to the mundane and everyday strategies used by cultural workers to consistently streamline and commodify the self. The affordances and culture of social media have not only opened up the avenues for artists to self-brand; they create a baseline expectation for artists to constantly do so in order to promote and sell their work.

Influencer creep sutures signature style and creative voice, fusing personality and practice. This chapter looks at how the platformization of art worlds, as well as the development of influencer cultures, has created opportunities and expectations for artists to augment art world conventions with personal branding. In this chapter, I will examine the ways that artists weave advertising and marketing techniques together with representations of a consistent self. Offline communications between art world intermediaries are carefully pitched based on the intended listener; however, conversations with collectors, galleries, and funders require different tones. But through Instagram, artists are required to consistently communicate to widespread and diverse audiences—customers, brands, galleries, magazine editors, and interior designers. The art-world-focused "thesis statement" sprawls into an accessible "elevator pitch" familiar to self-branding cultures.[3] I will examine how artists increasingly borrow from influencer self-branding strategies outlined in the previous chapter—consistent self-presentation, considerations of commercial suitability, and risk avoidance in the name of brand safety. I also reflect on the ways brand safety afforded by social media platforms like Instagram leads to increasing risk avoidance in the art world. I show how perceptions of each of these tenets of influencer creep are shaped by artists' identities, particularly looking at the possibilities and challenges of self-branding as shaped by gender.

## Consistency, Self-Branding, and Self-Promotion

Consistency is one of the core pillars of self-branding under influencer creep, but it also has a long history of being valued highly in art worlds. In her ethnographic study of visual artists working in New York City, sociologist Hannah Wohl found that artists would develop and use "style scripts" to "emphasize conceptual consistencies" within their work.[4] Artists identified specific form, themes, or materials as their own "iconicity" to communicate the continuity of their style to art world intermediaries like gallerists and curators.[5] Working artists were hesitant to vary their work because there was an important relationship between consistency and recognition. If they had achieved hard-won success (for example, a solo gallery show) by using specific iconography, then deviating from this conceptual focus could have real implications for their career. Artists working outside the contours of their expected practice were given poor reviews, were refused exhibitions, and even lost collectors. Works they produced deviating from existing style scripts were also priced at a lower rate than work that displayed their "established iconic elements."[6] The pressure to conform to art world consistency is now shaped by Instagram. How do artists use the tools and cultures identified by platform-dependent users like influencers to communicate consistency related to their work?

The artists I interviewed deliberately and consciously streamlined their Instagram profiles to communicate the consistency of their work. Cora, a metalworker, said, "We know consistency is really important," and Klara, a textile artist, described her "clear" Instagram style as "niche and specific." Jen Stark draws from language raised in her professional narrative materials within Instagram content, repeating and reiterating the consistent iconicity within her practice. Her official promotional narratives and exhibition notes describe themes and motifs like "organic, molecular, cloud-like structures" in addition to influences such as the "implausible patterns found in nature" and "vivid colors in conversation with the natural world." While chattier and more relaxed, she invokes comparable language in her Instagram videos. She addresses the camera in one of the videos to note, "I love mixing

FIGURE 9. Artist Jen Stark's Instagram images mix
geometric shapes with shots of the artist in motion.
Image courtesy of Jen Stark.

geometric shapes with designs in nature. . . . I'm inspired by fractals, plants, spirituality," and "so with my art work you'll see me use a lot of different colors."

Gertrude, who is an illustrator and painter, told me that she had decided to separate her online presence between two Instagram accounts to avoid dilution or confusion around her practice. She has one account for art objects, on which she paints dimensional abstract iconography across canvas, murals, and sculpture. She created a second Instagram account just for clothing, orders, and commissions. There she swirls suns and moons across shirts, jackets, and bags, which she sells via Instagram. "I really am glad I did that because it really streamlines it," she told me, "and it makes it very palatable and easy to navigate for people." Catching herself, she reflected on how instrumental she sounded here, commenting on the marketing language she was using: "It's a funny language to speak, isn't it?."

Despite streamlining her practice, Gertrude still found it challenging to ensure her Instagram presence was aesthetically coherent and consistent. While she viewed Instagram as a space to offer an overview of her creative vision, it was also the primary site where she was able share information about herself and her work. This meant that she was required to publicly post promotional materials for residencies, exhibitions, or shows she was a part of, some of which did not match the rest of her Instagram vibe. "If I'm reposting, say, something I'm involved in where I don't like the typeface or something, I'll post it for a week, or two weeks . . . [then] I'm going to take that square out because that doesn't work. In my mind that looks jarring." Artists are under pressure to communicate consistency across their artistic vision, but they are also realistically required to include practical, business-related information in their social media. These diverging pressures are reminiscent of the attempts by artists to forge consistency in physical spaces like their studios—for example, by hiding or removing outlier or experimental artworks to create a streamlined impression of their aesthetic. On Instagram, artists prune and edit in the direction of coherence and consistency, which complicates an understanding of the platform as a straightforward space for self-promotion.

## Branding and Iconography

The pitch is central to self-branding. It involves individuals summarizing their "value-add" through one pithy, hook-like statement.[7] The pitch must be accessible. To make it so, individuals often draw from a handful of related or unrelated cultural touchstones, in order stir up affective attachments and forge brand value. For example, Fern's pitch reads "an exploration of magic, ritual and clay." In figuring this out, Fern deliberately attached meaning to her practice through the iconography of spirituality and witchcraft.

I was particularly interested in the way Fern used the language of witchcraft in her self-branding. In our interview, she explained that tapping into spirituality allowed her to "offset" a commercially oriented sales pitch with the language of magic and personal power. This strategy dovetails with the contemporary fashionable appeal of the occult, particularly in queer spaces, with witchcraft viewed as the "natural inheritance of the outsider."[8] Fern told me that she deliberately drew from the language of witchcraft in her branding to refute the "fey nicety" of middle-class ceramics, which she disparagingly aligned with the feminized, pseudo-bohemian audiences of the Condé Nast publication *World of Interiors*. She found that engaging with the alternative space of witchcraft made self-promotion seemed "plausible." Otherwise she found the whole idea of self-promotion to be "sickening." In this case, witchcraft is a useful heuristic because it can be a shorthand and a vehicle for alternative politics and ways of being, sidestepping the normative power of capital and the state.

In practice, witchcraft and capitalism may not be as opposed as they initially seem. Sociologist Karen Gregory has drawn attention to the long history of individuals who sell "spiritual goods and services," a powerful side of the goods and service economy which dovetails neatly with aspirational labor, reputation work, and self-branding,[9] promising practitioners an ability to "gain power and perhaps even freedom."[10] Lured by this promise, Fern created an email newsletter that offered prompts and writing related to the occult. The newsletter follows the Wiccan wheel of the year, a calendar organized around seasonal phases of the sun and pagan festivals. While Fern could draw from the stylistic and visual iconography familiar to witchcraft, her newsletter aligned with the safe creative potential of Wiccan lore and nature, deliberately sidestepping their (brand-unsafe) "politicized and weird" connotations.

Fern's experiences capture the creative, labor-intensive strategies that individuals use to attempt to communicate values in self-branding. Engaging with cool and weird cultural touchstones, like witchcraft, were part of a deliberate strategy to reject the feminine and domestic implications of ceramics. This strategy can be understood better when we recognize the gendered nature of art worlds. Women artists are under greater pressure to engage in activities that reinforce membership within fine art professions, to claim and legitimize artistic identities.[11] Through these self-branding activities, female and nonbinary artists wanted to navigate the challenges they experienced when forging their identity as legitimate artists. They looked for values that had historical legitimacy. Maye, a metalworker, said, for example, that she was "obsessed with medieval history and Tudor history and ancient history." Sociologist Alison Bain has noted that art worlds are shaped around long-held stereotypical ideas of "heroic male" artists, as well as their leisure-seeking counterparts, "dabbling lady painters."[12] Artists used the tools made available to them by social media to align their pitch with iconography attached to serious and nonfrivolous (read: feminized, commercial) value to shore up their ability to reach for compelling and valuable references.

Fern told me that the original plan for her witchcraft newsletter was to drive interest and sales to her online shop—"if I got people understanding what I'm like, and what I do, and what my story is, then maybe they'll just click on the shop and see something they like and they buy it." In practice, the newsletter legitimized her expertise at the intersections of pottery and witchcraft, but it did not directly benefit sales of her art works. She told me that the newsletter ended up being a time-intensive effort for little monetary reward but "what it did do is give me exposure." For Fern, this was fine, because the newsletter was always intended as a promotional tool. However, she told me she was still anxious to find other ways to grow her audience and customer base, particularly as she had quit her second job as a university instructor: "[my practice] is a delight, but it is, essentially, to make money from making objects."

Despite the limited financial payoff, Fern considered her newsletter a worthy write-off in the service of aspirational labor, a live and ongoing project.[13] Influencers and artists work iteratively to try and test different ideas and strategies. The payoff for these kinds of strategies is often elusive, and if it's there, it's hard to track. In

Fern's case, the pagan-themed newsletter became a totally separate content-creation responsibility that she was required to maintain *in addition to* her artistic practice and her shop. She felt she had to keep it going, though, because her content baseline had been tweaked to accommodate it. It was now an expectation, even an obligation, of her online presence. Of course, art worlds have always been precarious, and individuals have always had to strategize their way through this precarity. What is arguably new is the way that artists navigate risk by turning to influencer-driven promotional strategies that are well to the side of their artistic practice, under the banner of influencer creep.

## Brand Safety and Good Behavior

In the previous chapter we saw how brand safety worked, how it compelled individuals to positively reproduce a brand's ideals, avoid controversy, and circumvent elements of sex, violence, and profanity. Judgements of brand safety are central to influencer economies, but they might seem less relevant to art world transactions. After all, branding has been historically positioned as a danger to art because of its appeal to the masses and "overt consumerism."[14] We expect artists to be shocking and edgy—brand unsafe. Artists are often given leeway to deal in profanity, sex, and violence, or to behave badly and take risks. The ideal type of artist is a creative genius, who refuses to bend for commercial conditions, being fueled instead by economic disinterest, unmanageability, and eccentricity. Stories about artists' bad behavior become an important part of their mythology. Andy Warhol was known as an "emotionless person, a sort of freak" with a "desire to shock."[15] Damien Hirst is also known for having an attitude problem. In one interview he bragged about being rude to a customer at Pharmacy, his restaurant. "Somebody came up to me while I was eating and said, 'Ah, Mr. Hirst I want to ask you what is this restaurant about?' And I just said, 'shut up!'"[16]

How would we ever expect mercurial creative genius types to be brand safe? How does the draw toward bad behavior clash with influencer creep, where artists are subject to digital commercial visibility economies? Common myths about artist identity dovetailing with "marginality, alienation, 'outsider' status and creative freedom" are still persuasive.[17] But in reality, a long-running formalization of art markets and the art school, peaking in the early 2000s, means that artists also must be marketable.[18] Now an additional mandate to perform brand safety has crept into the art world through the platformization of visual culture on Instagram and the techniques required to navigate these commercial cultures—in other words, influencer creep.

Gender is an important factor here. It is relevant that my participants are women and nonbinary individuals because women and nonbinary artists' behavior never actually brings about the professional, critical, or economic rewards that it does for men. Hannah Wohl suggests that, in practice, "eccentricity [is] associated with masculinity and male genius."[19] Behavior that is ideologically framed as unconventional and brilliant for male artists is perceived as odd or off-putting for their women counterparts. Sociologist Diana Miller similarly shows that the creative genius is symbolically masculinized because it has links with antisocial behaviors like "moodiness, sensitivity, eccentricity and a limited ability to function in ordinary society," which are "more acceptable in men than women."[20] Creative intermediaries can overlook, or even praise, unacceptable behaviors in men, but this tolerance or curiosity does not extend to women. This shapes the valuation of artwork, as women are less likely to seek out or attract the attention of intermediaries and stakeholders necessary to champion and promote their work.

Sociologists have shown that women working in (particularly feminized) contemporary creative industries are instead compelled to engage in a style of individualized self-presentation that cultural theorist Angela McRobbie calls "passionate work." This is a form of labor-intensive "exuberant enthusiasm," which is deployed to help navigate work in highly competitive and exploitative fields like art and fashion.[21] Creative workers use techniques of sustained cheerfulness even under conditions of uncertainty and risk within precarious forms of labor. Influencer work incorporates many of the same promises; influencers are expected to maintain an upbeat brand that communicates the idea of work as fun, flexible, and fulfilling. In line with these theories, the female and nonbinary artists I spoke to often used the language of love and care when describing their practice. Cora, a metalworker, told me that because Instagram offers an opportunity to attract the attention of intermediaries like gallerists, agents, and editors who are able to "elevate what you're doing," it is important to "[show] the world that you are about what you do and you care about your aesthetic and your little creative universe." Because they are aware that they are being monitored by creative intermediaries, artists express their passion publicly across their social media. Depicting one's work as passionate, or imbued with a higher purpose, is a useful strategy because it refutes the idea that work is for money, jeopardizing assessments of authenticity in the work.

A rejection of overt money-seeking behavior is a key tenet of brand safety. Recall the brand safety checks that L'Oréal engages in to ensure that influencers haven't worked with too many brands in the past. Brands like L'Oréal will also look to prevent influencers from engaging in more commercial partnerships in the future through an exclusivity clause. This is now a common feature of influencer marketing contracts, and it prevents influencers from engaging in commercial activities with other brands. Such a mandate is entwined with judgements about purity. As corporate law firm JMW's guide to influencer contracts puts it: "exclusivity is crucial for brands to ensure that the influencer's association with their product remains unique and undiluted by competitors' influences."[22] Influencers have long navigated the pressure of being judged as sellouts by agents of the very brands who want to hire them, for doing the very same work that those agents want to hire them to do. Similarly, the artists I interviewed all make a living by selling their work online; however, to be perceived as legitimate in the world of art, they have to come across as—you guessed it—not overtly wanting to sell their work online.

## Context Collapse

Self-branding within influencer creep brings together requirements to be consistent with requirements to be brand-safe. These dual pressures are exacerbated under *context collapse*, whereby individuals are forced to navigate disparate audiences within a single Instagram presence.[23] Lena, a textile artist, discussed the difficulty of maintaining one consistent online presence for art world intermediaries like gallerists or magazine editors and for customers looking to buy objects or to commission works. As she put it, "If you're trying to make industry connections no one wants to see you trying to sell your shit. It's the last thing they want to be spammed with. So it's confusing." I showed in chapter 2 that orienting content toward multiple audiences offers up a challenge when seeking algorithmic visibility; ultimately, however, there is a hierarchy of value in art worlds that Lena told me "pushes . . . the customer down to [a position of] less importance." In acknowledging their responsiveness to the market, artists get their hands dirty when they try to sell by engaging in self-branding. If artists do directly seek to promote themselves, this jeopardizes their valuation as appearing to be both "uninfluenced" by art world intermediaries and authentic.[24] If anyone is supposed to be selling art or the artist, it is professional intermediaries (agents, gallerists) who can do so at arm's length. Of course, very few individuals have access to these kinds of professional support, and such access is stratified by gatekeepers (and augmented by privilege).

Influencers, and now artists, navigate the pressure to self-brand while communicating authenticity through the language of passion. Communicating the fact that you would only sell a product because you *really love it* can valuably offset the commercial connotations of online activities. This style of communication has been finessed by influencers, who reiterate very frequently that they only engage in brand partnerships that they *really* love. Brooke Duffy sharply observes that influencers utilize the language of passion as a "buffer against critiques of crass commercialism" to support maintaining the "delicate balance between commercial pressures and one's own self branding."[25] A typical example of this framing comes from the former CEO of the influencer agency Gleam Futures, Dom Smales, speaking about influencer Victoria Magarath. Smales said, "[She will] hang out with the people at Dior because she loves that brand, she loves what they do, for no payment or anything like that," observing that "not everything is transactional, it's genuine, you know?"[26] Comments like this—expressing influencers' true passion and love for brands they work with—are an extremely common refrain in influencer content, press interviews, and podcasts. In 2022, *Forbes* named TikTokers Charli and Dixie D'Amelio as numbers 1 and 2 on their top creators list. Despite the *Forbes* write-up being centered around their $70 million family income, Dixie closes the interview by insisting, "With our true passions it's not about making money, but sharing what we love with the world."[27]

I have long studied the prevalence of passionate talk in influencer economies, but I was surprised how often this came up in my interviews with artists. Artists would talk about the challenges and anxieties of this work, but they would quickly mention their genuine or authentic love for artistic production. To take one example, Rose, who runs art markets, discussed how it was important for artists selling their work online to utilize the affordances of social media to highlight their creative joy, because this was one of the main sources of value and legitimacy for smaller artists and makers: "We might not be able to compete on price, we might not be able to compete on delivery time, but what we can compete on is personality, and we have real personalities, we're real people, and our businesses are really affecting, in a positive way, our livelihoods—we're living our dreams through these businesses."

Rose was not the only interviewee who specifically depicted an artistic career as dreamlike. As Cora put it, "We can really live our dreams and I don't mean that in a cheesy way." Other artists told me that they aspired to communicate their passion through their social media presence. Aoife told me that the artist Instagram accounts that she found inspiring gave "a cheery tone" in addition to communicating the "philosophy around their business."

Sometimes work that artists didn't love ended up being the work that sold really well; this could present serious challenges. Lena told me the following story, about the time one of her hand-knitted art works went viral. Although the increased visibility of this work on Instagram meant a bump in orders (and much-needed cash flow to her business), Lena felt ambivalent during this moment. She told me that she initially set to work on meeting this new demand by creating a stock of this work, because it was gaining online visibility, but went on as follows: "Then I was like, I don't want to share this image, I hate it. I don't like this piece." For Lena, the popularity of this work devalued it. She felt this object had been compromised. She ultimately decided to remove images of the work from social media, withdrawing it from sale. Navigating the hierarchies of fine art worlds is particularly challenging for textile artists like Ilana who make clothing, because of the delegitimization of fashion; in the context of high art, "designers are anxious to be taken seriously."[28] Lena's viral moment served as example when the pressures of art worlds collided with the commercially led visual economy of Instagram. Lena said, "It's funny, sometimes you get lots of interest. That's the problem with [Instagram], is you'll get interest in pieces that you actually don't like, and you don't respect, and you don't want anything to do with."

The artists I interviewed often invoked the push and pull of self-branding on Instagram, sometimes describing refusal in ways that, at least on the surface, seemed to harm them financially. Mary, a sculptor, said that her impulse was to limit the amount that she sold via Instagram wherever possible. "I feel a little bit of a refusal around it," she said. "I don't want to play this game." Similarly, Sarah, also a sculptor, told me that ensuring that still loving what one does as an artist requires maintaining interest and excitement in one's work: "with art you can't just make stuff that you know people are going to buy, because that would be really boring."

We can look here at the parallels between artists and influencers who publicly refute or refuse associations with economic success. In the previous chapter I discussed the influencer Michelle Phan, who dramatically left both YouTube and her cosmetics business because she no longer felt authentically connected to them. It is common for influencers to publicly brag about the lucrative partnerships or endorsements that they have turned down. For example, Molly Mae, a popular British influencer who rose to fame on the reality TV show *Love Island*, discussed this topic in a YouTube video with her manager Fran. In the video, Fran tells a story about a high street fashion brand that offered Molly Mae £2 million for a partnership deal. According to Fran, Molly Mae refused because, as she put it, "I don't buy my clothes from there." Her manager then said to her, "Well you can start!," which sent both of them into fits of laughter. Molly Mae looks on while Fran directly reinforces how passion underscores the business decisions that Molly Mae makes to their YouTube audience: "If you see 'AD'[29] on any of Molly's posts, you know that she genuinely uses, and wears, and believes in that brand." While it may seem counterintuitive to refuse to engage in lucrative brand deals or sell popular art works, avoiding associations that are overtly commercial can be a very important strategy for brand safety. Artists and influencers have both chosen highly individualized career paths, with few (if any) external sources of validation and verification. Creating and sustaining an effective and valuable self-brand can be precarious, and even if one is successful in doing so, self-branding can be difficult to manage. Communicating refusal shows a commitment to authenticity; it also reveals that an influencer is willing to walk away, as they seek to maintain legitimacy.

## Brand Safety, Art, and Nudes

The most commonly discussed brand safety issue in art worlds is the "allowability" of nudes and nudity on Instagram. Instagram's current policy on nudity is as follows: "we default to removing sexual imagery to prevent the sharing of non-consensual or underage content." However, the platform says it allows "photographs of paintings, sculptures and other art that depict nude figures."[30] Despite nude figures in art ostensibly being permitted, Instagram gives a confusing list of forbidden content, rife with contradictions and bizarre asides. For example, it does not permit "visible genitalia" or "fully nude close ups of buttocks," which makes sense initially, but maybe less so when this ban, explicitly stated, is followed by the unique exception expressed in the caveat "unless photoshopped on a public figure." Instagram also bans "uncovered female nipples," with the exception of "acts of protest." The list is followed by a catch-all restriction on "adult sexual activity in digital art."

Artists have criticized how Instagram presides over the difficult question of what counts as art, arguing there is excessive monitoring of legitimate artworks that they believe should be permitted on the platform. The Don't Delete Art coalition aims to draw attention to the moderation of artistic nudes on Instagram, with support from freedom-of-speech nonprofits like the National Coalition Against Censorship and PEN America.[31] Their mission is "dedicated to the protection and promotion of diverse forms of artist expression on social media platforms." They want to raise awareness about the consequences of social media moderation of art worlds through an online gallery Art Censored Online, for which artists are invited to submit removed artworks. The artist can also add the official reason Instagram gave them for removal, as well as any appeals they've lodged and whether these appeals were successful.

The gallery features banned images ranging in scope from traditional nudes to snippets of bodies reflected in mirrors, the blurred outlines of naked bodies in motion in sex acts like blow jobs, and abstract sculpture of genitalia shaped by hormone treatments. One photograph by Candelaria Deferrari depicts a joyful naked woman reclining on feathery green grass. The artist writes that they placed dried lilac flowers and pressed leaves onto the subject's "genitals and nipples" in order to "interrupt the skin and avoid the algorithm."[32] This explanation for the artist's inclusion of the flora and fauna in the image offers a neat example of social media governance shaping artistic practice. A piece in the *Art Newspaper* by artist Emma Shapiro offers a list of other techniques used by artists to circumvent Instagram moderation—for example, blurring body parts or casting them in shadow.[33] Sometimes artists just decide to play it safer through self-censorship, creating a schism between the artworks that can be shared on Instagram and other works that may be held back.[34]

The consequences of violating Instagram's policies can be severe, leading to post removal, shadow banning, and—for repeated violations—even permanent account deletion. In contemporary online discourse, shadow banning can be understood as the process of limiting content visibility through a platform's search features or suppressing the reach of content to an individual's followers.[35] Platform governance scholar Tarleton Gillespie suggests reduction and suppression techniques (like shadow ban-

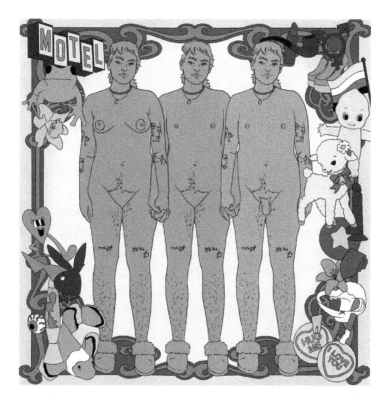

FIGURE 10. The image *How Am I Doing?* by artist Jodie Underwood is included in the Don't Delete Art Gallery. This image was removed from Instagram because it contained "adult content." Image credit: Jodie Underwood.

ning) are on the rise because they allow platforms the flexibility to reduce the visibility of content without confirming that moderation has taken place or publicly changing their policies. For Gillespie, "reduction is less politically harmful than removal."[36] However, suppression techniques are often enacted against content without explanation or opportunities for appeal, and in this sense they decrease the opportunities for accountability. Platforms have even flat-out denied using techniques like shadow banning, despite users accruing mountains of evidence and proof of this having taken place. This kind of intentional misdirection has been defined by Kelley Cotter as "black box gaslighting."[37] Submissions to the Art Censored Online gallery frequently cite feelings of anxiety and confusion related to suppression techniques. Sculptor Andy Lime writes, "I am constantly anxious that my account and access to community will be taken away."[38] As shadow banning comes without notification, artists do not know if or when they may permanently lose access to their account and Instagram presence. The consequences can be extremely severe. Painter Liza Shkirando points out in her explanation to the Art Censored Online gallery that because her work is a painting, it should be allowable under Instagram's guidelines. She explains the potentially dire consequences of Instagram's actions: "it was a painful process building up the audience and if my account gets deleted it will be the end of my career."[39]

The confusion leads to artists generating and sharing theories about how and when their content may have been reduced in visibility and reach, evocative of the shared algorithmic gossip discussed in chapters 1 and 2. In his submission to the gallery, Maurice Mechan wrote about recent changes that he had noticed on Instagram. He described his own form of algorithmic testing, uploading illustrations of a bare arm or leg and monitoring to see if these drawings were removed (they were).[40] As he put it, "I have deduced that since the start of this year, Meta has either begun a draconian tightening [of] its rules on nude art (without informing artists) or has introduced a new AI-led system of detection for nudity that has great problems in differentiating between photography and semi-realistic drawings. Perhaps both." Without explanations from Instagram, Mechan can only track the way each image he uploads is promoted or suppressed. He has no way of determining whether changes are permanent or temporary, which are unique to him, or whether such changes reflect wider experiences on the platform.

The risks of shadow banning or account deletion creep out beyond the act of sharing artworks on Instagram. Anxiety spills into the everyday experience of the backstage; it adds enormously to the pressures artists feel in depicting their artistic life. As discussed throughout this book, content documenting successful exhibitions, days out conducting research, or studio progress are required under the content baseline demanded by influencer creep. But glimpses of themes that violate Instagram's community guidelines open up the risks of removal and account deletion. The slightest hint of "unacceptable" content can cause a tumbling domino effect of consequences, leading to the loss of an account and the subsequent networks and audience this brings. So platform policy and governance are joined up with the cultural pressures to create content under influencer creep. Artists must represent their lives online but this must be sanitized and brand-safe; they are required to monitor everything they upload for potential violations. In this sense, influencer creep permeates beyond the platform. As Emma Shapiro puts it in the *Art Newspaper*, artists are required "to consider in 'real' life what might jeopardize their account."[41]

The blame for censorship is often squarely placed on Instagram. A typical headline in art journal 1 *Granary* reads "Instagram's Prudeness Is Ruining My Art."[42] Elsewhere, artist John Sheridan attributes the censorship of his art works to Meta, playing on the company's former name, Facebook, in tagging his post with the portmanteau "#fascistbook."[43] While the buck does stop with social media platforms, the policies they construct and the removals they enact are informed by the actions, desires, and political gerrymandering of complex networks of stakeholders.[44] For example, the increase in the moderation of nudity and sexual content can be traced back to 2018 legislation enacted in the United States titled the Allow States and Victims to Fight Online Sex Trafficking Act and the Stop Enabling Sex Traffickers Act, which together were given the acronym FOSTA-SESTA.[45] This legislation added caveats to the safe harbor laws enjoyed by social media platforms under section 230 of the 1996 Communications Decency Act, which, in short, exempted them from responsibility for the content that users posted on them. FOSTA-SESTA created an exception in this law for (even consensual) sex work, making platforms legally liable for the content posted on them. Media scholar Katrin Tiidenberg has noted that the "vague and uneducated wording of the law," which ultimately "conflates sex work with trafficking," makes it easier for "platforms to outlaw sexual content to take responsibility for differentiating exhibitionism from humour, from self-expression, from activism, from sex education, from sex-work and from 'promoting prostitution'."[46]

FOSTA-SESTA has had a huge impact on the kinds of content that can be shared on social media, but the moderation of sexual content is also informed by another stakeholder—namely, advertisers. The very first point of the World Federation of Advertisers' Global Alliance for Responsible Media's brand safety floor suggests that "explicit or gratuitous depiction of sexual acts, and/or display of genitals, real or animated," are "not appropriate for any advertising support."[47] We know that Meta uses this brand safety floor as the blueprint for its community guidelines. In other words, if advertisers do not accept the open display of genitals, neither will Instagram. Indeed, chapter 5 showed how advertisers tend to follow public morals, leading to an overly excessive designation of LGBTQ+ influencers as advertiser-unfriendly. In the Art Censored Online gallery, artists frequently suggested that LGBTQ+ content was more likely to be suppressed or removed. Photographer Adrian Alarcon Sanchez believes his artwork was removed because it featured two men kissing, suggesting "queer phobia [on Instagram] is still very present."[48] Similarly, photographer Gala Garrido writes that a photo of "two women kissing" was taken down by Instagram, even though the image only featured their faces. Tracking the definitions of suitability and safety as created by advertisers historically,[49] as well as examining how brand safety has become platformized via influencers, can offer an explanation for the excessive moderation of content by marginalized artists.

## Art versus Porn

As a response to censorship in online art worlds, Don't Delete Art suggests artists should be exempted from Instagram's moderation efforts.[50] Instagram should "verify artists and arts organisations and subject them to a different level of algorithmic scrutiny." They note that "the human nude has always been one of the central subjects of art," arguing that imagery "shared in the world's museums" should also be visible on social media. Artists writing in the Art Censored Online gallery are also incredulous that they have been lumped together with pornographers or sex workers. Digital artist Heather M suggests that the problem, for Instagram, is reducible to this understanding: "nudity equals pornography."[51] Or, as photographer Anita Acuman, put it: "I feel like they allow the most vulgar photos, but the aesthetic ones are always banned so nobody can see the real art."[52]

The comments by artists and the policy interventions suggested by Don't Delete Art are invested in a division between artwork (which, as the organization says, would be found in a museum) and pornography (which ostensibly would not be). This distinction between art and pornography has long been argued over by art critics and art historians, mostly wrapped up in a tedious moralizing or pseudo-philosophical framing.[53] Some critics offer deceptively simple recipes for decoding the differences—namely, that art is concerned with beauty and romance, whereas pornography is rooted in objectification and organs.[54] Such a simple definition is deceptive. There is a long list of works by established and admired artists that have been originally censored, criminalized, or destroyed because they were deemed to be pornographic only to be later redeemed and celebrated.[55] As art philosopher Hans Maes argues, the distinctions between these various things are not so absolute in practice, and "pornographic novels, photographs or films have many potential uses beyond the classic one-handed one."[56]

Some argue that pornography, specifically, is exploitative and immoral and that it harms women, but such an argument is fraught with contradictions and gray areas. This book has attended to the many ways that art worlds serve to exclude women, positioning them as hobbyists and enthusiasts rather than as serious artists. For feminist art historian Lynda Nead, the female nude is a sign of the "more hidden properties of patriarchal culture, possession, power and subordination."[57] Porn, on the other hand, is far from uniform, and can offer important reflection and insight into the diversities of female desire and sexuality.[58] And if we are going to delve into a moral argument, we can learn, as art philosophers Petra van Brabandt and Jesse Prinz teach us, that art is often made up of "morally problematic works" that are still regarded as "aesthetically good."[59] The differences between art and pornography have long captured the public's imagination, which gets philosophers hot and bothered because, as Maes observes, this discussion represents "one of the very few philosophical questions that regularly appear as a newspaper headline."[60] As these topics continue to be bickered over through the hallowed halls of academia, after decades of back and forth, it is no wonder that Instagram's moderation systems are unable to detangle their complexities. As artist Jessica Fairbrother writes, "the algorithm cannot distinguish between sex, sexuality, object and objectification."[61]

Here, I am not going to venture down a philosophical rabbit hole of what is and isn't art; this is a question I am not qualified to comment on, nor am I particularly interested in it. I am, rather, interested in "following around" words like "art" and "porn," and how they are being used functionally or as a means to an end.[62] By demanding that only nudity with an aesthetic or artistic justification be exempted from Instagram's community guidelines and moderation, groups like Don't Delete Art oversimplify the distinction between art and porn, falling into a normative (and moral) division between the two. Overfocusing on diagnosing and exempting art from platform moderation means artists sidestep opportunities for solidarity and shared struggle and common cause with a class of influencers who can be referred to as "sexual(ity) content creators."[63] Content creators who work across sexualized topics are an important piece of the puzzle in understanding platforms; they are the canaries in the coal mine of moderation, often the first to experience the stigma of social media platforms. Danielle Blunt, the cofounder of a New York–based sex worker collective, explains that sex workers pioneer platform features and develop strategies for working under the specific conditions that platforms demand.[64] Like influencers, sex workers are pioneering platform users who put information together and bootstrap solutions, sharing information about how to work within platform conditions.

In their comments, artists submitting to the Art Censored Online gallery suggest that art should be evaporated out of the slew of sexual content on Instagram. Photographer Roxanne Huber says she wishes there was a way for Instagram to determine the account of a "genuine" and an "authentic" artist.[65] But legitimization of one cultural form at the expense of another will do little to resolve the pressures, harms, and inequalities that influencer creep heightens and deepens. Instead, it reifies those power inequalities, which are at the heart of culture and cultural production. Lynda Nead suggests that the way we regard some nudity as high art is a symptom of the way cultural works are placed on a continuum of "cultural distinction," requiring an explicit denial of "lower, vulgar and venal enjoyment."[66] The ability to claim a legitimate art identity, and have one's nudes appointed as art, is stratified by race, gender, and class. Although artists are painfully subject to the risks and harms of moderation, they are also defended by some of the most significant free-speech activities and organizations in the United States. But on the subject of protecting those creating content deemed to be lesser or simply mass cultural nudity, organizations seeking to reduce censorship in art fall silent.

## Conclusion

Let's close by considering a review of Jen Stark's interactive art exhibition *Cascade* in New York City by immersive artist and critic Heather Gallagher.[67] Gallagher opens the review by letting the reader know her own disdain for the lucrative accessibility and consistency employed by Stark. She explains that she personally has "only ever been satisfied by the constant explorations of new themes, materials, media and structural challenges." But, she says, she does grudgingly hold respect for artists (like Stark) who are able to build a consistent niche. "If there's one thing this experience reminded me . . . is that it's important to have a shtick, and to shtick with it," she says, closing with the aside "hopefully it's done from joy and not obligation." Obligation, seemingly, would stem from a feeling that one has to maintain this style of work in order to make money. When artists continue to produce work with their recognizable formal qualities they may win success from dealers and gallerists, but they risk being judged as sellouts by their art world peers. To "win" in the competitive field, artists should successfully resist external pressures, like the need to sell work in order to make money. As Pierre Bourdieu writes, the "pure artist is indifferent to success and to the verdicts of the market."[68] Art world critiques, like Gallagher's here, raise further anxieties about artists' increasingly close relationships with the field of advertising.

Gallagher's comments recognize the pressures on artists to enact formal consistency to ensure their work generates and retains value, while denigrating those who engage in this kind of work as unpleasantly beholden to (presumably financial) obligation. This kind of criticism makes visible the tricky clash between economic success and legitimization in art worlds. Instagram may have sped up the commercialization of contemporary craft, but the dissolution of an apparent polarization between art worlds and branding has a longer history, which scholars attribute to a wider commodification of aesthetic culture and creative industries. Both fashion and design have become an "aesthetic practice," and ultimately, "art is more commercial than the art world is often prepared to admit."[69] As fashion studies scholars Nicola McCartney and Jane Tynan put it, "Many artists are working creatively with the fashion industry, but when the art world interprets this as a form of betrayal or plain foolishness, it is often couched in language that reveals fears of contamination, claims that, in a media age, sound increasingly hollow."[70] These kinds of comments make visible the pervasive complicated cultural hierarchies within art worlds, as well as the endemic imaginary of a pure, uncontaminated art, which arguably never existed in the first place.

But mythologies about who is a true artist prevail, and contemporary artists struggle to navigate a complicated, value-laden creative economy in order to successfully make a living. In a write-up in *ARTnews* about Damien Hirst's early career, Sir Norman Rosenthal, the exhibition secretary of the Royal Academy of Arts, said he was always impressed by Hirst's "enterprise."[71] But, as Rosenthal reflected, enterprise is not really a value that is aligned with the role of artist. As he tells it, Hirst's art world success therefore came as a surprise to art world stalwarts, who predicted that he would be a good "curator or gallerist." These kinds of statements reveal core judgments according to which art worlds are fraught sites of struggles over power relations, in which those directly producing for commercial audiences "[lose] in the game of prestige."[72] Those who are "responsive to external demands" (in other words, those thinking about making cash) are associated with mass production or the vulgar pursuit of profit.[73] Artists who create art for art's sake are, on the other hand, pure artists.

I have explored the shared trajectories and ties between artists and influencers throughout this chapter and I have shown how both are fields that are characterized by struggles to claim a legitimate identity. Artists draw from influencer practices to navigate these pressures: they use Instagram to showcase a streamlined consistency between their personal lives and their practice. They consciously build self-brands using the affordances of platforms, stitching together value-laden iconography in attempts to build a legitimized artistic identity. They also must navigate brand safety by refuting associations between bad behavior and art world legitimacy. I've shown how artists perform passion, love, and genuine attachment to their work, and how they use influencer practices to publicly reject an interest in economic success in the service of maintaining a safe reputation. I have also reflected on the ways platform policies cannot be thought of as existing outside the cultural pressures imposed by influencer creep. While platform policies limit the topics and content that can be safely posted on Instagram, it is influencer creep that mandates artists post their artwork and their backstage lives online, which often causes them to develop, consistently monitor, and perform a "safe" self-brand.

To elide the power inequalities baked into elitist art worlds is to forge solidarity across different categories of content creation. The labels of "influencer," "sex worker," and "artist" are not as disparate as one may imagine—there are many individuals who inhabit all three of these categories. Marginalized folks, especially, doing each of these jobs are all mandated to consistently create authentic, branded, platform-acceptable content to support their livelihoods. Instead of reifying divisions, this book on influencer creep is a rallying cry for a common cause, and an invitation to account for the many ways that social media platforms, together with the cultural expectations brought by influencer creep, may harm individuals by reducing workplace protections through the increase in demands for entrepreneurs to create content and put themselves online, by eroding an ability to take sick leave or parental leave under the threat of algorithmic invisibility, and through the threat of losing access to audiences, without explanation or recourse, that an individual has labored intensely to build. It doesn't make sense to examine these as solely influencer concerns, artist concerns, or entrepreneurial concerns; indeed, they affect us all.

# Conclusion

Time to Bring It Home with a Profound Conclusion

In early 2024, an Instagram story popped up on my feed from Los Angeles–based artist Jen Stark. The post was captioned "thank you for having me @simplybeverages #SimplyPartner." At the time, I didn't know what the brand Simply Beverages was, but after a quick search on Google I found out that it's a brand of fruit juices owned by the Coca-Cola Company. Stark's story showed a long table decorated in a white cloth punctuated by vivid floral arrangements, vintage martini glasses, and delicate bowls filled with oranges. I was growing used to artists posting their authentic artistic life on Instagram, but this was a different oeuvre. I have been studying influencers for nearly a decade, and this was clearly a product launch. The present company also diverged from a private view or art world event. Other brunch attendees included influencers like Ashley Torres, an entrepreneur who posts about "everyday fashion + beauty + mom life," and Helen Owen, a travel influencer with 1.5 million followers.

As my art world ethnography progressed, I started to notice a growing trend of artists advertising sponsored content on Instagram. I saw them shilling fashion, food, beverages, and cosmetics. I was particularly struck by the Instagram profile of New

York-based visual artist Zaria Forman, who uses it to document reputational work and works in progress, what she is wearing, mixed with sponsored artist/influencer marketing activities. Like Stark, she is legitimized in elite art worlds. She was the artist in residence aboard the *National Geographic Explorer* in Antarctica, and her work has been exhibited at international galleries in Iceland and Singapore as well as in British artist Banksy's immersive experience Dismaland. But—crucially for the case of influencer creep—she's also engaged in #SponCon.[1]

Forman's artworks document climate change with pastel drawings.[2] In line with her artworks, her collaborations with clothing brands tend to be more environmentally focused. One typical Instagram post shows Forman posing in a New York streetscape, a Canada Goose parka tossed effortlessly over her shoulder.[3] The video features the caption "honestly it's the backpack straps inside most of @canadagoose's winter coats that's had me hooked on them for years." Delving deeper into Forman's Instagram presence reveals more tableaux in Canada Goose, in addition to stylish shots inside a roomy Brooklyn apartment where she's wearing sweaters from ethical knitwear brand Eleven Six and underwear by sustainable womenswear brand KES NYC. Each of these posts is heavily tagged with featured brands and captioned with influencer vernacular—in this case, personal reflection and invocation of authenticity communicated through an upbeat sales pitch. There's plenty of art on her page too, of course. But this is mixed in with clearly monetized branded relationships that promote products using Forman's cool and climate-conscious self-brand. It is particularly striking how closely the blueprint for artist marketing collaborations matched the influencer partnership playbook, which, in many cases, was wholly irrelevant to individuals' artistic prac-

FIGURE 11. Artist Zaria Forman's Instagram mixes images of her personal style and her artistic practice. In an Instagram post featuring this image, she describes originally creating this diptych for her family, later choosing to include it for sale in her upcoming show to help make the deadline for a gallery show. Courtesy of Zaria Forman.

tices. Again, I was surprised that artists were doing influencer sponcon, arguably the neatest parallel with influencer work that I came across in this project. Was this the logical conclusion of influencer creep?

The artists I interviewed also discussed involvement in art/influencer partnerships, often with luxury brands that want to court associations with craft and art to increase the aura around their commercial goods. A couple of artists I spoke to had been part of a program for emerging artists run by a high-end British clothing brand. A handful of artists every year are invited to sell a limited number of their works via the brand's website. Importantly, they are provided with clothes—the denim workwear and linen apparel typical to the brand—and tag what they are wearing in Instagram posts. One artist I interviewed reflected on her involvement in the scheme, calling it a "a total greenwashing marketing strategy to make themselves look good" and saying, "They were twisting my words to suit their brand, that made me so angry." Another participant was more resigned to these kinds of activities, saying it was fine to work regularly with brands, as long as they want to "celebrate craft."

## Branded Histories

Listening to this, I hear my readers cry, "This can't be entirely new!" To be sure, there are long histories of artists collaborating with commercial brands in fashion industries and beyond. They may involve coproduction of a commodity object for sale, often in the area of fast-moving consumer goods like fashion, homewares, or beauty. In 1934, surrealist artist Salvador Dalí and designer Elsa Schiaparelli began a long partnership: they worked together to create a lobster dress for Wallis Simpson, the American socialite and partner of Edward VIII (who was forced to abdicate the throne when he made it clear he wanted to marry her). She collaborated on a scent called Le Roy Soleil, for which Dalí designed a spiky glass bottle shaped like a dawning sun.[4] More recently, Damien Hirst collaborated with Snapchat on a lens (an augmented reality filter) based on his multicolored Spin Art series. Artists are also commissioned by brands to create murals or street art as a form of cross-promotion. Japanese contemporary artist Yayoi Kusama was hired to engage in a showstopping version of this kind of artist/

brand collaboration for the famous London department store Harrods. Louis Vuitton bought Kusama's iconic dot-and-mirror exhibition "out of the gallery and onto the high street" with a fifteen-meter animated sculpture of the artist painting colorful dots across the facade of the building.

Artist/influencer brand partnerships are distinct from the collaborations highlighted above. They don't involve developing an art object for sale or an artist creating artwork for a brand's spaces or buildings. Instead, artist/influencer partnerships entirely hinge on the artist's personal and habitual attributes—their self-brand. The expansion of influencer/artist marketing practices, however, is concerning to me. This is not because I'm worried about the infiltration of brands within the art world—that kind of thinking is based on a gendered disdain for consumerism and its association with the frivolous, feminine pursuit of shopping. Art/brand collaborations have long been subject to the shopworn cultural hierarchies within art economies, and are (to put it mildly) not particularly celebrated, with their implications of selling out. I do not want to jump on this bandwagon, or to offer a moralistic critique of influencer marketing.

Instead, my concerns lie in the way that brands hope artists will attach *personal* meanings, values, and associations to their products. Firstly, artists engaging in influencer partnerships are nearly always hegemonically attractive white women; they are thin with clear skin, white teeth, and nice hair. They all neatly fit what sociologist Shirley Tate describes as the "dominant beauty paradigm," which she argues "privileges white/light skin, straight hair and what are seen to be European facial features."[5] Dovetailing with their beauty and racial capital is their cool artist look, haircuts, style, and sensibility. Sociologist Ashley Mears defines a "look" as a somewhat ineffable quality that is nonetheless an extremely important form of bodily capital that determines success within markets. The look does include physical attractiveness, but also evokes personality, reputation, and so on. It is temporally and culturally dependent, a "system of meanings, such as language or a code, tied to a social evaluation system."[6] Artists are seen by some scholars having a kind of special kind of cool value with them wherever they go. Urban studies scholar Richard Florida famously made the argument that it was the creative class that transformed the economic value of cities.[7] No longer were individuals moving to places because of transportation routes and tax breaks; rather, they wanted to live among other creative individuals, in spaces where there were thriving creative communities that "harness human creativity from all possible corners."[8] Florida's ideas on the creative class have been heavily criticized for an unbridled celebration of gentrification, ignoring structural harms that urban inequality sustains. Nonetheless, they're helpful here because they show us how the value of artists is perceived as cultivatable and harvestable by different stakeholders (for example, urban planners and, latterly, brand managers). It makes sense that a kind of cool that is specific to artists, particularly when matched with a healthy social media following, is attractive to commercial brands looking to deepen and expand their influencer marketing strategies.

Art world valuations are supposed to be based on the value of aesthetic work. Throughout this book, I have paid attention to the ways that influencer creep compels artists to hitch themselves (including their beauty and vibe) more closely to their work, by increasing time and affective commitment but also by opening up opportunities for discrimination. As sociologist Alison Bain has shown, "evaluations of women creative workers focus disproportionately on women's appearance and sexuality."[9] Those with a quirky, fashionable look and aspirational artistic life have an opportunity to capitalize on this further by working with brands online.[10] But participation is only available to a tiny handful of artists who have the beauty, time, and resources to grow a significant social media following. The opportunities and perils of this valuation affect women more acutely; as Ashley Mears writes, "the commonly accepted use of female bodies for their aesthetic value normalizes all women as display objects whether they enter into such an agreement or not."[11] Women's artwork is overshadowed—even devalued—by the hierarchies of gendered, embodied, and aesthetic capital within creative fields.

## Influencer Inequalities

Looking to the shifts within influencer culture can help us understand contemporary changes to labor conditions, compensation, and representation within art worlds. Like in art worlds, pay for most influencers is extremely low—the industry holds scant respect for minimum wage. When I was working in digital marketing in 2012, the lack of consistent standards in the influencer industry meant it was commonly described as a Wild West. Bloggers were expected to write lengthy posts, make videos, or attend public relations events in exchange for gifted or free products. That, however, was more than ten years ago, and brands nonetheless continue to expect influencers to work for free or in exchange for a gifted product. In 2024, Influencer Marketing Hub surveyed three thousand intermediaries working in influencer marketing and found that only 40 percent offer influencers monetary compensation for promotional posts, paying the remaining 60 percent with free samples, product discounts, or giveaways.[12] Brands have also bragged in marketing industry press about the ways they dangle the carrot of paid work by expecting influencers to post for free first. L'Oréal, for example, told the *Drum* that they send out product samples as part of their influencer recruitment process.[13] Should the brands be impressed with how an influencer presents a product, they may hire her in the future for a paid campaign. Gifted products, then, represent a "hopeful object."[14] A gift from a brand may represent a career opportunity, and ignoring such a gift can even harm one's career.

The influencer economy continues to be fueled by "aspirational labor," whereby participants are (ostensibly) voluntarily creating volumes of promotional content for little or even no pay.[15] Campaigners have set up transparency initiatives such as Fuck You Pay Me and Influencer Pay Gap, online spaces for influencers to publicly share and compare the pay rates that they are being offered by brands. Sociologists Angele Christin and Yingdan Liu analyzed 1,082 posts submitted to the Influencer Pay Gap's Instagram page, finding that influencers of color are significantly more likely to be asked to work for free than white influencers, in addition to experiencing hostility or even abuse in attempts to negotiate fees offered by brands.[16]

With these contextualizing snippets in mind, it's hard to imagine that influencer creep will improve pay or working conditions in art worlds. As influencer marketing partnerships may become a more significant income stream for artists, artists will be subject to the same opaque pay scales and contracts that influencers are. This is particularly concerning for artists without management or representation, who will be able to bargain on their behalf. Artists' pay rates will decrease in line with the (unacceptably) low pay scales normalized in the majority of the influencer economy. In evidence of this trend, one artist anonymously submitted a prototypical commission to Influencer Pay Gap:

> I'm paid $600 + art supplies to complete a full art project, 3 stories, 1 reel, 2 feed posts with process steps. $250 more if I make a 1 minute time lapse for YouTube. I am learning this is LOW especially since I am creating a complete art project PLUS making content. People are paid more to try on clothes ??
>
> Oh and this is by a MAJOR art supply chain.[17]

Creating an art project is time-consuming and labor-intensive—it involves consultation, planning, materials, and installation. Capturing the content demanded by this art supply chain would create a lot of work on top of art processes; it's not a simple or natural by-product of just doing the work. The brand wants Stories (which would be more ad hoc in tone) and sophisticated Reels (likely more polished and high quality), plus a selection of still images for an Instagram feed. Gathering all this content involves setting up, lighting, filming, narrating, and editing. It's difficult to compare the proposed pay rates to standard art world rates without context, but we can follow some clues. American painter Andrew Norman Wilson submitted an illuminating (entertaining, and distressing) account of his experiences of art work and commissions for *The Baffler* in 2024,[18] detailing a collaboration with Balenciaga paying $100,000. Of course, it's hard to know how much an artist should be paid without understanding contextual factors that we don't have access to in this case. But we do know that creating the influencer/art project described above would take some time, and thus likely falls well below the rates of pay guidelines set by the Artists' Union England, which convert to about 270 dollars per day for a newly graduated artist, or 353 dollars per day for an artist with three years' experience.[19] These scales also don't take into account other contractual concerns—for example, whether the work can be reshared by the brand or who owns the rights to the artwork.

## Entrepreneurship and Art Worlds

I'm far from the only person to notice that art worlds have been changed by individualistic cultural pressures, coupled with the proliferation of social media platforms. Writers in the popular press have discussed (and derided) the growth of "entrepreneurialism" in art worlds. In 2014, essayist William Deresiewicz observed what he called "the death of the artist and the birth of the entrepreneur" in the *Atlantic*,[20] arguing that cultural shifts toward online network building as a form of entrepreneurship cause the erasure of cultural intermediaries,[21] a lack of artistic focus, and the erasure of expert critics and tastemakers. In this piece, Deresiewicz predicts that this would lead to the worsening of art, meaning "no climactic masterwork of deep maturity, no *King Lear* or *Faust*, but rather many shifting interests and directions as the market forces blow you here or there." His concerns echo the fetishization of art as entirely unmotivated by economic forces, a fantasy critiqued by sociologist Pierre Bourdieu,[22] media theorist David Hesmondhalgh,[23] and many others, according to whom individual, transcendent creators can exist apart from the interconnected fields of economic and political power.

Critics also argue that time spent promoting oneself online takes away from time spent doing the pure and undistracted work of creation that being an artist demands. Deresiewicz raises a (now almost quaint) concern with how artists spend time networking instead of creating, taking away from the ten thousand hours he believes artists should spend perfecting their craft.[24] Building on these critiques, journalist Rebecca Jennings published a piece titled "Everyone's a Sellout Now" in *Vox* magazine, pointing out that the time investment required for platform promotional work takes away from time spent making art.[25] She argues that, as an artist, you must "spend your time doing this stuff on the off chance that the algorithm picks it up," suggesting that artists working in preceding decades, like Radiohead, would not have produced work of such quality if they had spent their early careers promoting their work by making TikToks.

Others have pointed out the ways that this affects the role and expertise of intermediaries in art worlds. When music review site Pitchfork was moved under the masthead of men's magazine *GQ*, journalist Israel Daramola raised concerns about a reduction in individuals qualified to determine the quality of art in society, speculating that laying off "actual journalists" means that "what has filled the vacuum left behind by actual music criticism is a loose collection of YouTubers and influencers who feed slop to their younger audiences."[26] The term "influencer" is invoked in the derisive way noted throughout this book, infantilized and associated with the promotion of mass cultural "slop."

In the pieces summarized above, the authors raise concerns about how cultural and platformized changes to creative work can lead to a loosening of shared standards in art, a reduction in the valuation of professional training, and a lack of time dedicated to artistic practice. They worry that the distinction between *real* artists who are trained and able to produce high art and those who do not have the standing, or the training, to participate in art worlds is being erased. They deride those one one side of this distinction as influencers who are wittingly or unwittingly serving out cultural sludge. The implication is that if artists can promote themselves via social media, away from the processes of legitimization linked to traditional art worlds, the quality of art plummets, meaning Shakespeare or Goethe or Radiohead would not exist in our time. For William Deresiewicz, this momentum may even lead to a philosophical crisis; he is deeply worried that entrepreneurial working conditions mean that the kind of "high art" that provides a "vessel for our inner life" may disappear.[27]

While I do share some of the worries raised—for example, about the time that workers are required to spend creating content for social media—I do not draw a line between influencer creep and a change in the quality of art. Following the work of sociologist Pierre Bourdieu, I see the work of art as a "fetish," a culturally constituted object "which exists as such only by virtue of the (collective) belief which knows and acknowledges it as a work of art."[28] Artworks are sites of struggle over legitimization, over whose work or opinion will be taken seriously, and over what has cultural and monetary value. These struggles are influenced by a particularly classed strain of elitism and reification of social privilege, in which those who can evince a lack of interest in economic rewards net the highest rewards.[29]

For me, the historic setup of art worlds is not actually something we should be romanticizing or trying to preserve. Research shows that art world inequalities are co-constructed, and called into being, by an interlinked number of stakeholders and intermediaries who reify privilege and exclude many.[30] At an institutional level, museum boards and sponsors tend to be majority-white, and they reproduce the dominant cultural narrative of whiteness within mainstream museum collections, separating and excluding artworks based on a racialized process of othering.[31] At the level of art markets, economist Richard Agnello shows that art by African American artists is not valued as highly as that of their white contemporaries,[32] is sold at high-end auction houses less frequently, and is subject to quicker depreciation. Art historian Martin A. Berger has shown the ways that art criticism, too, has been founded to be based on the internalization of "racial blindness characteristic of our society."[33] Art critics are generally representative of the cultural elite,[34] and are thus less able or qualified to recognize the contexts, narratives, and associations that may not be immediately familiar to them. In this sense, sociologist Phillipa Chong points out that critics similarly use "ethno-racial positions as a criterion for evaluating the author's creative work."[35] Stuart Hall, the British founder of the Birmingham School of Cultural Studies, traced the way that modern Black avant-garde artists in Britain were prohibited from artistic recognition, causing some retreat into "self-imposed internal exile."[36]

There are also staggering gaps related to gender, representation, and pay in art worlds. Art by women sells at auction for 42.1 percent less than art produced by men.[37] For every one pound earned by a man in art worlds, a woman earns ten pence.[38] These realities are propped up by the pervasive belief in art worlds as sites of meritocracy. Artist Georg Baselitz told the *Guardian*, "If women are ambitious enough to succeed, they can do so, thank you very much. But up until now, they have failed to prove that they want to. Normally, women sell themselves well, but not as painters."[39] For these (appalling!) comments, Baselitz has suffered very few consequences. His work continues to be exhibited in the Guggenheim,

MoMA, and the Tate Britain. If we reflect on the intersecting harms that occur to marginalized individuals within art worlds, we see that a study of influencer creep means an examination of the additional layers of inequality that influencer culture brings to this already highly unequal workplace.

One of the main contributing factors to art world inequalities is a loose organizational structure. Art worlds are based on subjective, classed forms of valuation—perfect recipes for ensuring the continuation of sexist and racist practices. Frances Morris, previously the director of the Tate Modern, has an illuminating take on art worlds as sites of reputational struggle. She says, "Everybody lacks confidence, everybody's looking for confirmation. So there's been a sort of confirmational history, which you could call the canon. And, of course, convention and history were framed by patriarchy."[40] I find this explanation especially useful, because it can also be very neatly applied to influencer economies. Influencer culture, too, is a field in motion. Like art worlds, influencer economies are spaces where reputation lies in flux, buoyed by a constant struggle for legitimization. They are underpinned by a feeling of risk, an affective atmosphere of anxiety. Platforms, advertisers, and influencers are engaged in laborious efforts to legitimize themselves through the strategies outlined in this book—algorithmic optimization, a convincing representation of occupational and emotional authenticity, and a consistent and commercially safe self-brand.

Influencers' legitimacy and success requires a significant amount of dedication and labor investment in social media platforms, their affordances, and their cultures. For influencers, such investment often leads to the formation of sophisticated techniques to help navigate their reality as platform-dependent cultural workers. Influencer practices are technically sophisticated and worthy of study: they are not ahistorical. To emphasize the lineage and connections within the practices I've observed, this book has drawn widely from scholarship in the fields of media and cultural studies to evince the ways that influencer work has deep histories entwined with broadcast production, journalism, marketing, music production, and many more kinds of work in creative industries. I've drawn attention to the specific ways that influencers assemble and cohere these historically informed responses to conditions, cultures, and expectations.

I've found that, because they experience platformized work first, influencers foreshadow contemporary working conditions in art worlds, a field of apparent independence that is ostensibly located at one of the furthest distances away from influencer culture. Throughout the book, I've also show how forms of precarity and anxiety calcified by influencer creep exacerbate inequalities related to class, race, sexuality, and gender in art worlds, with relevance to many other creative (and noncreative) fields of work. In closing, I want to note that neither social media platforms, influencer culture, nor art worlds remains static. Influencer creep is always on the move. Rather than being a complete guide to influencer culture, this book offers a snapshot of the phenomenon of influencer creep, but more importantly a critical framework, signposting toward taking influencers (and whatever cultural producers end up continuing this cultural lineage) seriously. While it's easy to dismiss influencer culture, I would recommend paying attention to it. Influencer culture is probably creeping into your life more acutely, deeply, and frequently than you might think.

# Methods Appendix

This book brings together two research projects, which, for ease of reference, I have titled the "influencer" and the "artist" projects. The influencer project extends the research undertaken during my PhD—a critical examination of the UK influencer industry through ethnography and interviews conducted between 2015 and 2018.[1] I have updated this work with new research, drawing from a messy web of research sites, including influencer content, news, entertainment media, trade press, and podcasts (2022–24).[2] In the "artist" project, I examined the ways that artists use social media to promote their work, through ethnography and interviews conducted between 2021 and 2024. I am a feminist researcher interested in the intersecting inequalities discussed throughout this book; thus, both projects primarily focus on the experiences of women and nonbinary people.

Bringing together different methods like interviews, digital ethnography, and ethnography is typically called mixed methods research. I've found this approach to be useful, as the methods inform each other. For example, fieldwork at influencer events allowed me to make a map of the people involved in the front and backstage areas of the beauty influencer industry, a map that could grow richer with online ethnography and interviews. Going to influencer meetups and conventions helped me see influencers' teams of public relations staff and talent agents, who are usually hiding backstage. In the interest of authenticity, influencers rarely discussed the role of their agents in their content, but I witnessed them flanking their clients at meet-and-greets, speaking on panels, and politely grimacing while taking questions from excitable aspiring creators. I could then approach agents for interviews, follow up on them in my online ethnography, and parse their roles and relationships in the influencer industry more fully.

## Ethnography

I conducted ethnographic research at influencer events over a three-year period. These events included VidCon EU,[3] Summer in the City,[4] and Twitter's invitation-only influencer event, Creator Day. I also attended a slate of specialist beauty networking events run by the glossy industry magazine *Blogosphere*,[5] which involved heavy brand rep attendance, panels, and lectures on content production. I also conducted participant observation at the YouTube Space between late 2017 and the early months of 2018, including a tour, events, and periods of hanging out at the Creator Café.[6]

Throughout my online ethnography of influencer industries I walked through social media platforms like YouTube, Instagram, and Twitter to identify influencers while following networks to build a holistic picture of influencer industries. Following algorithmic recommendations on social media platforms replicates the gender and race biases exacerbated by these sociotechnical systems and makes it challenging to find individuals who are under the radar,[7] or who are more likely to be from historically marginalized identities.[8] I sought to build a more holistic representation of influencer culture by looking beyond my top algorithmic recommendations. I used combinations of search strings related to influencer genres—for example, "what's in my bag," "tutorial," "smokey eye," "chatty vlog," and so on. I also followed individuals' collaborations, mentions, and recommendations to garner a wider viewpoint beyond the narrow scope of social media platform algorithms.

In early 2020, my research project into artists started and the Covid lockdowns began. Physical art world events like open views and markets were abruptly canceled. Art world schmoozing and sales shifted online, and my research followed suit. I followed one hundred UK artists and makers who had a public social media profile and participated in commercial art activities, such as selling work through an online store, participating in art markets, or inviting commissions. Those I interviewed had artistic practices like ceramics, illustration, metalwork, and textile art. To research the political and economic context of art worlds, I also followed upwards of fifty intermediary organizations on Instagram, such as galleries, markets, and art stores; I found these organizations by art-world-related search terms (ceramics, portraiture, art galleries), through social media posts and recommendations, and by checking which art organizations followed each other. I scrutinized the artists who were supported by these galleries, whose works were stocked in shops and markets, and who were followed by other artists in my sample. As I show throughout this book, influencer economies and art worlds are industries that often necessitate economic and networked privilege to access. The research I undertook in both these projects is limited by the lack of racial and class diversity in these research sites (see, for example, this book's conclusion).

During both projects, I kept research diaries or journals in which I noted and reflected on events, moments, and happenings in my field site. I built a corpus of screengrabs, including tweets, Instagram posts, and YouTube videos in addition to a folder of news articles, magazine coverage, and industry blog posts. Analyzing media texts across platforms afforded an attention to the wider meaning construction of my research site. These representations in turn enabled an analysis of multilayered "semantic networks" and "discursive formation,"[9] which the researcher can make visible to strengthen understandings of culture or a cultural artifact.

## Interviews

For the influencer project, I conducted semi-structured interviews with eighteen vloggers, experts, and intermediaries in total, including CEOs/directors of digital talent management organizations, founders of UK-based multichannel networks, and Twitter's community manager for the UK and Europe, who "works with creators worldwide alongside top brands to develop authentic and resonating branded content."[10] I also interviewed the director of the Internet Creators Guild, an international organization intended to promote and support full-time content creators. I asked them about their approach to creating content, their strategies for self-presentation, their relationships with brands, their working lives, and their feelings about algorithmic visibility.

Interview data has been extremely valuable to my analysis in many ways, but I didn't rush to update my data for the book project with new influencer interviews. This is partly because of the very real challenge in getting content creators to agree to interviews.[11] As I've discussed in this book, influencers are invested in appearing authentic and ordinary, which can mean they appear misleadingly accessible. In fact, many high-profile influencers have a star status that could parallel movie stars or other so-called traditional celebrities. They're booked and they're busy. What's more, I know that influencers are inundated with requests to participate in scholarly projects: one influencer I interviewed in 2018 said she received more than five emails a day from students hoping to speak to her for university research. I can only imagine this number has increased with time.

Of course, I do have good networks within influencer economies and I could have approached influencers for interviews. But I don't actually think interviews generate a truer or more authentic perspective than data found in video content, social media posts, press interviews, public talks, and nonverbal performances and representations. Each of these sources involves performance for an imagined audience, whether this is a researcher, fans, or potential talent agents.[12] The job of being an influencer is quite unique in that it entails constantly constructing a public-facing identity across multiple sites; in this sense, then, there's a lot of data out there in the ether to be plundered, which influencers have created on their own terms.

Moreover, influencers often approach interviews with academics the same way they do with journalists. As Brooke Duffy explains in her book *(Not) Getting Paid to Do What You Love: Gender, Social Media, and Aspirational Work*, aspiring and growing creators may see interviews for a book project as a potentially lucrative opportunity to pitch themselves and build their brand, similar to how they might see a press interview. One example of this kind of pitching can be found in an interview given to queer influencer Ingrid Nilsen by researchers Stuart Cunningham and David Craig. Nilsen tells Cunningham and Craig how she risked her relationship with cosmetics company Cover Girl when she came out: "[Nilsen] declared in our interview, she did not want to represent a brand that wouldn't accept who she is."[13] This point parallels the statements she has given to mainstream magazines such as *Women's Health*: "If [brands] I was working with had a problem with me being gay, I didn't want to work with them anyway."[14] Both these statements are equally valuable: they are slices of identity work that reinforce Nilsen's performance of authentic and noncommercial self-branding. Whether told to a journalist or academic, they show that she is an individual invested in publicly reinforcing her ethical standpoint toward brand collaborators, a huge plus in an industry that hinges on convincing performances of authenticity. One is not more real than the other.

Artists do not tend to discuss the topics I am interested in as publicly as influencers do, however, so interviews became very important to my second project. In total, I conducted semi-structured interviews over Zoom with twenty-five UK-based artists who self-identified as either nonbinary or female. Interviews focused on artistic practice, promotional strategies, and experiences of Instagram. I did not ask artists to identify their race or class position, although participants did frequently discuss these themes in interviews. Interviews lasted between sixty and ninety minutes and were recorded and fully transcribed.

In my work, I followed the analysis guidance set out by Ann Gray in the book *Research Practice for Cultural Studies*. As Gray so accurately puts it, "Analysis and interpretation became part of the process of research."[15] I immersed myself in the data from each of my projects, drawing together my corpus of ethnographic fieldnotes, screengrabs, and interview transcripts to identify themes important to my research. Examples included backstage, expertise, and algorithms. I also investigated Instagram posts as images with their own forms of storytelling and meaning-making, bearing in mind the particular contextual information enlightened by platform features and affordances, such as image captions and temporary images.[16] I analyzed collected content against an informed backdrop of literature related to the primary themes of this book: self-branding, optimization, and authenticity.

# Notes

## Introduction

1. Bishop (2022).
2. Nyce (2024).
3. Nyce (2023).
4. Cotter (2018).
5. For accounts of race in the early days of the feminized commercial blogosphere, see Lopez (2009, 2014); Pham (2011, 2013, 2015).
6. These inequalities will be discussed throughout this book but see Bishop (2018, 2021a); Christin & Lu (2023); Duffy & Meisner (2022); Glatt (2024); Sobande et al. (2019); Stevens (2021).
7. For information on my methodological approach, please see this book's Methods Appendix.
8. Becker (2008: 1).
9. Lena & Lindemann (2014).
10. Becker (1978: 863).
11. McRobbie (2015).
12. McRobbie (2015: 61).
13. Berlant (2011: 2).
14. Berlant (2011).
15. For examples, see Gill (2002, 2011); Hesmondhalgh & Baker (2015); Littler (2013); McRobbie (2011, 2015); Scharff (2015); Sobande (2020); Sobande et al. (2019).
16. Hund (2023: 32).
17. Nieborg & Poell (2018).
18. Nieborg & Poell (2018: 4276).
19. Nieborg & Poell (2018: 4282).
20. Duffy et al. (2019: 1).
21. See Poell et al. (2022) for a good summary of this research to date.
22. Glatt (2022).
23. Abidin (2016: 3).
24. Duffy (2021: 1).
25. Senft (2008: 25).
26. Marwick (2013: 13).
27. Ahmed (2012).
28. I wrote about this in *Real Life* magazine (Bishop, 2021b).
29. Du Gay et al. (2013).

30. See Duffy (2017) and Hund (2023) for valuable histories of feminized promotional media, as well as their relationships with influencer industries.
31. Becker (2008).

## Chapter 1. Influencers: The Canaries in the Algorithmic Coal Mine

1. Shaw & Bergen (2020).
2. Shadow banning is when content is hidden, or its visibility restricted, without content creators being notified. See Are (2021); Cotter (2021).
3. For examples of optimization strategies in creative industries, see chapter 2, or Morris et al. (2021); Patel (2020); Poell et al. (2021); Sobande et al. (2023).
4. See Ziewitz (2019).
5. Morris et al. (2021: 170).
6. For a doomsday-ish account of the "black box society," see Frank Pasquale's (2015) book *The Black Boxed Society*, which eerily suggests that platforms operate with a "mix of real and legal secrecy and scale" (8). *The Black Boxed Society* is concerned that automated forms of decision-making (like platform recommendations) may be animated by nefarious intentions: "the economic, political and cultural agen-

das behind [platform] suggestions are hard to unravel" (5). Pasquale raises the issue of power asymmetry inherent in platform functions: social media platforms collect information about us, but we cannot know anything about them.
7. See Bucher (2018); Cotter (2021); Meisner (2023); Noble (2018).
8. A typical use of this kind of logic can be found in an op-ed published by social media researchers in the popular science magazine *Scientific American* titled "It's Time to Open the Black Box of Social Media" (DiResta et al., 2022). In this piece, the authors argue that it is "time to require more transparency from social media companies" in order to "develop better, safer systems."
9. Bucher (2018).
10. Bucher (2018: 46).
11. See Benjamin (2019); Noble (2018); Seaver (2017).
12. Dourish (2016).
13. Ryan (1992).
14. Ryan (1992: 154).
15. Ryan (1992: 149).
16. Negus (1999: 19).
17. Negus (1999: 162).
18. Saha (2018: 111).
19. Havens (2014: 41).
20. Ananny & Crawford (2018); Gillespie (2014).
21. Covington et al. (2016).

22. The Game Theorists (2017).
23. As of late 2023.
24. Paddy Galloway (2021b).
25. Paddy Galloway (2022).
26. Paddy Galloway (2019).
27. Paddy Galloway (2021a).
28. Bouk (2015: 107).
29. Bouk (2015: 107).
30. Paddy Galloway (2022).
31. Ryan (1992: 178).
32. Saha (2018: 136).
33. Paddy Galloway (2019).
34. Caplan & Gillespie (2020: 7).
35. Paul (2018: 3).
36. The Game Theorists (2014).
37. Kendall (2011: 5016).
38. Duffy & Hund (2019: 4996).
39. Marwick (2021: 2).
40. Marwick (2021: 2).
41. Marwick (2021: 6).
42. Meisner (2023: 5).
43. Creator Insider (2023a).
44. Creator Insider (2023a).
45. Creator Insider (2023b).
46. Creator Insider (2023b).
47. Creator Insider (2023b).
48. Creator Insider (2023b).
49. Cotter (2021: 1227).
50. Petre et al. (2019: 2).
51. Mosseri (n.d., #dadlife).
52. Mosseri (n.d., #AMA).
53. Nulleparttousjours (2023).
54. Adkins (2002: 215).
55. Adkins (2002: 215).
56. For example, Taina Bucher (2017) has shown how individuals develop "algorithmic imaginaries," which shape and guide how they use social media platforms like Facebook.
57. Related to "algorithmic folk theories," which are ideas generated by "non-professionals" about how technical systems work (Eslami et al., 2017: 2).
58. Adkins (2002: 216).
59. McKelvey, Prey & Nieborg (2021).
60. Saha (2018: 140).

## Chapter 2. Artists: Optimization, but Make It Aesthetic

1. *The Artist Business Plan* (2021).
2. Becker (2008: 94).
3. DiMaggio (1987).
4. Bourdieu (2000).
5. Bourdieu (2000: 49).
6. Bourdieu (2000: 217).
7. Bourdieu (1983: 319).
8. Through my ethnography and interviews with artists, Instagram has regularly been mentioned as the most important platform of focus. Although artists certainly do maintain a presence on TikTok, art economies focus on Instagram because of their emphasis on visual culture and the perception that audiences on Instagram are older, and are thus likely to be able to afford to buy art.

9. Seaver (2022:12).

10. Seaver (2022:152).

11. Morris et al. (2021).

12. Morris (2020:1).

13. Hodgson (2021); Morris et al. (2021).

14. Seaver (2022:154).

15. Jobin & Ziewitz (2018:4).

16. See Abidin (2018); Leaver et al. (2020).

17. See Leaver et al. (2020).

18. Epps-Darling (2020).

19. See Benjamin (2019).

20. Agostinho (2018:136).

21. Duffy (2019).

22. Bsquared.social (2024).

23. Bsquared.social (2024).

24. Design Trust (2021).

25. Poell et al. (2022).

26. Hund & McGuigan (2019).

27. Hund & McGuigan (2019:32).

28. Baym (2018).

29. Abidin (2015:5).

30. Abidin (2015:8).

31. Cotter (2021).

32. Petre et al. (2019).

33. Glatt (2022:19).

34. See Caplan & Gillespie (2020); Duffy & Meisner (2022); Glatt (2022); Meisner (2023).

35. Bucher (2012).

36. Wohl (2021:45).

37. Wohl (2021:69).

38. Becker (2008:94).

39. Becker (2008).

40. Becker (2008:94).

41. Negus (1999:206).

Chapter 3. Making Soup, Eating Dino Nuggets: Authenticity within Influencer Cultures

1. emma chamberlain (2021b).

2. Grazian (2003).

3. Peterson (1997:3).

4. Helmond (2015); Nieborg & Poell (2018).

5. Banet-Weiser (2012:45).

6. Duffy (2017:133).

7. Marwick (2013:120).

8. Cunningham & Craig (2018).

9. Findlay (2015); Pham (2011); Rocamora (2011).

10. Duffy (2015:54).

11. Lorenz (2019).

12. Abidin (2017:1).

13. Abidin (2017:6).

14. Burgess & Green (2018:25).

15. emma chamberlain (2021a).

16. Guilbault (2023).

17. Glyde (2012).

18. Guilbault (2023).

19. Steele (2021:74).

20. Pitcan et al. (2018:171).

21. Banet-Weiser & Higgins (2022:4).

22. Specter (2023).

23. Vogue (2016).

24. Genz (2015); Skeggs (2009).

25. The D'Amelio Family (2020).

26. McRobbie (2009:15).

27. *Saturday Night Live* (2021).

28. Hochschild (2012: 91).
29. Hochschild (2012: 54).
30. Hochschild (2012: 55).
31. Hochschild (2012: 90).
32. Hochschild (2012: 92).
33. Caplan & Gillespie (2020: 6).
34. Caplan & Gillespie (2020: 2).
35. James Charles (2019).
36. Olivia Jade (2018).
37. Logan Paul (2018).
38. Banet-Weiser (2021 :144).
39. Anthony Padilla (2019).
40. Cotter (2021: 2).
41. Cotter (2021: 13).
42. E.g., Duffy (2017); Glatt (2022).
43. Duffy & Meisner (2022: 12).
44. Duffy & Pruchniewska (2017: 855).
45. Marchese (2023).
46. DiMaggio (1987: 450).
47. Negus (1999: 363).
48. Ahmed (2014: 4).
49. "SA" is an initialism for "sexual assault" and "SH" is an initialism for "sexual harassment." Platform users deploy abbreviations because they believe that social media platforms will make content with unsafe themes less visible. For more on brand safety, see chapters 5 and 6.
50. Illouz (2003).
51. Illouz (2003).
52. Grazian (2003).
53. Grazian (2003: 42).
54. Stuart (2020: 9).
55. Stuart (2020: 6).
56. Stuart (2020: 12).

Chapter 4. Linen, Looms, and Limestone Cottages: Being an "Authentic" Artist on Social Media

1. See Abidin (2017); Duffy & Wissinger (2017).
2. Benjamin (2017: 3).
3. Becker (2008: 356).
4. Becker (2008: 357).
5. Menger (2014: 294).
6. Menger (2014: 313).
7. Patel (2020: 62).
8. Luckman (2013: 254).
9. Manovich (2016).
10. Manovich (2016: 54).
11. For example, as outlined in the previous chapter in relation to practices used by American influencer Emma Chamberlain.
12. A. Marwick (2013).
13. Duffy (2017: 107).
14. Poell et al. (2022: 151).
15. Goffman (1990: 210).
16. Goffman (1990: 116).
17. Goffman (1990: 116).
18. Abidin (2017).
19. Duffy & Hund (2015: 5).
20. Patel (2020: 69).
21. Bain (2004: 80).
22. The video was coproduced by Elin Wretlund in a partnership with Swedish brand Björk and Berries.

23. Patel (2022: 1559).
24. White (2015: 13).
25. Mamidipudi (2019: 242).
26. Cohen (1998).
27. Baym (2018); Poell et al. (2021).
28. Miller (2016).
29. Miller (2016).
30. Brook et al. (2020b); Gill (2011).
31. Brook et al. (2020a).
32. Toft & Friedman (2021: 91).
33. Banet-Weiser (2021: 143).
34. Nunn & Biressi (2010: 50).
35. Ringrose & Walkerdine (2008).
36. Gill & Elias (2014).

Chapter 5. No Historic Nudes
Allowed: Influencer Self-Branding
and Brand Safety

1. Alison Hearn (2008) defines self-branding as the "self-conscious construction of a meta-narrative and meta-image of the self" (21).
2. Baym & boyd (2012); Marwick (2013); Marwick & boyd (2011).
3. Wagoner (2020).
4. Phm (2015: 87).
5. Phan (2013).
6. Banet-Weiser (2012: 7).
7. Hearn (2008: 198).
8. Duffy & Hund (2015: 4).
9. Duffy & Hund (2015: 6).
10. Kilbane (2021).
11. Born in 1987, Phan was thirty-seven at the time of writing.
12. Michelle Phan (2017b).

13. Michelle Phan (2017b).
14. Michelle Phan (2017a).
15. Hou (2017).
16. Michelle Phan (2017b).
17. A video genre popular on YouTube in the early to mid-2000s, in which creators would use a whiteboard to draw and narrate key moments of their life prior to YouTube stardom.
18. Michelle Phan (2013).
19. Michelle Phan (2017b).
20. Neff (2012); Neff, Wissinger & Zukin (2005).
21. Beck (2009: 4).
22. Marwick (2013: 167).
23. Marwick (2013: 166).
24. Marwick (2013: 167).
25. Marwick (2013: 193).
26. Nieborg & Poell (2018: 4275).
27. Poell et al. (2022: 122).
28. Fahey (1991).
29. Bagdikian (1997: 133
30. Andrejevic (2009: 412).
31. Lobato (2016: 357–58).
32. Burgess & Green (2018: 111).
33. Andrejevic (2009: 413).
34. Mahdawi (2017).
35. Creator Insider (2022).
36. Creator Insider (2018).
37. Meta (2024b).
38. Kopf (2022: 13).
39. Creator Insider (2018).
40. Duffy & Meisner (2023: 13).
41. Creator Insider (2018).
42. Carty (2022: 570).

43. Carty (2022: 576).
44. Meta (2024a).
45. YouTube (2023).
46. Unilever (2018).
47. Influencer Marketing Hub (2024: 43).
48. Wiley (2023).
49. Faull (2018).
50. Are & Briggs (2023: 4).
51. Gerrard & Thornham (2020).
52. Gamson (1995: 392).
53. Sender (2002: 20).
54. Fahey (1991: 678).
55. Sender (2003: 336).
56. Oakley (2017).
57. Russo (2017).
58. Willson (2017: 5).
59. Eubanks (2017: 178).
60. Benjamin (2019: 8).
61. Sender (2003: 344).
62. BBC News (2019).
63. Waldman (2022).
64. Ragusa (2005: 666).
65. Budweiser's decline was also probably caused by simultaneous boycotts of the brands by LGBTQ+ groups, who criticized their decision to not speak out in support of transgender issues or of Mulvaney. See Guynn (2023); Gologi (2023).
66. Dylan Mulvaney (2023).
67. Carroll (2023).
68. Whitworth (2023).
69. Jefferson (2022).
70. Phạm (2015: 93).
71. Phạm (2015: 96).
72. Sobande (2022: 4).
73. Sobande et al. (2022: 1579).
74. Sobande et al. (2022: 1681).
75. Marwick (2013: 192).

Chapter 6. When Naked Becomes Nude: Artist Self-Branding and Brand Safety

1. Kerrigan et al. (2011: 1512).
2. Lury (2005: 95).
3. For explanations of the elevator pitch and the collapse of different audiences online, see Marwick (2013); Marwick & boyd (2011).
4. Wohl (2021: 136).
5. Wohl (2021: 142).
6. Wohl (2021: 151).
7. See Marwick (2013); Neff (2012); Neff et al. (2005).
8. Sheedy (2022: 2).
9. Gregory (2019).
10. Gregory (2012: 267).
11. Bain (2004, 2005).
12. Bain (2004: 173).
13. Duffy (2017).
14. Radford (1998: 146).
15. Acocella (2020).
16. Restany (2023).
17. Wohl (2021: 29).
18. McRobbie (2015).
19. Wohl (2021: 26).
20. Miller (2016: 123).
21. McRobbie (2015: 113).
22. "10 Critical Components of Influencer Engagement Contracts

through the Eyes of the Influencer and the Brand," jmw, January 25, 2025, https://www.jmw.co.uk/articles/corporate/10-critical-components-of-influencer-engagement-contracts.

23. Marwick and boyd (2011).
24. Fine (2006).
25. Duffy (2017: 175).
26. Elmhirst (2019).
27. Bertoni (2023).
28. McCartney & Tynan (2021: 149).
29. Short for "advertisement."
30. Meta (2024c).
31. Don't Delete Art (2023a).
32. Don't Delete Art (2022a).
33. Shapiro (2022).
34. Shapiro (2022).
35. See Are (2021); Are & Paasonen (2021); Myers West (2018).
36. Gillespie (2022: 6).
37. Cotter (2021).
38. Don't Delete Art (2023e).
39. Don't Delete Art (2023d).
40. Don't Delete Art (2023b).
41. Shapiro (2022).
42. Bachmann (2022).
43. Don't Delete Art (2022c).
44. Caplan (2023).
45. Are & Paasonen (2021); Tiidenberg (2021).
46. Tiidenberg (2021: 386).
47. Don't Delete Art (2025).
48. Don't Delete Art (2023c).
49. McGuigan (2023).
50. Don't Delete Art (2023a).

51. Don't Delete Art (2019).
52. Don't Delete Art (2023c).
53. Maes & Levinson (2012).
54. Maes (2011); Nead (1990).
55. Maes & Levinson (2012).
56. Maes (2011: 388).
57. Nead (1990: 326).
58. Paasonen (2021); Paasonen et al. (2019); Smith & Attwood (2014).
59. van Brabandt & Prinz (2012: 176).
60. Maes & Levinson (2012: 39).
61. Don't Delete Art (2023c).
62. This is inspired by Sara Ahmed's approach. See Ahmed (2012).
63. Stegeman et al. (2024).
64. Blunt & Stardust (2021).
65. Don't Delete Art (2022b).
66. Nead (2010: 84).
67. Gallagher (2021).
68. Bourdieu (1983: 342).
69. McCartney & Tynan (2021: 158).
70. McCartney & Tynan (2021: 158).
71. Holmes (2007).
72. Mears (2023: 2).
73. Bourdieu (1983: 322).

Conclusion: Time to Bring It Home with a Profound Conclusion

1. Sponsored content.
2. Forman (2025).
3. Canada Goose was previously criticized by activists like People for the Ethical Treatment of Animals (PETA) for their use of fur and down (Peta, 2025), but the com-

pany has recently started to pursue sustainability. Ethical fashion watchdog Good on You has changed their Canada Goose sustainability ranking from "Not Good Enough" to "It's a Start" (Good on You, 2023).

4. Yotka (2017).
5. Tate (2007: 301).
6. Mears (2011: 7).
7. Florida (2014).
8. Florida (2014: 317).
9. Bain (2005: 125).
10. Both Jen Stark and Zaria Forman live in well-decorated lofts located in art world centers like New York and LA.
11. Mears (2014: 1339).
12. Influencer Marketing Hub (2024).
13. Faull (2018).
14. Berlant (2011).
15. Duffy (2017).
16. Christin & Lu (2023).
17. Influencer Pay Gap (2021).
18. Wilson (2024).
19. Artists Union (2024).
20. Deresiewicz (2014).
21. G's argument posits that "mediating figures" like publishing companies and record labels serve to shield creators from market logic, although many critical media industries scholars have shown that these intermediaries shape art in the direction of market logic in practice. See, e.g., Hesmondhalgh

& Baker (2010); Negus (1999); Saha (2018).
22. Bourdieu (1983, 2000).
23. Hesmondhalgh (2006).
24. Ten thousand hours is a figure proposed by Canadian journalist Malcolm Gladwell.
25. Jennings (2024).
26. Daramola (2024).
27. Deresiewicz (2014).
28. Bourdieu (1983: 317).
29. Bourdieu (1983).
30. Blackwood & Purcell (2014); Domínguez et al. (2020).
31. See Hall (1992); Hall et al. (2013); Said (1978).
32. Agnello (2010).
33. Berger (2005: 14).
34. Bourdieu (2000).
35. Chong (2011: 2).
36. Hall (2006: 16).
37. Adams et al. (2021).
38. Sieghart (2022).
39. Connolly (2015).
40. Sieghart (2022).

## Methods Appendix

1. See Bishop (2018b).
2. Postill & Pink (2012).
3. VidCon is an annual convention for social media stars and their fans, founded by YouTube stars Hank and John Green in 2010. VidCon takes place in Anaheim, California, but hosted events in the

United Kingdom and the Netherlands between 2017 and 2020. Events have also been run in Singapore, Mexico, and the United Arab Emirates.

4. Summer in the City (now called Social in the City) is a UK-based social media convention, first organized as an ad hoc meetup in a London park in 2009. The event gradually became professionalized, and it was held at the ExCel Center in London between 2015 and 2019; the center has a capacity for ten thousand attendees.

5. Now called *bCreator* magazine.

6. At one point, there were ten physical YouTube Spaces across the world, which included facilities and resources to support creators in producing content. These involved a creator café, production studios, equipment rentals, workshops, and classes. The London YouTube Space was open from 2012 on. Seven of these Spaces were closed in 2021 following the Covid-19 pandemic. Spaces remain open in São Paulo, Mumbai, and Dubai.

7. Bishop (2018a); Noble (2018); Sobande (2017).

8. Abidin (2021).

9. Du Gay et al. (2013: 15).

10. Niche (2018).

11. Cunningham & Craig (2016).

12. Marwick & boyd (2011).

13. Abber (2016).

14. Gray (2002).

15. Gray (2002: 133).

16. Highfield & Leaver (2016: 53).

# References

Abidin, C. (2015). Communicative ♥ intimacies: Influencers and perceived interconnectedness. *Ada: A Journal of Gender, New Media, & Technology 8*, 1–16. https://scholarsbank.uoregon.edu/server/api/core/bitstreams /a18cd997-772b-42f9-acb3-096dadfa2eae/content

Abidin, C. (2016). "Aren't these just young, rich women doing vain things online?": Influencer selfies as subversive frivolity. *Social Media + Society*, 2(2), 2056305116641342. https://doi.org/10.1177/2056305116641342

Abidin, C. (2017). #familygoals: Family influencers, calibrated amateurism, and justifying young digital labor. *Social Media + Society*, 3(2), 2056305117707191.

Abidin, C. (2018). From internet celebrities to influencers. In *Internet celebrity: Understanding fame online* (pp. 71–98). Emerald Publishing Limited. https://www.emerald.com/insight/content/doi/10.1108/978 -1-78756-076-520181004/full/html

Acocella, J. (2020, June 1). Untangling Andy Warhol. *The New Yorker*. https:// www.newyorker.com/magazine/2020/06/08/untangling-andy-warhol

Adams, R. B., Kräussl, R., Navone, M., & Verwijmeren, P. (2021). Gendered prices. *The Review of Financial Studies*, 34(8), 3789–3839. https://doi.org /10.1093/rfs/hhab046

Adkins, K. C. (2002). The real dirt: Gossip and feminist epistemology. *Social Epistemology*, 16(3), 215–232. https://doi.org/10.1080/0269172022000025598

Agnello, R. (2010). Race and art: Prices for African American painters and their contemporaries. *Journal of Black Studies*, 41(1), 56–70. https://doi .org/10.1177/0021934708328444

Agostinho, D. (2018). Chroma key dreams: Algorithmic visibility, fleshy images and scenes of recognition. *Philosophy of Photography*, 9(2), 131–155. https://doi.org/10.1386/pop.9.2.131_1

Ahmed, S. (2012). *On being included: Racism and diversity in institutional life*. Duke University Press.

Ahmed, S. (2014). *The cultural politics of emotion* (2nd ed.). Edinburgh University Press.

Ananny, M., & Crawford, K. (2018). Seeing without knowing: Limitations of the transparency ideal and its application to algorithmic accountability. *New Media & Society*, 20(3), 973–989. https://doi.org/10.1177/1461444816676645

Andrejevic, M. (2009). Exploiting YouTube: Contradictions of user-generated labor. In P. Snickars & P. Vonderau (Eds.), *The YouTube reader* (Vol. 413). National Library of Sweden. http://forskning.blogg.kb.se/files/2012/09/YouTube_Reader.pdf#page=204

Anthony Padilla. (2019, April 2). I spent a day with TEEN YOUTUBE STARS (ft. Tanner Fox, Big Nik & Bryce Hall) [video]. YouTube. https://www.youtube.com/watch?v=pd0qhcpDRsc

Are, C. (2021). The Shadowban cycle: An autoethnography of pole dancing, nudity and censorship on Instagram. *Feminist Media Studies*, 0(0), 1–18. https://doi.org/10.1080/14680777.2021.1928259

Are, C., & Briggs, P. (2023). The emotional and financial impact of de-platforming on creators at the margins. *Social Media + Society*, 9(1), https://doi.org/10.1177/20563051231155103

Are, C., & Paasonen, S. (2021). Sex in the shadows of celebrity. *Porn Studies*, 8(4), 411–419. https://doi.org/10.1080/23268743.2021.1974311

*Artist Business Plan*. (2021, September 30). *Six figure artist with Isaac Pelayo*. https://the-artist-business-plan.captivate.fm/episode/six-figure-artist-with-isaac-pelayo

Artists Union. (2024). Rates of pay. https://www.artistsunionengland.org.uk/

Bachmann, L. (2022, June 10). Instagram's prudeness is ruining my art. *1 Granary*. https://1granary.com/opinion/instagrams-prudeness-is-ruining-my-art/

Bagdikian, B. H. (1997). *The media monopoly* (5th ed.). Beacon Press.

Bain, A. (2004). Female artistic identity in place: The studio. *Social & Cultural Geography*, 5(2), 171–193. https://doi.org/10.1080/1464936041000169204

Bain, A. (2005). Constructing an artistic identity. *Work, Employment and Society*, 19(1), 25–46. https://doi.org/10.1177/0950017005051280

Banet-Weiser, S. (2012). *Authentic™*. New York University Press.

Banet-Weiser, S. (2021). Gender, social media, and the labor of authenticity. *American Quarterly*, 73(1), 141–144.

Banet-Weiser, S., & Higgins, K. C. (2022). Television and the "honest" woman: Mediating the labor of believability. *Television & New Media*, 23(2), 127–147. https://doi.org/10.1177/15274764211045742

Baym, N. K. (2018). *Playing to the crowd: Musicians, audiences, and the intimate work of connection*. New York University Press.

Baym, N. K., & boyd, danah. (2012). Socially mediated publicness: An introduction. *Journal of Broadcasting & Electronic Media*, 56(3), 320–329. https://doi.org/10.1080/08838151.2012.705200

BBC News. (2019, February 21). AT&T and Hasbro pull YouTube ads over abuse claims. BBC News. https://www.bbc.com/news/business-47325893

Beck, U. (2009). *World at risk*. Polity.

Becker, H. S. (1978). Arts and crafts. *American Journal of Sociology*, 83(4), 862–889.

Becker, H. S. (2008). *Art worlds* (25th anniversary ed.). University of California Press.

Benjamin, R. (2019). *Race after technology: Abolitionist tools for the new Jim code*. Polity.

Benjamin, W. (2017). The work of art in the age of mechanical reproduction (1936). In *Aesthetics* (pp. 66–69). Routledge.

Berger, M. A. (2005). *Sight unseen: Whiteness and American visual culture*. University of California Press.

Berlant, L. G. (2011). *Cruel optimism*. Duke University Press.

Bertoni, S. (2023, December 1). Top creators 2023. *Forbes*. https://www.forbes.com/sites/stevenbertoni/2023/09/26/top-creators-2023/

Bielby, W. T., & Bielby, D. D. (2003). Controlling prime-time: Organizational concentration and network television programming strategies. *Journal of Broadcasting & Electronic Media*, 47(4), 573–596. https://doi.org/10.1207/s15506878jobem4704_6

Bishop, S. (2018). Anxiety, panic and self-optimization: Inequalities and the YouTube algorithm. *Convergence: The International Journal of*

*Research into New Media Technologies*, 24(1), 69–84. https://doi.org/10.1177/1354856517736978

Bishop, S. (2021a). Influencer management tools: Algorithmic cultures, brand safety, and bias. *Social Media + Society*, 7(1), https://doi.org/10.1177/20563051211003066

Bishop, S. (2021b, June 14). Name of the game. *Real Life*. https://reallifemag.com/name-of-the-game/

Bishop, S. (2022, June 9). Influencer creep. *Real Life*. https://reallifemag.com/influencer-creep/

Blackwood, A., & Purcell, D. (2014). Curating inequality: The link between cultural reproduction and race in the visual arts. *Sociological Inquiry*, 84(2), 238–263. https://doi.org/10.1111/soin.12030

Blunt, D., & Stardust, Z. (2021). Automating whorephobia: Sex, technology and the violence of deplatforming. *Porn Studies*, 0(0), 1–17. https://doi.org/10.1080/23268743.2021.1947883

Bourdieu, P. (1983). The field of cultural production, or: The economic world reversed. *Poetics*, 12(4–5), 311–356. https://doi.org/10.1016/0304-422X(83)90012-8

Bourdieu, P. (2000). *Distinction: A social critique of the judgement of taste* (Reprint 1984 ed.). Harvard University Press.

Brook, O., O'Brien, D., & Taylor, M. (2020). Art workers, inequality, and the labour market: Values, norms, and alienation across three generations of artists. In Andrea Glauser, Patricia Holder, Thomas Mazzurana, Olivier Moeschler, Valérie Rolle, Franz Schultheis (Eds.), *The sociology of arts and markets* (pp. 75–96). Springer.

Brook, O., O'Brien, D., & Taylor, M. (2020b). Culture is bad for you. In *Culture is bad for you*. Manchester University Press.

Bsquared.social. (2024, May 1). Social media management & coaching services. B Squared Social. https://www.bsquared.social/reels-report

Bucher, T. (2012). Want to be on the top? Algorithmic power and the threat of invisibility on Facebook. *New Media & Society*, 14(7), 1164–1180. https://doi.org/10.1177/1461444812440159

Bucher, T. (2017). The algorithmic imaginary: Exploring the ordinary affects of Facebook algorithms. *Information, Communication & Society*, 20(1), 30–44. https://doi.org/10.1080/1369118X.2016.1154086

Bucher, T. (2018). *If . . . then: Algorithmic power and politics.* Oxford University Press.

Burgess, J., & Green, J. (2018). *YouTube: Online video and participatory culture.* Polity Press. http://ebookcentral.proquest.com/lib/kcl/detail.action ?docID=5502950

Caplan, R. (2023). *Networked platform governance: The construction of the democratic platform.*

Caplan, R., & Gillespie, T. (2020). Tiered governance and demonetization: The shifting terms of labor and compensation in the platform economy. *Social Media + Society*, 6(2), 2056305120936636. https://doi.org/10.1177 /2056305120936636

Carroll, N. (2023, June 16). Bud Light brand health shows no sign of recovery as impact of backlash persists. *Marketing Week.* https://www.marketingweek .com/bud-light-brand-health/

Carty, A. W. (2022). Cancelled: Morality clauses in an influencer era. *Lewis & Clark Law Review*, 26, 565.

Chong, P. (2011). Reading difference: How race and ethnicity function as tools for critical appraisal. *Poetics*, 39(1), 64–84. https://doi.org/10.1016 /j.poetic.2010.11.003

Christin, A., & Lu, Y. (2023). The influencer pay gap: Platform labor meets racial capitalism. *New Media & Society*, https://doi.org/10.1177 /14614448231164995

Cohen, J. H. (1998). Craft production and the challenge of the global market: An artisans' cooperative in Oaxaca, Mexico. *Human Organization*, 57(1), 74–82.

Connolly, K. (2015, May 19). Georg Baselitz: Why art's great shock merchant has set his sights on opera. *The Guardian.* https://www.theguardian.com /artanddesign/2015/may/19/georg-baselitz-artist-glyndebourne-opera -festival-exhibition-white-cube

Cotter, K. (2018). Playing the visibility game: How digital influencers and algorithms negotiate influence on Instagram. *New Media & Society*, online first, 19. https://doi.org/10.1177/1461444818815684

Cotter, K. (2021). "Shadowbanning is not a thing": Black box gaslighting and the power to independently know and credibly critique algorithms. *Information, Communication & Society*, 1–18. https://doi.org/10.1080/136 9118X.2021.1994624

Covington, P., Adams, J., & Sargin, E. (2016). Deep neural networks for YouTube recommendations. *Proceedings of the 10th ACM Conference on Recommender Systems—RecSys '16*, 191–198. https://doi.org/10.1145/2959100.2959190

Creator Insider. (2018, March 6). Ads friendly guidelines—Barbara's take [video]. YouTube. https://www.youtube.com/watch?v=x58Ff1-joeU

Creator Insider. (2022, September 29). Monetization policies at YouTube: How are they made? [video]. YouTube. https://www.youtube.com/watch?v=iMfGS2MGjZY

Creator Insider. (2023a, May 25). YouTube algorithm 2023: What creators need to know [video]. YouTube. https://www.youtube.com/watch?v=67TkpHKv9tE

Creator Insider. (2023b, August 23). YouTube shorts algorithm—explained! [video]. YouTube. https://www.youtube.com/watch?v=n3jsYK_-aRU

Cunningham, S., & Craig, D. R. (2018). *Social media entertainment: The new intersection of Hollywood and Silicon Valley*. New York University Press.

D'Amelio Family. (2020, November 16). Our first mystery guest: Dinner with the D'Amelios [video]. YouTube. https://www.youtube.com/watch?v=eiOKp2RAcvs

Daramola, I. (2024, January 18). Music journalism can't afford a hollowed-out Pitchfork. *Defector*. https://defector.com/music-journalism-cant-afford-a-hollowed-out-pitchfork

Deresiewicz, W. (2014, December 29). The death of the artist—and the birth of the creative entrepreneur. *The Atlantic*. https://www.theatlantic.com/magazine/archive/2015/01/the-death-of-the-artist-and-the-birth-of-the-creative-entrepreneur/383497/

Design Trust. (2021, June 20). How do I grow my business? https://www.thedesigntrust.co.uk/

DiMaggio, P. (1987). Classification in art. *American Sociological Review*, 52(4), 440–455. https://doi.org/10.2307/2095290

DiResta, R., Endelson, L., Nyham, B., & Zuckerman, E. (2022, April 28). It's time to open the black box of social media. *Scientific American*. https://www.scientificamerican.com/article/its-time-to-open-the-black-box-of-social-media/

Domínguez, S., Weffer, S. E., & Embrick, D. G. (2020). White sanctuaries: White supremacy, racism, space, and fine arts in two metropolitan

museums. *American Behavioral Scientist*, 64(14), 2028–2043. https://doi
.org/10.1177/0002764220975077

Don't Delete Art. (2019, April 18). Heather M. *Don't Delete Art*. https://www
.dontdelete.art/gallery/heather-m

Don't Delete Art. (2021, September 9). Gala Garrido. *Don't Delete Art*. https://
www.dontdelete.art/gallery/gala-garrido

Don't Delete Art. (2022a, April 20). Candelaria Deferrari. *Don't Delete Art*.
https://www.dontdelete.art/gallery/candelaria-deferrari

Don't Delete Art. (2022b, November 17). Roxanne Huber. *Don't Delete Art*.
https://www.dontdelete.art/gallery/roxanne-huber

Don't Delete Art. (2022c, December 3). John Sheridan. *Don't Delete Art*.
https://www.dontdelete.art/gallery/john-sheridan

Don't Delete Art. (2023a). Don't Delete Art. *Don't Delete Art*. https://www
.dontdelete.art

Don't Delete Art. (2023b, May 7). Maurice Mechan. *Don't Delete Art*. https://
www.dontdelete.art/gallery/maurice-mechan

Don't Delete Art. (2023c, September 19). Jessa Fairbrother. *Don't Delete Art*.
https://www.dontdelete.art/gallery/jessa-fairbrother

Don't Delete Art. (2023d, October 4). Liza Shkirando. *Don't Delete Art*.
https://www.dontdelete.art/gallery/liza-shkirando

Don't Delete Art. (2023e, December 10). Andy Lime. *Don't Delete Art*. https://
www.dontdelete.art/gallery/andy-lime

Don't Delete Art. (2025). Adrian Alarcon Sanchez. *Don't Delete Art*. https://
www.dontdelete.art/gallery-archive

Dourish, P. (2016). Algorithms and their others: Algorithmic culture in context.
*Big Data & Society*, 3(2), https://doi.org/10.1177/2053951716665128

Du Gay, P., & Pryke, M. (2002). Cultural economy: An introduction. In
*Cultural economy: Cultural analysis and commercial life* (pp. 1–20). SAGE.
https://doi.org/10.4135/9781446218440.n1

Duffy, B. E. (2015). Amateur, autonomous, and collaborative: Myths of
aspiring female cultural producers in web 2.0. *Critical Studies in Media
Communication*, 32(1), 48–64. https://doi.org/10.1080/15295036.2014
.997832

Duffy, B. E. (2016). The romance of work: Gender and aspirational labour in
the digital culture industries. *International Journal of Cultural Studies*,
19(4), 441–457. https://doi.org/10.1177/1367877915572186

Duffy, B. E. (2017). *(Not) getting paid to do what you love: Gender, social media, and aspirational work*. Yale University Press.

Duffy, B. E. (2021). Social media influencers. *The international encyclopedia of gender, media, and communication*. https://osf.io/gcj3r/download

Duffy, B. E., & Hund, E. (2015). "Having it all" on social media: Entrepreneurial femininity and self-branding among fashion bloggers. *Social Media + Society*, 1(2). https://doi.org/10.1177/2056305115604337

Duffy, B. E., & Hund, E. (2019). Gendered visibility on social media: Navigating Instagram's authenticity bind. *International Journal of Communication*, 13, 20.

Duffy, B. E., & Meisner, C. (2023). Platform governance at the margins: Social media creators' experiences with algorithmic (in)visibility. *Media, Culture & Society*, 45(2), 285–304. https://doi.org/10.1177/01634437221111923

Duffy, B. E., Poell, T., & Nieborg, D. B. (2019). Platform practices in the cultural industries: Creativity, labor, and citizenship. *Social Media+ Society*, 5(4), https://doi.org/10.1177/2056305119887967

Duffy, B. E., & Pruchniewska, U. (2017). Gender and self-enterprise in the social media age: A digital double bind. *Information, Communication & Society*, 20(6), 843–859. https://doi.org/10.1080/1369118X.2017.1291703

Duffy, B. E., & Wissinger, E. (2017). Mythologies of creative work in the social media age: Fun, free and "just being me." *International Journal of Communication*, 11, 4625–4671. https://doi.org/1932–8036/20170005

Du Gay, P., Hall, S., Janes, L., Madsen, A. K., MacKay, H., & Negus, K. (2013). *Doing cultural studies: The story of the Sony Walkman* (2nd ed.). SAGE.

Elmhirst, S. (2019, April 5). "It's genuine, you know?": Why the online influencer industry is going "authentic." *The Guardian*. https://www.theguardian.com/media/2019/apr/05/its-genuine-you-know-why-the-online-influencer-industry-is-going-authentic

emma chamberlain. (2021a, November 20). It will be ok [video]. YouTube. https://www.youtube.com/watch?v=-gBfn6LBh-E

emma chamberlain. (2021b, December 14). U totally caught me making soup [video]. YouTube. https://www.youtube.com/watch?v=Xl1iR47dzes

Epps-Darling, A. (2020, October 24). How the racism baked into technology hurts teens. *The Atlantic*. https://www.theatlantic.com/family/archive/2020/10/algorithmic-bias-especially-dangerous-teens/616793/

Eslami, M., Vaccaro, K., Karahalios, K., & Hamilton, K. (2017). "Be careful; things can be worse than they appear": Understanding biased algorithms and users' behavior around them in rating platforms. *ICWSM*, 62–71.

Eubanks, V. (2017). *Automating inequality: How high-tech tools profile, police, and punish the poor*. St. Martin's Press.

Fahey, P. M. (1991). Advocacy group boycotting of network television advertisers and its effects on programming content. *University of Pennsylvania Law Review*, 140(2), 647–709. https://doi.org/10.2307/3312353

Faull, J. (2018, September 13). L'Oreal is doing "background checks" as part of a new influencer vetting process. *The Drum*. https://www.thedrum.com/news/2018/09/13/l-oreal-doing-background-checks-part-new-influencer-vetting-process

Findlay, R. (2015). The short, passionate, and close-knit history of personal style blogs. *Fashion Theory*. https://doi.org/10.2752/175174115X14168357992319

Fine, G. A. (2006). *Everyday genius self-taught art and the culture of authenticity*. University of Chicago Press.

Florida, R. (2014). *The rise of the creative class—revisited*. Basic Books.

Forman, Z. (2025). Zaria Forman. https://www.zariaforman.com/

Game Theorists. (2014, December 22). Game theory: Yes, PewDiePie. YouTube IS broken [video]. YouTube. https://www.youtube.com/watch?v=HLJQogFHM8s&t=23s

Game Theorists. (2017, June 15). Game theory: Beyond fidget spinners—how to create a YouTube trend [video]. YouTube. https://www.youtube.com/watch?v=GTuso_IRQWg&t=9s

Gamson, J. (1995). Must identity movements self-destruct? A queer dilemma. *Social Problems*, 42(3), 390–407.

Genz, S. (2015). My job is me: Postfeminist celebrity culture and the gendering of authenticity. *Feminist Media Studies*, 15(4), 545–561. https://doi.org/10.1080/14680777.2014.952758

Gerrard, Y., & Thornham, H. (2020). Content moderation: Social media's sexist assemblages. *New Media & Society*, 22(7), 1266–1286. https://doi.org/10.1177/1461444820912540

Gill, R. (2002). Cool, creative and egalitarian? Exploring gender in project-based new media work in Europe. *Information, Communication & Society*, 5(1), 70–89. https://doi.org/10.1080/1369118011011766

Gill, R. (2011). Life is a pitch: Managing the self in new media work. In M. Deuze (Ed.), *Managing Media Work* (pp. 249–262). Sage.

Gill, Rosalind, R., & Elias, A.S. (2014). "Awaken your incredible": Love your body discourses and postfeminist contradictions. *International Journal of Media & Cultural Politics*, 10(2), 179–188. https://doi.org/10.1386/macp .10.2.179_1

Gillespie, T. (2014). The relevance of algorithms. In P. Boczkowski J., T. Gillespie, & K.A. Foot (Eds.), *Media technologies: Essays on communication, materiality, and society* (pp. 167–194). MIT Press.

Gillespie, T. (2022). Do not recommend? Reduction as a form of content moderation. *Social Media + Society*, 8(3), https://doi.org/10.1177 /20563051221117552

Glatt, Z. (2022). "We're all told not to put our eggs in one basket": Uncertainty, precarity and cross-platform labor in the online video influencer industry. *International Journal of Communication*, 20.

Glatt, Z. (2024). The intimacy triple bind: Structural inequalities and relational labour in the influencer industry. *European Journal of Cultural Studies*, 27(3), 424–440. https://doi.org/10.1177/13675494231194156

Glyde, C. (2012, August 13). The cult of Michelle Phan. *Vogue Australia*. https://www.vogue.com.au/beauty/makeup/the-cult-of-michelle-phan /news-story/1325f0ee5a4db7060b52c3ed6493de11

Goffman, E. (1990). *The presentation of self in everyday life* (Reprint). Penguin.

Grazian, D. (2003). *Blue Chicago: The search for authenticity in urban blues clubs*. University of Chicago Press.

Gregory, K. (2012). Negotiating precarity: Tarot as spiritual entrepreneurialism. *Women's Studies Quarterly*, 40(3/4), 264–280.

Gregory, K. (2019). Pushed and pulled to the internet: Self employment in the spiritual marketplace. *American Behavioral Scientist*, 63(2), 208–224. https://doi.org/10.1177/0002764218794768

Guilbault, L. (2023, January 12). In strategy shift, Lancôme names Emma Chamberlain as new brand ambassador. *Vogue Business*. https://www .voguebusiness.com/beauty/in-strategy-shift-lancome-names-emma -chamberlain-as-new-brand-ambassador

Guynn, J. (2023, May 15). Bud Light maker stripped of LGBTQ+ rating for caving to Dylan Mulvaney backlash. *USA Today*. https://www.usatoday

.com/story/money/2023/05/18/bud-light-loses-lgbtq-score-after-dylan-mulvaney-transgender-campaign/70229893007/

Hall, S. (1992). Race, culture, and communications: Looking backward and forward at cultural studies. *Rethinking Marxism*, 5(1), 10–18. https://doi.org/10.1080/08935699208657998

Hall, S. (2006). Black diaspora artists in Britain: Three "moments" in post-war history. *History Workshop Journal*, 61(1), 1–24. https://doi.org/10.1093/hwj/dbi074

Hall, S., Evans, J., & Nixon, S. (Eds.). (2013). *Representation* (2nd ed.). Sage; The Open University.

Havens, T. (2014). Towards a structuration theory of media intermediaries. In D. Johnson, A. Santo, & D. Kompare (Eds.), *Making media work: Cultures of management in the entertainment industries* (pp. 39–62). New York University Press.

Hearn, A. (2008). "Meat, mask, burden": Probing the contours of the branded "self." *Journal of Consumer Culture*, 8(2), 197–217. https://doi.org/10.1177/1469540508090086

Helmond, A. (2015). The platformization of the web: Making web data platform ready. *Social Media+ Society*, 1(2), https://doi.org/10.1177/2056305115603080

Hesmondhalgh, D. (2006). Bourdieu, the media and cultural production. *Media, Culture & Society*, 28(2), 211–231. https://doi.org/10.1177/0163443706061682

Hesmondhalgh, D., & Baker, S. (2010). "A very complicated version of freedom": Conditions and experiences of creative labour in three cultural industries. *Poetics*, 38(1), 4–20. https://doi.org/10.1016/j.poetic2009.10.001

Hesmondhalgh, D., & Baker, S. (2015). Sex, gender and work segregation in the cultural industries. In B. Conor, R. Gill, & S. Taylor (Eds.), *Gender and creative labour* (1st ed., pp. 23–37). Wiley-Blackwell.

Hesmondhalgh, D., Valverde, R.C., Kaye, D.B.V., & Li, Z. (2023). Digital platforms and infrastructure in the realm of culture. *Media and Communication*, 11(2), 296–306.

Hochschild, A.R. (2012). *The managed heart: Commercialization of human feeling* (4th ed.). University of California Press.

Hodgson, T. (2021). Spotify and the democratisation of music. *Popular Music*, 40(1), 1–17. https://doi.org/10.1017/S0261143021000064

Holmes, P. (2007, October 1). The branding of Damien Hirst. ARTnews.Com. https://www.artnews.com/art-news/artists/the-branding-of-damien-hirst-176/

Hou, K. (2017, June 2). Why Michelle Phan left YouTube to find "true happiness." *The Cut*. https://www.thecut.com/2017/06/why-michelle-phan-left-youtube-to-find-true-happiness.html

Hund, E. (2023). *The influencer industry: The quest for authenticity on social media*. Princeton University Press.

Hund, E., & McGuigan, L. (2019). A shoppable life: Performance, selfhood, and influence in the social media storefront. *Communication, Culture and Critique*, 12(1), 18–35. https://doi.org/10.1093/ccc/tcz004

Illouz, E. (2003). *Oprah Winfrey and the glamour of misery: An essay on popular culture*. Columbia University Press.

Influencer Marketing Hub. (2024). The state of influencer marketing 2024. Influencer Marketing Hub. https://influencermarketinghub.com/ebooks/Influencer_Marketing_Benchmark_Report_2024.pdf

Influencer Pay Gap [@influencerpaygap]. (2021, 26 March) #influencerpaygap. Instagram. https://www.instagram.com/influencerpaygap/?hl=en

James Charles. (2019, May 18). No More Lies [video]. YouTube. https://www.youtube.com/watch?v=uFvtCUzfyL4

Jefferson, M. (2022, March 25). Munroe Bergdorf: L'Oréal controversy was a "masterclass" in dialogue and humility. *Marketing Week*. https://www.marketingweek.com/munroe-bergdorf-loreal-controversy/

Jennings, R. (2024, February 1). Everybody has to self-promote now. Nobody wants to. *Vox*. https://www.vox.com/culture/2024/2/1/24056883/tiktok-self-promotion-artist-career-how-to-build-following

Jobin, A., & Ziewitz, M. (2018). *Organic search: How metaphors help cultivate the web*. HIIG.

Kendall, L. (2011). "White and nerdy": Computers, race, and the nerd stereotype. *The Journal of Popular Culture*, 44(3), 505–524. https://doi.org/10.1111/j.1540-5931.2011.00846.x

Kerrigan, F., Brownlie, D., Hewer, P., & Daza-LeTouze, C. (2011). "Spinning" Warhol: Celebrity brand theoretics and the logic of the celebrity brand.

*Journal of Marketing Management*, 27(13-14), 1504-1524. https://doi.org
/10.1080/0267257X.2011.624536

Kilbane, B. (2021, February 20). Michelle Phan on influence—and how to use
it. *Allure*. https://www.allure.com/story/michelle-phan-the-original
-beauty-vlogger-interview

Kopf, S. (2022). Corporate censorship online: Vagueness and discursive
imprecision in YouTube's advertiser-friendly content guidelines. *New
Media & Society*, https://doi.org/10.1177/14614448221077354

Leaver, T., Highfield, T., & Abidin, C. (2020). *Instagram: Visual social media
cultures*. Polity.

Lena, J.C., & Lindemann, D.J. (2014). Who is an artist? New data for an old
question. *Poetics*, 43, 70-85. https://doi.org/10.1016/j.poetic.2014.01.001

Littler, J. (2013). Meritocracy as plutocracy: The marketising of "equality"
under neoliberalism. *New Formations*, 80(80), 52-72. https://doi.org/10
.3898/NewF.80/81.03.2013

Lobato, R. (2016). The cultural logic of digital intermediaries: YouTube
multichannel networks. *Convergence: The International Journal of Research
into New Media Technologies*, 22(4), 348-360. https://doi.org/10.1177
/1354856516641628

Logan Paul. (2018, January 2). So Sorry [video]. YouTube. https://www.youtube
.com/watch?v=QwZT7T-TXT0

Lopez, L.K. (2009). The radical act of "mommy blogging": Redefining
motherhood through the blogosphere. *New Media & Society*, 11(5), 729-747.
https://doi.org/10.1177/1461444809105349

Lopez, L.K. (2014). Blogging while angry: The sustainability of emotional
labor in the Asian American blogosphere. *Media, Culture & Society*, 36(4),
421-436. https://doi.org/10.1177/0163443714523808

Lorenz, T. (2019, July 3). Emma Chamberlain is the most important YouTuber
today. *The Atlantic*. https://www.theatlantic.com/technology/archive
/2019/07/emma-chamberlain-and-rise-relatable-influencer/593230/

Luckman, S. (2013). The aura of the analogue in a digital age: Women's crafts,
creative markets and home-based labour after Etsy. *Cultural Studies
Review*, 19(1), 249-270.

Lury, C. (2005). "Contemplating a self-portrait as a pharmacist": A trade
mark style of doing art and science. *Theory, Culture & Society*, 22(1),
93-110. https://doi.org/10.1177/0263276405048435

Maes, H. (2011). Drawing the line: Art versus pornography. *Philosophy Compass, 6*(6), 385–397. https://doi.org/10.1111/j.1747-9991.2011.00403.x

Maes, H. L., & Levinson, J. (2012). *Art and pornography: Philosophical essays.* Oxford University Press.

Mahdawi, A. (2017, February 15). PewDiePie thinks "Death to all Jews" is a joke. Are you laughing yet? *The Guardian.* https://www.theguardian.com /commentisfree/2017/feb/15/youtube-pewdiepie-thinks-death-to-all -jews-joke-laughing-yet

Mamidipudi, A. (2019). Crafting innovation, weaving sustainability. *Comparative Studies of South Asia, Africa and the Middle East, 39*(2), 241–248. https://doi.org/10.1215/1089201X-7586764

Manovich, L. (2016). *Instagram and contemporary image.* https://manovich .net/index.php/projects/instagram-and-contemporary-image

Marchese, D. (2023, February 20). YouTube made Emma Chamberlain a star. Now she's leaving it behind. *The New York Times.* https://www.nytimes.com /interactive/2023/02/20/magazine/emma-chamberlain-interview.html

Marwick, A. (2013). *Status update: Celebrity, publicity, and branding in the social media age.* Yale University Press.

Marwick, A., & boyd, danah. (2011). To see and be seen: Celebrity practice on Twitter. *Convergence: The International Journal of Research into New Media Technologies, 17*(2), 139–158. https://doi.org/10.1177/1354856510394539

Marwick, A. E. (2021). Morally motivated networked harassment as normative reinforcement. *Social Media + Society, 7*(2), https://doi.org/10.1177 /20563051211021378

Marwick, A. E., & boyd, danah. (2011). I tweet honestly, I tweet passionately: Twitter users, context collapse, and the imagined audience. *New Media & Society, 13*(1), 114–133. https://doi.org/10.1177/1461444810365313

McCartney, N., & Tynan, J. (2021). Fashioning contemporary art: A new interdisciplinary aesthetics in art-design collaborations. *Journal of Visual Art Practice, 20*(1–2), 143–162. https://doi.org/10.1080/14702029.2021 .1940454

McGuigan, L. (2023). *Selling the American people: Advertising, optimization, and the origins of adtech.* MIT Press.

McRobbie, A. (2009). *The aftermath of feminism: Gender, culture and social change.* SAGE.

McRobbie, A. (2011). Reflections on feminism, immaterial labour and the post-Fordist regime. *New Formations*, 70(70), 60–76.

McRobbie, A. (2015). *Be creative: Making a living in the new culture industries.* Polity Press.

Mears, A. (2011). *Pricing beauty: The making of a fashion model.* University of California Press.

Mears, A. (2014). Aesthetic labor for the sociologies of work, gender, and beauty. *Sociology Compass*, 8(12), 1330–1343. https://doi.org/10.1111/soc4.12211

Mears, A. (2023). Bringing Bourdieu to a content farm: Social media production fields and the cultural economy of attention. *Social Media + Society*, 9(3), https://doi.org/10.1177/20563051231193027

Meisner, C. (2023). The weaponization of platform governance: Mass reporting and algorithmic punishments in the creator economy. *Policy & Internet.* https://doi.org/10.1002/poi3.359

Menger, P.-M. (2014). *The economics of creativity: Art and achievement under uncertainty.* Harvard University Press.

Meta. (2024a, March 4). Brand safety and integrity. Meta for Business [Facebook page]. Facebook. https://en-gb.facebook.com/business/brand-safety

Meta. (2024b, March 4). Partner monetization policies. Meta business help center [Facebook page]. Facebook. https://en-gb.facebook.com/business/help/169845596919485

Meta. (2024c, May 17). Adult nudity and sexual activity. Transparency Centre. Meta. https://transparency.meta.com/en-gb/policies/community-standards/adult-nudity-sexual-activity/

Miller, D. L. (2016). Gender and the artist archetype: Understanding gender inequality in artistic careers. *Sociology Compass*, 10(2), 119–131. https://doi.org/10.1111/soc4.12350

Morris, J. W. (2020). Music platforms and the optimization of culture. *Social Media + Society*, 6(3), 205630512094069. https://doi.org/10.1177/2056305120940690

Morris, J. W., Prey, R., & Nieborg, D. B. (2021). Engineering culture: Logics of optimization in music, games, and apps. *Review of Communication*, 21(2), 161–175. https://doi.org/10.1080/15358593.2021.1934522

Mosseri, A [@mosseri] (n.d.) #AMA What's 1 thing you wish people knew about IG? [video]. Instagram. https://www.instagram.com/stories/highlights/17849103598598460/?hl=en

Mosseri, A [@mosseri] (n.d.) #dadlife [video] Instagram. https://www.instagram.com/stories/highlights/17880752587420022/?hl=en

Mulvaney, Dylan. (2023, June 29). Trans people like beer too ??????? [video]. TikTok. https://www.tiktok.com/@dylanmulvaney/video/7250155134087449898

Myers West, S. (2018). Censored, suspended, shadowbanned: User interpretations of content moderation on social media platforms. *New Media & Society*, 1–18. https://doi.org/10.1177/1461444818773059

Nead, L. (1990). The female nude: Pornography, art, and sexuality. *Signs*, 15(2), 323–335.

Nead, L. (2010). *The female nude: Art, obscenity and sexuality*. Routledge.

Neff, G. (2012). *Venture labor: Work and the burden of risk in innovative industries*. MIT Press.

Neff, G., Wissinger, E., & Zukin, S. (2005). Entrepreneurial labor among cultural producers: "Cool" jobs in "hot" industries. *Social Semiotics*, 15(3), 307–334. https://doi.org/10.1080/10350330500310111

Negus, K. (1999). *Music genres and corporate cultures*. Routledge.

Nieborg, D. B., & Poell, T. (2018). The platformization of cultural production: Theorizing the contingent cultural commodity. *New Media & Society*, 18. https://doi.org/10.1177/1461444818769694

Noble, S. U. (2018). *Algorithms of oppression: How search engines reinforce racism*. New York University Press.

Nulleparttousjours. (2023, June 25). Mosseri states that if your reach has dropped it is because your followers are no longer interested in your content. [Reddit post]. R/Instagram. www.reddit.com/r/Instagram/comments/14ip8y6/mosseri_states_that_if_your_reach_has_dropped_it/

Nunn, H., & Biressi, A. (2010). "A trust betrayed": Celebrity and the work of emotion. *Celebrity Studies*, 1(1), 49–64. https://doi.org/10.1080/19392390903519065

Nyce, C. M. (2023, November 26). Watching a line cook flip eggs for six hours. *The Atlantic*. https://www.theatlantic.com/technology/archive/2023/11/tiktok-live-livestreaming-work/676098/

Nyce, C. M. (2024, March 28). You can't even rescue a dog without being bullied online. *The Atlantic*. https://www.theatlantic.com/technology/archive/2024/03/dog-fosters-social-media-harassment/677910/

Oakley, Tyler. (2017, March 19). Still not fixed. One of my recent videos "8 Black LGBTQ+ Trailblazers Who Inspire Me" is blocked because of this. I'm perplexed, @YouTube. https://twitter.com/PopCrave/status/843229803540959232 . . . [Twitter post]. @tyleroakley. X. https://twitter.com/tyleroakley/status/843544801916010496?lang=en

Olivia Jade. (2018, August 16). Im sorry [video]. YouTube. https://www.youtube.com/watch?v=LAJArLC6v7o

Gogoi, P. (2023, June 28). How the Bud Light boycott shows brands at a crossroads: Use their voice, or shut up? NPR. https://www.npr.org/2023/06/28/1184309434/bud-light-boycott-lgbtq-pride

Paasonen, S. (2021). "We watch porn for the fucking, not for romantic tiptoeing": Extremity, fantasy and women's porn use. *Porn Studies*, 1–14. https://doi.org/10.1080/23268743.2021.1956366

Paasonen, S., Jarrett, K., & Light, B. (2019). *NSFW: Sex, humor, and risk in social media*. MIT Press.

Paddy Galloway. (2019, December 31). Here's how Mr Beast BLEW UP—how he grew his YouTube channel (part 2) [video]. YouTube. https://www.youtube.com/watch?v=M-Z7VDyLw4c

Paddy Galloway. (2021a, October 10). How Beluga gained 4 million subscribers in 3 months (genius strategy) [video]. YouTube. https://www.youtube.com/watch?v=c5-3g0tpgz8

Paddy Galloway. (2021b, November 27). How MrBeast's Squid Game broke YouTube (genius strategy) [video]. YouTube. https://www.youtube.com/watch?v=o8ZbGnwXjj4

Paddy Galloway. (2022, June 30). How Ryan Trahan's $0.01 series broke YouTube (forever) [video]. YouTube. https://www.youtube.com/watch?v=EYah62QBLCQ

Pasquale, F. (2015). *The black box society: The secret algorithms that control money and information*. Harvard University Press.

Patel, K. (2020). *The politics of expertise in cultural labour: Arts, work, and inequalities*. Rowman & Littlefield.

Patel, K. (2022). "I want to be judged on my work, I don't want to be judged as a person": Inequality, expertise and cultural value in UK craft.

*European Journal of Cultural Studies, 25*(6), 1556–1571. https://doi.org/10.1177/13675494221136619

Paul, C. A. (2018). *The toxic meritocracy of video games: Why gaming culture is the worst.* University of Minnesota Press.

Peterson, R. A. (1997). *Creating country music: Fabricating authenticity.* University of Chicago Press.

Petre, C., Duffy, B. E., & Hund, E. (2019). "Gaming the system": Platform paternalism and the politics of algorithmic visibility. *Social Media + Society, 5*(4), 2056305119879995. https://doi.org/10.1177/2056305119879995

Pham, M.-H. T. (2011). Blog ambition: Fashion, feelings, and the political economy of the digital raced body. *Camera Obscura, 26*(1 76), 1–37. https://doi.org/10.1215/02705346-2010-013

Pham, M.-H. T. (2013). "Susie Bubble is a sign of the times": The embodiment of success in the Web 2.0 economy. *Feminist Media Studies, 13*(2), 245–267. https://doi.org/10.1080/14680777.2012.678076

Phạm, M.-H. T. (2015a). *Asians wear clothes on the internet: Race, gender, and the work of personal style blogging.* Duke University Press.

Phan, M. (2013, May 19). Draw my Life—Michelle Phan [video]. YouTube. https://www.youtube.com/watch?v=05KqZEqQJ40

Phan, M. (2017a, April 11). Michelle Phan: Why I dropped everything & traveled for a year. *Refinery29.* https://www.refinery29.com/en-gb/2017/04/149725/michelle-phan-ipsy-em-cosmetics-relaunch

Phan, M. (2017b, June 1). Why I left [video]. YouTube. https://www.youtube.com/watch?v=UuGpmo1SPcA

Pitcan, M., Marwick, A. E., & boyd, danah. (2018). Performing a vanilla self: Respectability politics, social class, and the digital world. *Journal of Computer-Mediated Communication, 23*(3), 163–179. https://doi.org/10.1093/jcmc/zmy008

Poell, T., Nieborg, D. B., & Duffy, B. E. (2021). *Platforms and cultural production.* Polity Press.

Radford, R. (1998). Dangerous liaisons: Art, fashion and individualism. *Fashion Theory.* https://doi.org/10.2752/136270498779571103

Ragusa, A. T. (2005). Social change and the corporate construction of gay markets in the New York Times' advertising business news. *Media, Culture & Society, 27*(5), 653–676. https://doi.org/10.1177/0163443705055721

Restany, P. (2023, June 6). Damien Hirst, Pierre Restany, and a pharmacy-inspired restaurant. *Domus*. https://www.domusweb.it/en/from-the-archive/2023/06/06/pierre-restany-interviews-damien-hirst-on-domus-pages.html

Ringrose, J., & Walkerdine, V. (2008). Regulating the abject: The TV make-over as site of neo-liberal reinvention toward bourgeois femininity. *Feminist Media Studies*, 8(3), 227–246. https://doi.org/10.1080/14680770802217279

Rocamora, A. (2011). Personal fashion blogs: Screens and mirrors in digital self-portraits. *Fashion Theory*, 15(4), 407–424. https://doi.org/10.2752/175174111X13115179149794

Russo, K. (2017, March 20). YouTube restricts LGBTQ+ content to "protect children" and pisses me the f*ck off. *Autostraddle*. https://www.autostraddle.com/youtube-restricts-lgbtq-content-to-protect-children-and-pisses-me-the-fck-off-373214/

Ryan, B. (1992). *Making capital from culture: The corporate form of capitalist cultural production*. Walter de Gruyter.

Saha, A. (2018). *Race and the cultural industries*. Polity.

Said, E. W. (1978). *Orientalism*. Pantheon Books.

Saturday Night Live. (2021, April 4). Viral apology video—SNL [video]. YouTube. https://www.youtube.com/watch?v=UV0_6rGSiyI

Scharff, C. (2015). Blowing your own trumpet: Exploring the gendered dynamics of self-promotion in the classical music profession. In B. Conor, R. Gill, & S. Taylor (Eds.), *Gender and creative labour* (pp. 97–112). Wiley-Blackwell.

Seaver, N. (2017). Algorithms as culture: Some tactics for the ethnography of algorithmic systems. *Big Data & Society*, 4(2) https://doi.org/10.1177/2053951717738104

Seaver, N. (2022). *Computing taste: Algorithms and the makers of music recommendation*. University of Chicago Press.

Sender, K. (2002). Business, not politics: Gays, lesbians, bisexuals, transgender people and the consumer sphere. Departmental Papers (ASC). https://repository.upenn.edu/items/5d072efa-7d90-4a0d-9a99-bcba0552a4bd

Sender, K. (2003). Sex sells: Sex, taste, and class in commercial gay and lesbian media. *GLQ: A Journal of Lesbian and Gay Studies*, 9(3), 331–365.

Senft, T. M. (2008). *Camgirls: Celebrity and community in the age of social networks*. Peter Lang.

Shapiro, E. (2022, January 19). Is Instagram censorship changing art itself? The Art Newspaper—International Art News and Events. https://www .theartnewspaper.com/2022/01/19/is-instagram-censorship-changing -art-itself

Shaw, L., & Bergen, M. (2020, December 22). The North Carolina kid who cracked YouTube's secret code. Bloomberg.com. https://www.bloomberg .com/news/articles/2020-12-22/who-is-mrbeast-meet-youtube-s-top -creator-of-2020

Sheedy, S. (2022). Folk survivals, spurned witches, and thwarted inheritance, or, what makes the occult queer? *Arc: The Journal of the School of Religious Studies*, 50, 1–42.

Sieghart, M. A. (2022, August 2). "Mind-blowing": Why do men's paintings cost 10 times more than women's? *The Guardian*. https://www .theguardian.com/artanddesign/2022/aug/02/painting-gender-pay-gap -recalculating-art

Skeggs, B. (2009). The moral economy of person production: The class relations of self-performance on "reality" television. *The Sociological Review*, 57(4), 626–644. https://doi.org/10.1111/j.1467-954X.2009 .01865.x

Smith, C., & Attwood, F. (2014). Anti/pro/critical porn studies. *Porn Studies*, 1(1–2), 7–23. https://doi.org/10.1080/23268743.2014.887364

Sobande, F. (2020). *The digital lives of Black women in Britain*. Palgrave Macmillan.

Sobande, F. (2022). The celebrity whitewashing of Black Lives Matter and social injustices. *Celebrity Studies*, 13(1), 130–135. https://doi.org/10.1080 /19392397.2022.2026147

Sobande, F., Fearfull, A., & Brownlie, D. (2019). Resisting media marginalisation: Black women's digital content and collectivity. *Consumption Markets & Culture*, 1–16. https://doi.org/10.1080/10253866 .2019.1571491

Sobande, F., Hesmondhalgh, D., & Saha, A. (2023). Black, Brown and Asian cultural workers, creativity and activism: The ambivalence of digital self-branding practices. *The Sociological Review*, 71(6), 1448–1466. https:// doi.org/10.1177/00380261231163952

Sobande, F., Kanai, A., & Zeng, N. (2022). The hypervisibility and discourses of "wokeness" in digital culture. *Media, Culture & Society*, 44(8), 1576–1587. https://doi.org/10.1177/01634437221117490

Specter, E. (2023, January 12). Emma Chamberlain takes on French girl beauty as the new face of Lancôme. *British Vogue*. https://www.vogue.co.uk/beauty/article/emma-chamberlain-lancome-interview

Steele, C. K. (2021). *Digital Black feminism*. New York University Press.

Stegeman, H. M., Are, C., & Poell, T. (2024). Strategic invisibility: How creators manage the risks and constraints of online hyper(in)visibility. *Social Media + Society*, 10(2). https://doi.org/10.1177/20563051241244674

Stevens, W. E. (2021). Blackfishing on Instagram: Influencing and the commodification of Black urban aesthetics. *Social Media + Society*, 7(3), https://doi.org/10.1177/20563051211038236

Stuart, F. (2020). *Ballad of the bullet: Gangs, drill music, and the power of online infamy*. Princeton University Press.

Tate, S. (2007). Black beauty: Shade, hair and anti-racist aesthetics. *Ethnic and Racial Studies*, 30(2), 300–319. https://doi.org/10.1080/01419870601143992

Tiidenberg, K. (2021). Sex, power and platform governance. *Porn Studies*, 8(4), 381–393. https://doi.org/10.1080/23268743.2021.1974312

Toft, M. & Friedman, S. (2021). Family wealth and the class ceiling: The propulsive power of the bank of mum and dad. *Sociology*, 55(1), 90–109. https://doi.org/10.1177/0038038520922537

Unilever. (2018, June 18). Unilever calls on industry to increase trust, transparency and measurement in influencer marketing. Unilever. https://www.unilever.com/news/press-releases/2018/unilever-calls-on-industry-to-increase-trust-transparency-and-measurement-in-influencer-marketing.html

van Brabandt, P., & Prinz, J. (2012). Why do porn films suck? In H. L. Maes & J. Levinson (Eds.), *Art and pornography: Philosophical essays* (pp. 161–191). Oxford University Press.

Vogue. (2016, September 25). Ciao, Milano! Vogue.com's editors discuss the week that was. *Vogue*. http://www.vogue.com/article/milan-fashion-week-spring-2017-vogue-editors-chat

Wagoner, M. (2020, February 14). Is this the second coming of beauty vlogger Michelle Phan? *Elle*. https://www.elle.com/uk/beauty/a30923191/michelle-phan/

Waldman, A. E. (2022). Disorderly content. *Washington Law Review*, 97(4), 907–976.

White, M. (2015). *Producing women: The internet, traditional femininity, queerness, and creativity*. Routledge.

Whitworth, B. (2023, April 14). Our responsibility to America. Anheuser-Busch. https://www.anheuser-busch.com/newsroom/our-responsibility-to-america

Wiley, D. (2023, March 13). Council post: Why smaller influencers outshine mega-influencers in the age of social media. *Forbes*. https://www.forbes.com/sites/forbesagencycouncil/2023/03/13/why-smaller-influencers-outshine-mega-influencers-in-the-age-of-social-media/

Willson, M. (2017). Algorithms (and the) everyday. *Information, Communication & Society*, 20(1), 137–150. https://doi.org/10.1080/1369118X.2016.1200645

Wilson, A. N. (2024, April 1). It's not what the world needs right now. *The Baffler*. https://thebaffler.com/odds-and-ends/its-not-what-the-world-needs-right-now-norman-wilson

Wohl, H. (2021). *Bound by creativity: How contemporary art is created and judged*. The University of Chicago Press.

World Federation of Advertisers. (2022, June 17). GARM brand safety floor + suitability framework. https://wfanet.org/knowledge/item/2022/06/17/GARM-Brand-Safety-Floor—Suitability-Framework-3

Yotka, S. (2017, October 13). Dalí & Schiaparelli, in daring fashion proves they were the best at art-fashion collaborations. *Vogue*. https://www.vogue.com/article/dali-schiaparlli-in-daring-fashion-exhibit-dali-museum

YouTube. (2023, June 1). YouTube channel monetization policies — YouTube help. Google. https://support.google.com/youtube/answer/1311392?hl=en#zippy=%2Ccreator-responsibility

Ziewitz, M. (2019). Rethinking gaming: The ethical work of optimization in web search engines. *Social Studies of Science*, 49(5), 707–731. https://doi.org/10.1177/0306312719865607

# Index

and, 9–10, 47–50, 52–54, 55*fig.*,
56–58, 59*fig.*, 66–74, 111–20, 121*fig.*,
122*fig.*, 123, 126–30, 159–60,
164–65, 166*fig.*, 167, 176, 182–83,
189, 191, 195*fig.*, 196, 213, 217n8;
intermediaries and, 173; labor
involved and, 58, 61–62, 112–13,
169, 201; legitimization and, 10,
17, 49, 52, 65, 82, 114, 169–70, 174,
176, 179, 188, 190–91, 194; love for
the craft and, 173, 175–78, 189, 191;
male artists and, 172, 205;
marginalization and, 185, 191,
206; marketing strategies and,
115–16; networking and, 126, 203;
nonbinary artists, 8, 11, 129,
169–70, 172–73, 213; paid
advertising and, 70; partnerships/
sponsorships and, 193–97;
personal/domestic lives and, 16,
119–20, 121*fig.*, 122*fig.*, 123–26,
128–29, 160, 183, 191; platformization and, 46, 172; platforms, trust/
anxiety and, 70–75, 183; race and,
123–24, 204–205, 213; reputation
and, 110; studios and, 8–10, 58, 62,
106, 108*fig.*, 109*fig.*, 111–12, 119,
126, 129, 168, 183; truth/verifica-
tion, expectations for, 110–14;
uncertainty and, 129; unfinished
work, documentation of, 111. *See
also* brands; brand safety; Design
Trust; platforms; self-branding;
women
Artists' Union England, 202
*ARTnews*, 190
*Art Newspaper*, 180, 183
art worlds, 7–12, 66, 74, 80, 107, 110,
189, 193, 204, 210; audience

identity and, 69; authenticity and,
105, 107, 206; blogs and, 65;
branding and, 162–63, 189;
consistency and, 164–65; cultural
hierarchies and, 190; definition of,
8; distribution and, 57; elites and,
17, 49, 191, 194; gender and,
169–70, 186, 207; governmentality
and, 73; income and, 199–200;
inequalities and, 126, 191,
206–207; Instagram, impact of,
56–57, 74–76, 165, 177, 189;
intermediaries and, 49–50, 65, 69,
164, 174–75; legitimization and,
189, 191, 194; marginalization in,
206; moderation of, 179–80;
networking and, 57; optimization
and, 46; platformization of, 164;
precarity of, 171; race and,
204–205, 207; risk avoidance and,
19, 164; sexuality and, 207;
sociality and, 69; social media,
impact on, 8, 17; taste-making
and, 50; truth/verification,
expectations for, 110–14; value
and, 198–99, 206
*Atlantic* (magazine), 1–2, 81, 202
AT&T, 152
audiences, 2–4, 15–16, 21, 73, 79, 93,
107, 118, 192; audience analytics
and, 66, 68–69; audience
meaning and, 15; audience
sharing and, 65; context collapse
and, 138; engagement and, 66–68,
74, 126–27; free vs. paid access
and, 67; gay audiences and, 149;
influence and, 155; management
of, 86; reach and, 5, 40–41; time
of day, engagement and, 43; value

GQ, 203
Gray, Ann, 213
Grazian, David, 78, 104
Green, Josh, 83, 140
Gregory, Karen, 169
Guggenheim, 206

Hall, Stuart, 14, 205
Harrods, 197
hashtags, 15, 43, 151. *See also*
    Facebook; Twitter
Havens, Timothy, 27
Hearn, Alison, 132
Hesmondhalgh, David, 202
Higgins, Kat, 86
Hirst, Damien, 163, 171–72, 190, 196
Hochschild, Arlie, 94
Hollywood, 26, 143
Huber, Roxanne, 188
Hund, Emily, 11, 34, 38, 66, 71, 119,
    132

identity formation, 14–15
Illouz, Eva, 103
inauthenticity, 18, 76, 113, 117, 155
income, 2, 13, 16, 18, 37; anxiety and,
    98–99; audience, dependence on,
    23; brand partnerships and, 13,
    178; lack of, for partnerships, 4–5;
    revenue-sharing and, 13; stipends
    and, 5. *See also* artists; art worlds;
    content creators; influencer creep;
    influencer economy; influencer
    industry; influencers; visibility
influencer creep: amateur aesthetic
    and, 78–79; anxiety/stress and,
    129–30, 207; artistic production,
    impact on, 17, 47, 65, 69, 73–75,
    125, 171, 183, 188, 194, 198, 200,

204; authenticity and, 80,
104–105, 107, 119–20; content
creation, constant demand and,
75; definition of, 1; eccentricity/
bad behavior and, 171–72;
emotional vulnerability and,
78–79; frustrations of, 63; income
and, 200; mission creep and, 1;
personal life, sharing of and, 125,
128–29, 160; platform policies and,
191; platform work, inequality
and, 44; self-branding, influence
on, 136, 154, 158, 174; sociality
and, 69; women, pressure on and,
11

influencer culture, 6, 8, 27, 75, 103,
105, 156, 164, 206–207, 210;
advertising and, 128; amateurism
and, 106; anxiety and, 10, 99–100;
audiences and, 110, 128; authenticity and, 128; blogs, decline of in,
65; curation and, 15; emotions
and, 101, 117; feminized genres of,
89; professionalization of, 7; risk
and, 89, 91, 98, 100, 126; risk
avoidance and, 154
influencer economy, 7, 12, 18, 27, 79,
132, 146, 206, 210, 212; aspirational
labor and, 200; brand safety and,
171; ethical concerns and, 88;
gender inequality and, 11;
impression management in, 119;
income in, 200–201; legitimization and, 206; passionate talk
and, 175–76; risk and, 206;
self-branding and, 132–33
influencer industry, 6, 13, 78, 199,
209; participation and, 7; pay and,
7; platformization of, 65;

professionalization of, 12

Influencer Marketing Hub, 145, 199–200

Influencer Pay Gap (campaign), 200–201; Instagram page of, 200

influencers: account hopping and, 43, 66; anxiety and, 3, 96, 136; apology content and, 90–94, 96–97, 100; apology content (influencers of color) and, 101–103; audiences and, 15–16, 21–22, 39–41, 43, 45–46, 65, 104, 212; beauty influencers and, 90, 209; consumerism and, 2, 174–76, 191; contracts and, 174; conventions and, 209; crying and, 97; culture, impact on, 14; definitions of, 12–14; derision/ stereotypes of, 13–14, 16, 38, 87, 203; emotional vulnerability and, 91–96, 126; feminized output and, 42; filler content and, 82–83; gendered view of, 14, 91; importance of, 22; intimacy and, 69; labor involved and, 3; legitimization and, 16, 32–33, 104, 114, 132, 190–91, 206; livelihoods/income of, 2, 13, 16, 22, 37, 148, 199–200; marginalization and, 191; marketing and, 174, 194, 197–200; multivariate testing and, 43; ordinariness and, 83, 97, 100, 103, 110, 114, 119, 135, 211; platformized work and, 12, 15, 25, 44, 206–207; platforms, trust/anxiety and, 70–72, 74, 98–100, 207; race and, 200; risk and, 21–22, 27, 35, 89, 91, 98, 100, 136; self-identification as, 13; self-presentation and, 173, 213; self-surveillance and, 157; skill and,

1–2, 88; sponsorships/paid partnerships and, 91–92, 178, 194–95, 200; technological development, impact of, 15; third-party tools and, 43–44; truth/ verification, expectations for, 110–14; vanity and, 2, 14; visibility and, 7, 37–41, 46; visibility (algorithmic) and, 22, 27, 35, 42, 93. *See also* algorithms; artists; authenticity; content creators; labor, emotional; mental health; platforms

influencer work, 3, 12, 69, 88, 95, 101, 153, 195, 207; upbeat self-presentation and, 173, 194

Instagram: affordances and, 52–54, 70, 120, 162; algorithms of, 47, 56–57, 62, 66–67, 180, 187; appeals and, 180–81; as artistic intermediary, 50; artworks, removal of, 179–81, 181*fig.*, 182–83; audiences and, 10, 47, 50–52, 54, 66–68, 70–74, 117, 183; blogs and, 65; B-Roll content and, 61, 84; business/commercial features and, 66–68; censorship and, 183; creator reach and, 39; creator resources and, 11; deletion of accounts and, 71–72, 180, 182–83; feed of, 71; grid posts and, 43, 114, 159; increased use of during COVID-19, 9; Influencers in the Wild, account of, 88–89; insiders and, 38–39; Instagram Live, 90; moderation and, 180, 185, 187; monetization and, 142; nudity, policy on, 179, 182–84, 187; punishment and, 180–83;

Instagram *(continued)*
racialized visibility and, 56, 74; recommendation algorithms and, 50–51; Reels and, 3, 43, 201; removal of posts and, 180; reshared/reposted content, visibility of, 62–63; r/Instagram Subreddit, 40, 44; rules/ governance and, 152, 183; sexual content, policy on, 179, 188; shadow bans and, 180, 183; sponsorships/paid partnerships and, 91–92, 193–94; Stories and, 40, 43, 51, 62, 160, 193, 201; terms and conditions of, 70–71; time lapses and, 58; trust/anxiety and, 70–75; user support and, 70–74; videos and, 58, 59*fig.*, 60*fig.*, 61, 108*fig.*, 109*fig.*, 120, 121*fig.*, 122*fig.*, 165–66; views and, 43; vox pop and, 162. *See also* advertisers; art; artists; art worlds; fakeness
Internet Creators Guild, 211
*Interview* (magazine), 82, 162
invisibility, 21, 56, 136, 192; algorithmic invisibility and, 192; threat of, 72, 99

Jade, Olivia (YouTuber), 96–97
Janes, Linda, 14
Jennings, Rebecca, 203
Jobin, Anna, 52

Kaluuya, Daniel, 93
Kenworthy, Gus, 148
Kid Rock, 153
Kjelberg, Felix (YouTuber), 141. *See also* PewDiePie (YouTuber)
Kopf, Susanne, 142

Koval, Matt, 35–36
KSI (YouTuber), 33
Kusama, Yayoi, 196–97

Labato, Ramon, 140
labor, emotional, 91, 94, 100, 129
Lee, Laura (YouTuber), 97
Le Roy Soleil, 196
LGBTQ+ community, 35, 148–50, 152, 154–55, 185; AIDS crisis (1980s) and, 149; Christians/ conservatives and, 149; LGBTQ+ consumers and, 149; LGBTQ+ themes and, 34, 152; queer (term), use of, 148. *See also* brands; social media; YouTube
Lime, Andy, 182
Lissette, 93
Liu, Yingdan, 200
Logan Paul (YouTuber), 33–35, 97
London, Scarlett (Instagram Creator), 91–92
London Fashion Week, 5
L'Oréal, 134–35, 154–55, 200. See also brand safety
Lorenz, Taylor, 81
Louis Vuitton, 197
Lovato, Demi, 159
*Love Island*, 178
Luckman, Susan, 113
Lury, Celia, 163

Mae, Molly (YouTuber), 178
Maes, Hans, 186–87
Magarath, Victoria (YouTuber), 175
makeup, 5, 85, 131, 133; minimal/lack of, 91, 96, 106; self-empowerment and, 135
Mamidipudi, Annapura, 124

Owen, Helen (Instagram Creator), 193

Padilla, Anthony (YouTuber), 98
Patel, Karen, 111, 119, 124
Patreon, 13
Paul, Christopher, 32–33
Paytas, Trisha (YouTuber), 90
Pelayo, Isaac, 47–48
PEN America, 179
*People*, 82
Peterson, Richard A., 78
Petre, Caitlin, 38, 71
PewDiePie (YouTuber), 33–35
Pham, Minh-Ha T., 132, 154–55
Phan, Michelle (YouTuber), 85,
    131–35, 156, 178; Ipsy and, 134;
    makeup and, 131, 133–34, 178;
    mental health and, 134; ordinari-
    ness and, 135, 156; personal stories
    and, 133–34; proto-influencer
    strategies of, 132; self-branding
    and, 132–35, 137; self-presentation,
    131–33
Pitcan, Mikaela, 86
Pitchfork, 203
platform cultures, 15, 92, 98, 100,
    157
platformization, 11–12, 38, 46, 65–66,
    78, 139; audiences, impact on, 69;
    culture and, 48; pressures of, 12.
    *See also* artists; authenticity;
    creative industries
platforms, 7, 11, 14–15, 21, 26–28, 31,
    101, 203, 216n6; affordances and,
    15, 131, 191; appeals and, 180–81;
    capitalism and, 17; culture of, 15;
    economy and, 18; engagement
    with, lack of, 117; engineers and,

62; features, constant changes to,
37; inconsistency and, 21, 45–46,
70, 98; influencers, impact on,
42, 107; insiders/outsiders and,
35–41, 44–45; marginalization
and, 33–34; moderation and, 19,
21, 98, 143–44, 180–81, 187;
nudity/sexual content, increase
in concern over, 184; platform
dependency and, 72–73; platform
effects and, 51; platform paternalism and, 71; platform users, 12, 15,
33, 44–45, 70–72, 103; punishment
and, 18, 54, 57, 143–44; requirements and, 1, 23, 45; risk and, 46,
98; rules and governance of, 11–12,
19, 72–73, 79, 98, 180–84; scrutiny
and, 18; sex-negative governance
and, 146; shadow bans and, 21, 43,
98, 180–82, 216n2; transparency/
opacity and, 36, 48, 73, 98, 100,
216n8; trust issues/uncertainty
and, 70–74, 129; workplace
protections and, 191–92. *See also*
advertisers; algorithms; brand
safety; platformization; visibility
Poell, Thomas, 11–12, 117, 138
pornography, 185–87; artwork,
    contrast with, 186–87; exploitative
    nature of, 186; sexuality, insights
    into, 186. *See also* women
Prey, Robert, 23
Prinz, Jesse, 186
privacy, 69, 125, 129
profanity, 96, 139, 147–48, 171
Pruchniewska, Ursula, 99

queer community, 35, 148–50, 152,
    156–57, 212; queer phobia and, 185;

queer spaces and, 168; queer theory, 148

racism, 56, 97, 152; othering and, 205; racial slurs and, 147
Radiohead, 203–204
rationalization, 27, 45. *See also* optimization
*Real Life* (magazine), 1–2
Reddit, 40, 43–44, 92. *See also* Instagram
risk society, concept of, 136–37
Ritchie, Rene, 36–37
Robertson, Ro, 111–12
Rosenthal, Norman, 190
Ross, Bob, 133
Royal Academy of Arts, 190
Russo, Kristin, 150
Ryan, Bill, 25–26, 31

Saha, Anamik, 27, 31, 45
Sanchez, Adrian Alarcon, 185
*Saturday Night Live*, 93
Schiaparelli, Elsa, 196
search engine optimization (SEO), 22, 63
Seaver, Nick, 50–51
self, the, 7, 22, 137; authenticity and, 119; brand safety and, 18, 136; commercial suitability and, 18, 136; consistent identity and, 7, 18, 131, 136; editing of, 18; failed self and, 103; genuine self and, 107; online versions of, 138; race and, 86; sense of, 98
self-branding, 7, 18–19, 21, 27, 125, 130–39, 156–58, 178, 194, 213; anxiety/risk, response to, 137; artists and, 159, 164, 175–77, 183,

191, 197; brand safety and, 7, 136, 139, 174; challenges to, 156; commercial concerns and, 19; commercial suitability and, 7, 136, 164; consistency and, 164–65, 174; context collapse and, 138, 174; definition of, 132; gender and, 164; history of, 137–39; labor involved and, 169; pitching and, 168. *See also* authenticity; Phan, Michelle (YouTuber); self, the; witchcraft
self-censorship, 96, 180
self-help, 130
selfies, 4
self-improvement, 136–37
self-management, 137
self portraits, 55*fig.*
self-presentation, 86, 164, 173; feminized genres of, 89; impression management and, 118–19; strategies for, 114, 118. *See also* artists; influencers; influencer work; women
self-promotion, 117, 131, 137, 139, 168–69; dislike of, 169
self-representation, 13, 21
self-validation, 129
Sender, Katherine, 149
Senft, Terri, 13
*Seventeen* (magazine), 90
sexual assault (SA), 102, 219n49
sexual harassment (SH), 102, 219n49
sex workers, 87, 184, 187–88, 191; collectives and, 187; marginalization and, 191
Shakespeare, William, 204
Shapiro, Emma, 180, 183
Sheridan, John, 183
Shkirando, Liza, 182

Silicon Valley, 137–38
Smales, Dom, 175
Snapchat, 196
social media: advertisers and, 98, 139; advice on, 64; affordances and, 83, 113, 163, 176; artists and, 10, 19; art worlds and, 8; audiences and, 23; backstages and, 123; cultural work and, 11; culture of, 18, 52, 80, 105, 163; entrepreneurship and, 105; haphazard use of, 117; idealism and, 95; individual vs. collectives, promotion of, 138; influencers, lack of control over, 3; as intermediaries, 35; legitimacy and, 65; LGBTQ+ themes and, 34, 152; malicious flagging of content and, 35; managers and, 4–5; marketing and, 68, 116; mental health and, 129; online popularity and, 13; personal life, presentation of, 125; personal lives and, 125; personal risk and, 2, 35; platform employees and, 6, 36–37, 52; posts, ideas for, 64; promotional, 1; recommendations and, 24; risks of, 3; rules and governance and, 11–12, 152, 180; safe harbor laws and, 184; safety and, 16, 144, 156, 164; sponsorship and, 2–3. *See also* advertisers; algorithms; audiences; blogs and bloggers; Design Trust; Facebook; income; Instagram; Meta; platformization; platforms; TikTok; visibility; women; YouTube
software developers, 7
Spotify, 23, 51; listens, counting of, 51

*Squid Game*, 20
Stark, Jen, 159–60, 162, 165, 167, 188–89, 193–94, 223n10; Instagram presence of, 159–60, 161*fig.*, 166*fig.*; self-branding of, 162
start-up culture, 137–38; networking and, 137
Steele, Catherine Knight, 86
Stuart, Forrest, 104–105
Summer in the City, 6, 210, 224n4
Swoll, Joey (Instagram Creator), 102

talent agents, 4, 101, 209–10
talent managers, 6
Tate, Shirley, 197
Tate Britain, 206
Tate Modern, 206
tech bro image, 39
Tiidenberg, Katrin, 184
TikTok, 23, 37, 82, 90, 102, 106, 153, 176, 203; artists and, 217n8; policy and, 152; vox pop content and, 162
TikTok live, 2; working-class content creators and, 2
Torres, Ashley, 193
transgender community, 35, 87, 152–54, 157; transphobia and, 152–53
Twitch, 102
Twitter, 6, 23, 82, 92, 102, 210; Creator Day, 210; hashtags and, 15, 151
Tynan, Jane, 190

Underwood, Jodie, 181*fig.*
unemployment, 9, 126–27
United Kingdom, 4

Xanga, 132

YouTube, 6, 12, 20, 23, 28, 32–33, 36–38, 72, 81, 90, 131–35, 140, 178, 210; accessibility of, 88; advertiser-friendliness and, 141; affordances and, 37; algorithms of, 21, 28–30, 33, 151; apology videos and, 93–94, 96; backlashes against, 151–52; beauty content and, 85; Black male content creators and, 104–105; B-Roll content and, 84; content guidelines and, 141–44; creator liaison, position of, 35–36; creator responsibility policy and, 143; "draw my life" videos and, 135, 220n17; employees of, 36–38, 141; family-friendly/restricted mode and, 150–52; feminized content on, 131; idealism and, 95; LGBTQ+ creators and, 142–43, 148–50; moderation and, 151–52; monetization and, 95, 141–43; original content/form of, 83, 140; promotional content and, 95; purchase of, by Google, 131; revenue sharing and, 96; rules/governance of, 95–96, 141–42, 144, 150, 152; self, representation of and, 137; views, counting of and, 37; viral content on, 20–21, 93; visibility and, 96; #YouTubeIsOverParty and, 151–52; YouTube Shorts and, 37. *See also* advertisers; blogs and bloggers; Creator Insider channel; YouTube Creator Café; YouTube Partner Program (YPP)

YouTube Creator Café, 210

YouTube Partner Program (YPP), 140–41, 143–44; eligibility for, 141

YouTube Space, 210, 224n6

Zietwitz, Malte, 52

Instagram *(continued)*
  racialized visibility and, 56, 74;
  recommendation algorithms and,
  50–51; Reels and, 3, 43, 201;
  removal of posts and, 180;
  reshared/reposted content,
  visibility of, 62–63; r/Instagram
  Subreddit, 40, 44; rules/
  governance and, 152, 183; sexual
  content, policy on, 179, 188;
  shadow bans and, 180, 183;
  sponsorships/paid partnerships
  and, 91–92, 193–94; Stories and,
  40, 43, 51, 62, 160, 193, 201; terms
  and conditions of, 70–71; time
  lapses and, 58; trust/anxiety and,
  70–75; user support and, 70–74;
  videos and, 58, 59*fig.*, 60*fig.*, 61,
  108*fig.*, 109*fig.*, 120, 121*fig.*, 122*fig.*,
  165–66; views and, 43; vox pop
  and, 162. *See also* advertisers; art;
  artists; art worlds; fakeness
Internet Creators Guild, 211
*Interview* (magazine), 82, 162
invisibility, 21, 56, 136, 192; algorithmic invisibility and, 192; threat of,
  72, 99

Jade, Olivia (YouTuber), 96–97
Janes, Linda, 14
Jennings, Rebecca, 203
Jobin, Anna, 52

Kaluuya, Daniel, 93
Kenworthy, Gus, 148
Kid Rock, 153
Kjelberg, Felix (YouTuber), 141. *See
  also* PewDiePie (YouTuber)
Kopf, Susanne, 142

Koval, Matt, 35–36
KSI (YouTuber), 33
Kusama, Yayoi, 196–97

Labato, Ramon, 140
labor, emotional, 91, 94, 100, 129
Lee, Laura (YouTuber), 97
Le Roy Soleil, 196
LGBTQ+ community, 35, 148–50,
  152, 154–55, 185; AIDS crisis
  (1980s) and, 149; Christians/
  conservatives and, 149; LGBTQ+
  consumers and, 149; LGBTQ+
  themes and, 34, 152; queer (term),
  use of, 148. *See also* brands; social
  media; YouTube
Lime, Andy, 182
Lissette, 93
Liu, Yingdan, 200
Logan Paul (YouTuber), 33–35, 97
London, Scarlett (Instagram
  Creator), 91–92
London Fashion Week, 5
L'Oréal, 134–35, 154–55, 200. See also
  brand safety
Lorenz, Taylor, 81
Louis Vuitton, 197
Lovato, Demi, 159
*Love Island*, 178
Luckman, Susan, 113
Lury, Celia, 163

Mae, Molly (YouTuber), 178
Maes, Hans, 186–87
Magarath, Victoria (YouTuber), 175
makeup, 5, 85, 131, 133; minimal/lack
  of, 91, 96, 106; self-empowerment
  and, 135
Mamidipudi, Annapura, 124

professionalization of, 12
Influencer Marketing Hub, 145,
199–200
Influencer Pay Gap (campaign),
200–201; Instagram page of, 200
influencers: account hopping and, 43,
66; anxiety and, 3, 96, 136; apology
content and, 90–94, 96–97, 100;
apology content (influencers of
color) and, 101–103; audiences
and, 15–16, 21–22, 39–41, 43, 45–46,
65, 104, 212; beauty influencers
and, 90, 209; consumerism and, 2,
174–76, 191; contracts and, 174;
conventions and, 209; crying and,
97; culture, impact on, 14;
definitions of, 12–14; derision/
stereotypes of, 13–14, 16, 38, 87,
203; emotional vulnerability and,
91–96, 126; feminized output and,
42; filler content and, 82–83;
gendered view of, 14, 91; importance of, 22; intimacy and, 69;
labor involved and, 3; legitimization and, 16, 32–33, 104, 114, 132,
190–91; livelihoods/income
of, 2, 13, 16, 22, 37, 148, 199–200;
marginalization and, 191;
marketing and, 174, 194, 197–200;
multivariate testing and, 43;
ordinariness and, 83, 97, 100, 103,
110, 114, 119, 135, 211; platformized
work and, 12, 15, 25, 44, 206–207;
platforms, trust/anxiety and,
70–72, 74, 98–100, 207; race and,
200; risk and, 21–22, 27, 35, 89, 91,
98, 100, 136; self-identification as,
13; self-presentation and, 173, 213;
self-surveillance and, 157; skill and,

1–2, 88; sponsorships/paid
partnerships and, 91–92, 178,
194–95, 200; technological
development, impact of, 15;
third-party tools and, 43–44; truth/
verification, expectations for,
110–14; vanity and, 2, 14; visibility
and, 7, 37–41, 46; visibility
(algorithmic) and, 22, 27, 35, 42, 93.
*See also* algorithms; artists;
authenticity; content creators;
labor, emotional; mental health;
platforms
influencer work, 3, 12, 69, 88, 95,
101, 153, 195, 207; upbeat
self-presentation and, 173, 194
Instagram: affordances and, 52–54,
70, 120, 162; algorithms of, 47,
56–57, 62, 66–67, 180, 187; appeals
and, 180–81; as artistic intermediary, 50; artworks, removal of,
179–81, 181*fig.*, 182–83; audiences
and, 10, 47, 50–52, 54, 66–68,
70–74, 117, 183; blogs and, 65;
B-Roll content and, 61, 84;
business/commercial features
and, 66–68; censorship and, 183;
creator reach and, 39; creator
resources and, 11; deletion of
accounts and, 71–72, 180, 182–83;
feed of, 71; grid posts and, 43, 114,
159; increased use of during
COVID-19, 9; Influencers in the
Wild, account of, 88–89; insiders
and, 38–39; Instagram Live, 90;
moderation and, 180, 185, 187;
monetization and, 142; nudity,
policy on, 179, 182–84, 187;
punishment and, 180–83;

www.ingramcontent.com/pod-product-compliance
Lightning Source LLC
Chambersburg PA
CBHW031218050326
40689CB00009B/1378